Pro Dynamic .N Applications
Applications

Data-Driven Programming for the .NET Framework

Carl Ganz, Jr.

Apress®

Pro Dynamic .NET 4.0 Applications: Data-Driven Programming for the .NET Framework

ISBN-13 (pbk): 978-1-4302-2519-5

ISBN-13 (electronic): 978-1-4302-2520-1

Printed and bound in the United States of America 9 8 7 6 5 4 3 2 1

President and Publisher: Paul Manning
Lead Editor: Matthew Moodie
Technical Reviewer: Ryan Follmer
Editorial Board: Clay Andres, Steve Anglin, Mark Beckner, Ewan Buckingham, Gary Cornell, Jonathan Gennick, Jonathan Hassell, Michelle Lowman, Matthew Moodie, Duncan Parkes, Jeffrey Pepper, Frank Pohlmann, Douglas Pundick, Ben Renow-Clarke, Dominic Shakeshaft, Matt Wade, Tom WelshProject Manager: Anita Castro
Copy Editor: Tiffany Taylor
Compositor: Bronkella Publishing LLC
Indexer: John Collin
Artist: April Milne
Cover Designer: Anna Ishchenko

Distributed to the book trade worldwide by Springer-Verlag New York, Inc., 233 Spring Street, 6th Floor, New York, NY 10013. Phone 1-800-SPRINGER, fax 201-348-4505, e-mail orders-ny@springer-sbm.com, or visit http://www.springeronline.com.

For information on translations, please e-mail info@apress.com, or visit http://www.apress.com.

Apress and friends of ED books may be purchased in bulk for academic, corporate, or promotional use. eBook versions and licenses are also available for most titles. For more information, reference our Special Bulk Sales–eBook Licensing web page at http://www.apress.com/info/bulksales.

The source code for this book is available to readers at http://www.apress.com. You will need to answer questions pertaining to this book in order to successfully download the code.

With all paternal love, to Carl John III, Rose Veronica, and our unborn baby, either Paul Christian or Emily Anne, whichever one you turn out to be.

Contents at a Glance

Contents

About the Author

Carl Ganz, Jr. is a Senior Software Developer at Innovatix, LLC., in New York. He has an M.B.A in Finance from Seton Hall University and is the author of four other books on software development as well as dozens of articles on Visual Basic, C#, and Microsoft .NET technology. He is the president and founder of the New Jersey Visual Basic User Group and has been a featured speaker at software development conferences in both the U.S. and Germany. Carl and his wife Wendy, live in Raritan, New Jersey, with their son Carl III, their daughter Rose, and their cats Jack and Jake. Contact Carl at

`seton.software@verizon.net.`

About the Technical Reviewer

Ryan Follmer is a technical architect for CIBER Inc., an international system integration consultancy. He specializes in user interface development using the Microsoft .NET framework. As a consultant for nearly 10 years, Ryan has developed multi-platform applications for the financial, life science and service industry markets. Ryan lives in Pittsburgh, Pennsylvania and can be reached at ryanfollmer@gmail.com

Acknowledgments

There are several people whom I would like to thank for making this book possible:

Ryan Follmer performed his usual brilliant and thorough technical review to make sure that everything within is complete and accurate. This is the second time I've had the pleasure of working with Ryan. I can't imagine a successful book project without his dedication and professionalism.

The PCRS development staff at the Visiting Nurse Service of New York – Juan Maluf, Vinod Ramnani, Chris Ricciardi, Jose Lopez, Sheryl Feng, and LJ Li. It was their .NET application that finally induced me to write this volume which I've had on the back burner for more than a decade.

The editors at Apress – specifically Ewan Buckingham, Matt Moodie, and Anita Castro – for their professional guidance and overall kindness in steering this project through to completion.

My wife, Wendy, son, Carl III, and daughter, Rose, for providing me with the love, affection, and support that makes all these efforts worthwhile.

Most importantly, thanks be to God for the ability to do this kind of intellectually demanding work.

Introduction

Data-driven, or dynamic, programming is a series of techniques for modifying an application at runtime. You can accomplish this by storing screen definitions, business rules, and source code in a data source and then restoring them at runtime to alter the functionality of an application. The technology to perform data-driven programming encompasses many areas of software development. Language-specific source code is used as well as the metadata from whatever RDBMS you are using for the back end. Data-driven development is used in code generation, for adding features to an installed application, and for altering the user interface and application response based on previously selected choices.

This book explains the hows and whys of data-driven development. Here's how it's structured:

- Chapter 1 introduces the technology and explains the use of database metadata and its role in code generation.

- Chapter 2 explains Reflection, which is needed to examine the internals of a compiled assembly and manipulate objects at runtime.

- Chapter 3 shows how to compile .NET source code at runtime, thus altering its response completely.

- Chapters 4 , 5, and 6 explain the specifics of data-driven programming as it relates to WinForms, WebForms, and WPF development, respectively.

- Chapter 7 explains data-driven reports. It covers output to Excel, PDF, Crystal Reports, and SQL Server Reporting Services.

- Finally, Chapter 8 reviews optimal database design for data-driven applications.

Carl Ganz Jr
Raritan, New Jersey
seton.software@verizon.net

CHAPTER 1

■■■

Introducing Data-Driven Programming

Data-driven development focuses on storing application structures in a database and deriving application functionality from the data structure itself, though few applications are entirely data-driven. A Laboratory Information Management System (LIMS) system is one such type of application. Users of a LIMS system need to create definitions for various data elements they require in the process of laboratory research. It is, in effect, a scaled-down version of the Visual Studio IDE. You must dynamically generate data tables and drag and drop controls on a form. Each of the data elements may require data validation that's written in C# or VB.NET source code and compiled at runtime to check the data and provide feedback to those performing data entry to the system.

Normally, you'll never need to use data-driven programming in such an extensive fashion. A more common use of these techniques is found in off-the-shelf applications that give you some level of customization that the software publisher couldn't foresee. For example, an accounting system may have a data-entry form for entering invoices. Suppose the user's business model requires that each invoice be associated with a given delivery truck, but no delivery truck field is available. Using data-driven programming techniques, you can let the user define a text box (or a combo box) for entry and storage of a truck number, position it on the accounts receivable screen, and establish rules for validating the data entered into it. Then, whenever the accounts receivable form is displayed, it will include a delivery-truck field ready for data entry.

Perhaps the most common use of data-driven programming is found when user controls are instantiated at runtime depending on selections made by the user. For example, two check boxes may appear on a screen. Checking the first one displays one set of controls underneath, and checking the second one displays a completely different set. Granted, you can accomplish this by creating group boxes or panels to act as containers for the appropriate controls created at design time. In this case, the group boxes are made visible and invisible as appropriate. In many scenarios, this suffices because the controls collections belong to either one set or another. Suppose, however, that the controls to be displayed form too many permutations to place all the possibilities in group boxes. Dynamic instantiation of the controls then makes sense, and the implementation is far simpler.

Report criteria screens are a prime candidate for data-driven techniques. They're also needed in almost every application. I've seen applications with more than 30 different reports that have an equal number of criteria forms created to support them. This is unnecessary. By storing the criteria definitions in a data source, you can pass the report ID to one criteria form that dynamically creates and populates the needed controls. One form can then support every report in the application.

You start your examination of data-driven programming by learning about database metadata and how to harness it. Then, you examine code generation, both by writing your own code-generation utilities and by using tools like CodeSmith. You also explore the code-generation namespace offered by

.NET, known as the CodeDOM, to learn how to create templates that generate language-independent code.

Database Metadata

To dynamically generate many data-driven applications, you need to retrieve data definitions from an RDBMS. If your application is table driven—that is, if it generates output for a given table—you can accomplish this by retrieving table and column information from your database's metadata tables. Given that SQL Server and Oracle are the most popular databases on the market, this section examines these RDBMSs in detail. This serves to illustrate that these techniques are RDBMS independent and that using them in something other than SQL Server isn't difficult.

SQL Server

SQL Server stores its metadata in a series of system tables that can be joined with one another to retrieve information about tables and columns. Before you go too far down this road, be aware that you can obtain the same information from INFORMATION_SCHEMA views, which provide a much simpler access method.

System tables such as sys.tables and sys.columns return the data that their names suggest. However, you likely need to JOIN them to achieve the results you're looking for. Suppose you want a list of the table names, column names, and data types of every column in a given table. You can obtain this information by creating a JOIN between the sys tables like this:

```
SELECT SCHEMA_NAME(t.schema_id) AS SchemaName, t.name AS TableName,
c.name AS ColumnName, y.name as type, c.max_length
FROM sys.columns c
LEFT OUTER JOIN sys.tables t ON c.object_id = t.object_id
LEFT OUTER JOIN sys.types y ON c.system_type_id = y.system_type_id
WHERE t.type = 'U'
ORDER BY TableName, c.column_id
```

This SQL produces the output shown in Figure 1-1.

	SchemaName	TableName	ColumnName	type	max_length
1	dbo	Categories	CategoryID	int	4
2	dbo	Categories	CategoryName	nvarchar	30
3	dbo	Categories	CategoryName	sysname	30
4	dbo	Categories	Description	ntext	16
5	dbo	Categories	Picture	image	16
6	dbo	CustomerCustomerDemo	CustomerID	nchar	10
7	dbo	CustomerCustomerDemo	CustomerTypeID	nchar	20
8	dbo	CustomerDemographics	CustomerTypeID	nchar	20
9	dbo	CustomerDemographics	CustomerDesc	ntext	16
10	dbo	Customers	CustomerID	nchar	10
11	dbo	Customers	CompanyName	nvarchar	80
12	dbo	Customers	CompanyName	sysname	80

Figure 1-1. SQL Server table and column metadata

Because the INFORMATION_SCHEMA views already perform these JOINs for you, you can obtain the same information like this:

```
SELECT TABLE_SCHEMA AS SchemaName, TABLE_NAME AS TableName,
COLUMN_NAME AS ColumnName, DATA_TYPE as type,
CHARACTER_MAXIMUM_LENGTH AS max_length
FROM INFORMATION_SCHEMA.COLUMNS
ORDER BY TABLE_NAME, ORDINAL_POSITION
```

This SQL produces the output shown in Figure 1-2.

	TABLE_SCHEMA	TABLE_NAME	COLUMN_NAME	DATA_TYPE	CHARACTER_MAXIMUM_LENGTH
1	dbo	Alphabetical list of products	ProductID	int	NULL
2	dbo	Alphabetical list of products	ProductName	nvarchar	40
3	dbo	Alphabetical list of products	SupplierID	int	NULL
4	dbo	Alphabetical list of products	CategoryID	int	NULL
5	dbo	Alphabetical list of products	QuantityPerUnit	nvarchar	20
6	dbo	Alphabetical list of products	UnitPrice	money	NULL
7	dbo	Alphabetical list of products	UnitsInStock	smallint	NULL
8	dbo	Alphabetical list of products	UnitsOnOrder	smallint	NULL
9	dbo	Alphabetical list of products	ReorderLevel	smallint	NULL
10	dbo	Alphabetical list of products	Discontinued	bit	NULL
11	dbo	Alphabetical list of products	CategoryName	nvarchar	15
12	dbo	Categories	CategoryID	int	NULL

Figure 1-2. SQL Server table and column metadata from the INFORMATION_SCHEMA view

As you can see, taking advantage of the INFORMATION_SCHEMA views is much easier. It does, however, have one drawback. INFORMATION_SCHEMA shows the maximum length values only for string data types. Other values show as NULL. This shouldn't be a burden, because the other data types have lengths that are specific to their data type and can't be changed.

WORKING WITH TABLE JOINS

If you need to generate output for the results of a JOIN between many tables, create a table structure that holds the structure of the JOIN results like this example from Northwind:

```
SELECT TOP 0 o.OrderID, o.OrderDate, c.CompanyName, e.LastName, e.FirstName
INTO MyStructure
FROM Orders o
LEFT OUTER JOIN Customers c ON o.CustomerID = c.CustomerID
LEFT OUTER JOIN Employees e ON o.EmployeeID = e.EmployeeID
WHERE e.EmployeeID = 5
```

You can then generate your code from the MyStructure table and DROP it when you're done.

Oracle

Like SQL Server, Oracle has its own metadata tables, which are made accessible by a series of views whose names begin with `all_`. You can see a list of these tables and views by running this command:

```
SELECT table_name, comments
FROM dictionary
ORDER BY table_name;
```

The Oracle Dictionary table contains the list of all tables and views. Figure 1-3 shows the list of the main metadata tables along with their descriptions.

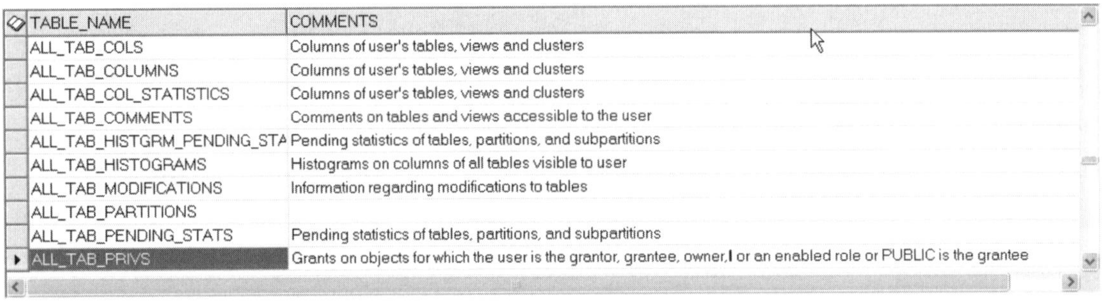

TABLE_NAME	COMMENTS
ALL_TAB_COLS	Columns of user's tables, views and clusters
ALL_TAB_COLUMNS	Columns of user's tables, views and clusters
ALL_TAB_COL_STATISTICS	Columns of user's tables, views and clusters
ALL_TAB_COMMENTS	Comments on tables and views accessible to the user
ALL_TAB_HISTGRM_PENDING_STA	Pending statistics of tables, partitions, and subpartitions
ALL_TAB_HISTOGRAMS	Histograms on columns of all tables visible to user
ALL_TAB_MODIFICATIONS	Information regarding modifications to tables
ALL_TAB_PARTITIONS	
ALL_TAB_PENDING_STATS	Pending statistics of tables, partitions, and subpartitions
ALL_TAB_PRIVS	Grants on objects for which the user is the grantor, grantee, owner,I or an enabled role or PUBLIC is the grantee

Figure 1-3. *Oracle table metadata*

The information for the various tables is stored in the `all_tables` view. You can extract the names and row counts of the sample employee tables (Oracle's equivalent of Northwind) belonging to the user `SCOTT` using this SQL:

```
SELECT table_name, num_rows
FROM all_tables
WHERE owner = 'SCOTT'
ORDER BY table_name;
```

The results of this query are shown in Figure 1-4.

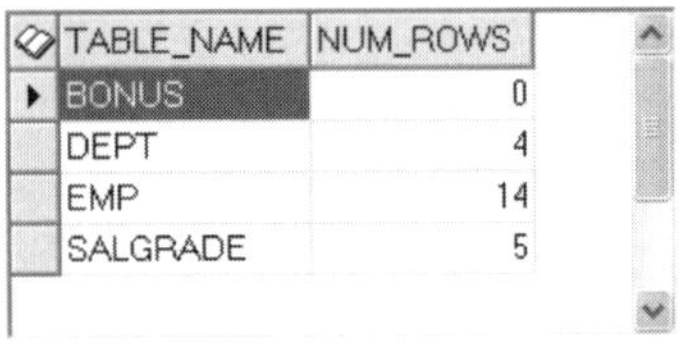

TABLE_NAME	NUM_ROWS
BONUS	0
DEPT	4
EMP	14
SALGRADE	5

Figure 1-4. *List of Oracle tables*

If you're generating code, you most likely require the details about the various columns of a table. This example returns the column name, data type, length, precision, and scale for the columns in the `EMP` table:

```
SELECT column_name, data_type, data_length, data_precision, data_scale
FROM all_tab_columns
WHERE table_name = 'EMP';
```

The output of this command is shown in Figure 1-5.

COLUMN_NAME	DATA_TYPE	DATA_LENGTH	DATA_PRECISION	DATA_SCALE
EMPNO	NUMBER	22	4	0
ENAME	VARCHAR2	10		
JOB	VARCHAR2	9		
MGR	NUMBER	22	4	0
HIREDATE	DATE	7		

Figure 1-5. Oracle column metadata

To extract information about constraints like primary keys and referential integrity rules, you can join the all_constraints and all_cons_columns tables. This SQL returns the output shown in Figure 1-6:

```
SELECT cc.table_name, cc.column_name, c.constraint_type
FROM all_constraints c
INNER JOIN all_cons_columns cc ON c.constraint_name = cc.constraint_name
WHERE cc.owner = 'SCOTT'
AND c.status = 'ENABLED'
ORDER BY cc.table_name, cc.position;
```

TABLE_NAME	COLUMN_NAME	CONSTRAINT_TYPE	
DEPT	DEPTNO	P	
EMP	DEPTNO	R	
EMP	EMPNO	P	

Figure 1-6 Oracle constraint metadata

You can perform the same operation for SQL Server via this SQL:

```
SELECT OBJECT_NAME(parent_object_id) AS TableName,
OBJECT_NAME(OBJECT_ID) AS ConstraintName,
type_desc AS ConstraintType
FROM sys.objects
WHERE type_desc LIKE '%CONSTRAINT'
```

Practical Applications

SQL Server metadata can provide data-driven solutions to many practical problems. Most developers work with at least three sets of data: production, test, and development. The problem with the latter two data sets is that the information in them becomes so mangled from testing and development efforts that you soon lose any semblance of comparison to real data. Moreover, if you need to have users perform evaluation testing against these mangled data sets, the users become frustrated when the data doesn't looks like what they've recently been working with.

It's very easy to back up and restore the production data over the test and development versions. The problem is that new tables, columns, views, and stored procedures would be overwritten by doing so. This section shows a data-driven stored procedure that copies the data from one server to another while leaving existing objects and structures intact.

The key idea is to determine which table/column combinations exist on both the source and the target, and then migrate the data in just those tables and columns. You must deal with a number of issues when you're migrating data in this fashion, especially when foreign key constraints enter the picture. First, you need to turn off the table constraints. This doesn't remove the constraints—it ignores them until they're turned back on so as to avoid any further unintended consequences. Likewise, if you have any triggers on your tables, you may wish to disable them as well. The final goal is to create a list of the SQL commands that will affect the migration. These commands are added to a temp table and then executed in sequence.

To begin, you must decide if any of the tables shouldn't be migrated. For example, user permissions tables probably aren't appropriate, because your permissions on the production database will be far less than those available for you on development. You can prepare a list of these table by creating a table variable and populating it, as shown in Listing 1-1.

Listing 1-1. Excluding Tables from Migration

```
DECLARE @SkipTables TABLE
(
   TableName varchar(100)
)
INSERT INTO @SkipTables (TableName) VALUES ('User_Permission')
```

Next, you can pull a list of all the constraints from the INFORMATION_SCHEMA view and suspend them by applying the NOCHECK option to them. You can accomplish this via the code in Listing 1-2.

Listing 1-2. Turning Off the Constraints

```
INSERT INTO #SQLtemp
   SELECT 'ALTER TABLE [' + SCHEMA_NAME(schema_id) + '].' +
OBJECT_NAME(parent_object_id) +
   ' NOCHECK CONSTRAINT ' + OBJECT_NAME(OBJECT_ID)
   FROM sys.objects
   WHERE type_desc LIKE '%CONSTRAINT'
```

Then, you need to delete the data in the target tables. Unfortunately, you can't use the TRUNCATE statement here because these tables may have foreign key constraints, and TRUNCATE doesn't work in these cases. You must perform the much slower process of DELETEing the data. You can create these commands via the SQL in Listing 1-3.

Listing 1-3. Deleting the Data in the Target Tables

```
INSERT INTO #SQLtemp
    SELECT 'DELETE FROM ' + t1.TABLE_SCHEMA + '.[' + t1.TABLE_NAME + ']'
    FROM INFORMATION_SCHEMA.tables t1
    INNER JOIN [PRODUCTION].[Contracts].INFORMATION_SCHEMA.tables t2
ON t1.TABLE_NAME = t2.TABLE_NAME
    WHERE t1.TABLE_TYPE = 'BASE TABLE'
    AND t1.TABLE_NAME NOT IN (SELECT TABLE_NAME
        FROM INFORMATION_SCHEMA.columns
        WHERE DATA_TYPE = 'xml')
    AND t1.TABLE_NAME NOT IN (SELECT TableName FROM @SkipTables)
    ORDER BY t1.TABLE_NAME
```

You only need to DELETE data from those tables that exist in both the source and target databases. Tables that don't exist in both are assumed to be works in progress and are left alone. Another major consideration is the issue of referential integrity. If there is, say, a Dictionary table that contains foreign key references to a series of other tables, those other tables must be deleted before the Dictionary table is deleted. Otherwise, a referential integrity error occurs. You can avoid this by using the extended properties of the table objects to establish a sort-order value so that objects like Dictionary tables are cleaned out last.

■ **Note** Tables with XML columns are excluded because of their inability to participate in distributed queries. Even pulling only the non-XML columns isn't permitted. You can handle such tables by creating views that pull all but the XML columns. By extracting the data from these views, you can successfully perform the migration.

Because your database may be quite large, you should speak with your DBA about allocating the required space or turning off the logging that accompanies such massive data deletions and inserts. You can easily exceed the allocated space for the database, in which case your migration will end in the middle. A data migration is normally far too large to wrap a transaction around for a rollback, so you're left with sections of your data missing. Although this example doesn't show it, you may wish to use SQL Server's e-mail features to send a message if the migration terminates before it completes.

After the data has been cleaned out of the target, the next step is to create a temp table of those tables and column combinations that exist in both databases. The code in Listing 1-4 performs this feat.

Listing 1-4. Creating a List of Table/Column Names

```
INSERT INTO #Tabletemp
    SELECT c1.TABLE_SCHEMA, c1.TABLE_NAME, c1.COLUMN_NAME
    FROM [Contracts].INFORMATION_SCHEMA.columns c1
    INNER JOIN INFORMATION_SCHEMA.tables t1 ON c1.TABLE_NAME = t1.TABLE_NAME
    INNER JOIN [PRODUCTION].[Contracts].INFORMATION_SCHEMA.columns c2
ON c1.TABLE_NAME +    c1.COLUMN_NAME = c2.TABLE_NAME + c2.COLUMN_NAME
    WHERE t1.TABLE_TYPE = 'BASE TABLE'
    AND c1.TABLE_NAME NOT IN (SELECT TABLE_NAME
```

```
     FROM INFORMATION_SCHEMA.columns
     WHERE DATA_TYPE = 'xml')
  AND c1.TABLE_NAME NOT IN (SELECT TableName FROM @SkipTables)
  ORDER BY c1.TABLE_NAME, c1.ORDINAL_POSITION
```

With this in place, you can iterate through each column in a given table to create a SQL statement that looks like this:

```
INSERT INTO Employees (EmployeeID, LastName, FirstName)
SELECT EmployeeID, LastName, FirstName
 FROM [SourceServer].[MyDB]. Employees WITH (NOLOCK)
```

If this table has an IDENTITY key, the INSERT..SELECT statement is preceded by SET IDENTITY_INSERT Employees ON and followed by SET IDENTITY_INSERT Employees OFF. This allows migration of the primary key column. Here, as well, the INSERT...SELECTs must be performed in a certain order so as to avoid referential integrity conflicts. Tables like the Dictionary example with all the foreign key pointers need to be populated first this time.

In the final step, you must turn all the constraints back on. Now that you have a temp table filled with all the SQL statements to perform a data migration, you can execute these SQL statements in sequence. The code in Listing 1-5 iterates through the SQL commands in the temp table and executes them one by one.

Listing 1-5. Executing Each SQL Statement in Turn

```
SELECT @Cnt = MAX(ID) FROM #SQLtemp

SET @x = 1

WHILE @x <= @Cnt
BEGIN

   SELECT @SQL = SQL
   FROM #SQLtemp
   WHERE ID = @x

   BEGIN TRY
     SET @StartTime = GETDATE()

     EXEC(@SQL)

     SET @ElapsedTime = DATEDIFF(SECOND, @StartTime, GETDATE())

     --Write every successfully executed SQL command to SyncLog
     INSERT INTO SyncLog
     (ErrorNumber, Message, SQL, ErrorDate, ElapsedTime)
     VALUES
     (Null, 'OK', @SQL, GETDATE(), @ElapsedTime)
   END TRY
   BEGIN CATCH
```

```
    SET @SQLError = @@ERROR

    --If an error was found, write it to the SyncLog table.
    --One of the most common errors will be caused by trying to insert a value
    --from a larger column into that of a smaller column. This will happen
    -- if you reduced the size of a column in your target to less than that of your
    -- source. In other cases, the data type may have changed
    --and this will throw an error as well.
    IF @SQLError <> 0
        INSERT INTO SyncLog
        (ErrorNumber, Message, SQL, ErrorDate)
        VALUES
        (@SQLError, Error_Message(), @SQL, GETDATE())
    END CATCH

    SET @x = @x + 1

END
```

For each table, the stored procedure executes SQL statements similar to those shown in Listing 1-6.

Listing 1-6. SQL Statements to Migrate Data

```
ALTER TABLE [dbo].MyTable NOCHECK CONSTRAINT PK_MyConstraint
DELETE FROM dbo.[MyTable]
SET IDENTITY_INSERT dbo.[MyTable] ON (if applicable)
INSERT INTO dbo.[MyTable] ([MyColumn1],[MyColumn2])
SELECT [MyColumn1],[MyColumn2]
FROM [MyServer].[MyDataBase].dbo.[MyColumn1]
SET IDENTITY_INSERT dbo.[MyTable] OFF (if applicable)
ALTER TABLE [dbo].MyTable CHECK CONSTRAINT PK_MyConstraint
```

Because this stored procedure is completely data-driven, it works with any SQL Server database. The only customization required is altering the name of the source server and database and enumerating the tables you wish to exclude.

Code Generation

Probably the most commonly used data-driven applications on the market today are code generators. A substantial amount of software development involves the creation of class wrappers, SQL statements, data-access methods, and variable initializations, and property accessors. Writing this code is a repetitive task that you can easily automate, because the code is a reflection of existing data structures.

Code-generation tools attach to data tables and, using the RDBMS's metadata, use data-driven techniques to output source code according to a template. You can then paste this code into your application and modify it as needed. A properly tuned code-generation template can produce about 80 percent of the code needed for a typical CRUD screen. You only need to add the data validation and business rules. The most popular commercial code generator is CodeSmith (www.codesmithtools.com); but if your needs are simple, you can very easily write your own.

Custom Code Generators

I once needed to generate class wrappers for a SQL Server application that had more than 200 user tables collectively containing thousands of fields. Each table needed its own class that held property wrappers for the various columns. The final code looked like Listing 1-7.

Listing 1-7. Code Generated from SQL Server Metadata

```
public class CustomerDemographics
{
    private string _szCustomerTypeID;

    public string CustomerTypeID
    {
        get { return _szCustomerTypeID; }
        set { _szCustomerTypeID = value; }
    }

    private string _szCustomerDesc;

    public string CustomerDesc
    {
        get { return _szCustomerDesc; }
        set { _szCustomerDesc = value; }
    }
}
```

To accomplish this, I pulled the data from the `INFORMATION_SCHEMA.COLUMNS` view and iterated the results, generating the source code in an ASCII file. Listing 1-8 shows the code that made this happen.

■ **Note** I use the Microsoft Enterprise Library here, mainly to save space by avoiding all the routine database code that would only get in the way of the example. You should use your favorite data-access technique to retrieve the data from the database. Also note the `CSharpDataType()` method. This is available in the code download; its function is fairly obvious and I didn't want to take up space with it.

Listing 1-8. Code Generator

```
SqlDatabase oDatabase;
DbCommand oDbCommand;
DataTable oDT;
string szTableName = string.Empty;
string szColumnName = string.Empty;
string szDataType = string.Empty;
string szSQL = @"SELECT TABLE_NAME, COLUMN_NAME,
```

```
                        DATA_TYPE, CHARACTER_MAXIMUM_LENGTH
                      FROM INFORMATION_SCHEMA.COLUMNS
                    ORDER BY TABLE_NAME, ORDINAL_POSITION";

oDatabase = new SqlDatabase("Data Source=(local);Initial catalog=OASIS;
Integrated security=SSPI");

oDbCommand = oDatabase.GetSqlStringCommand(szSQL);

oDT = oDatabase.ExecuteDataSet(oDbCommand).Tables[0];

using (StreamWriter oStreamWriter = new StreamWriter(@"c:\temp\source.cs"))
{
foreach (DataRow oDR in oDT.Rows)
{
    //if a new table, begin a class declaration
    if (szTableName != oDR["TABLE_NAME"].ToString())
    {
        //add a parens to close the previous class, but not
        //for the first one
        if (szTableName != string.Empty)
        {
            oStreamWriter.WriteLine("}");
            oStreamWriter.WriteLine(string.Empty);
        }

        szTableName = oDR["TABLE_NAME"].ToString();

        //declare the class
        oStreamWriter.WriteLine("public class " + szTableName);
        oStreamWriter.WriteLine("{");

    }

    szColumnName = oDR["COLUMN_NAME"].ToString();
    szDataType = oDR["DATA_TYPE"].ToString();

    //declare the internal class variable
    oStreamWriter.WriteLine("\tprivate " + CSharpDataType(szDataType) + " _" +
        CSharpPrefix(szDataType) + szColumnName + ";");

    //declare the property
    oStreamWriter.WriteLine("\tpublic " + CSharpDataType(szDataType) + " " +
        szColumnName);
    oStreamWriter.WriteLine("\t{");
    oStreamWriter.WriteLine("\t\tget { return _" + CSharpPrefix(szDataType) +
        szColumnName + "; }");
```

```
    oStreamWriter.WriteLine("\t\tset { _" + CSharpPrefix(szDataType) +
        szColumnName + " = value; }");
    oStreamWriter.WriteLine("\t}");
}

//close the last table class
oStreamWriter.WriteLine("}");

oStreamWriter.Flush();
oStreamWriter.Close();

}
```

In less than 100 lines of code, you can generate unlimited lines of source instructions with no effort, no variations from standards, and no bugs.

Commercial code generators function in a similar fashion. The advantage is that they're template driven so it's a bit easier to output code. The screen in Figure 1-7 shows the template to generate the same code using CodeSmith.

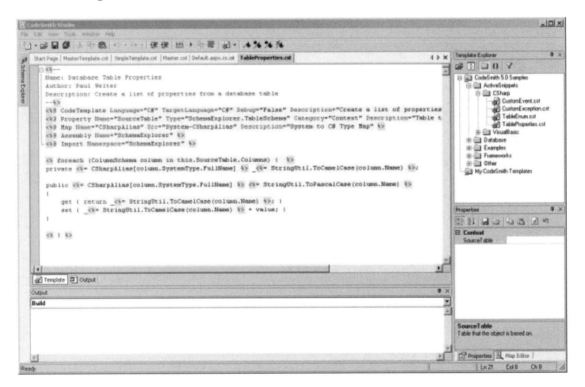

Figure 1-7 CodeSmith template

Although you can generate substantial amounts of code by writing your own code generator, CodeSmith ships with an object model that indicates things like primary and foreign keys. Armed with this information, you can implement the additional efficiencies that make code generation that much more worthwhile. If you know the primary keys to a table, you can, for example, create a perfect UPDATE statement because you know exactly what is needed for the WHERE clause. Granted, you can extract the primary key information from the metadata tables without CodeSmith, but using a code-generation tool shields you from dealing with all the plumbing needed to do this. Of course, when you start generating your own code, you'll most likely want to automate other tasks such as generating SELECT, INSERT, and UPDATE SQL, middle-tier classes, and user interfaces. Properly used, code generation can save you countless hours of development time and slash costs dramatically.

Using the CodeDOM

The System.CodeDom (DOM = Document Object Model) and System.CodeDom.Compiler namespaces encompass a series of classes that allow you to generate source code according to a language-independent template. The key advantage of doing it in this fashion is that you can easily output the code to C#, VB, C++, or any other language for which you possess the supporting language assemblies. These assemblies describe to the compiler the specific syntax of the language you wish to output.

Suppose you wish to offer your users a language-independent code generator that outputs code from a series of options they select in a rules screen. Rather than write an output generator that is customized for the syntax of every possible .NET language, you can use the CodeDOM to construct one syntax-independent template that generates the code based on the language you select. You may also wish to use the CodeDOM to generate proxy methods that bind parameters to stored procedures or, perhaps, generate web service methods for all the public methods in a class.

■ **Note** It's important to understand that the CodeDOM allows you to create a code framework. Because of its language independence, the code for setting up this framework can be complex. Although the code for setting up repetitive patterns like properties, methods declarations, constructor declarations, and variables assignments is simple, more involved coding constructs like if…else and for…next logic can get very hairy, as you see later in the chapter.

Namespaces, Classes, and Fields

Suppose you want to generate a simple abstract class named MyClass, contained within a namespace called CodeDOM, which has one private field called _szCustomerName. The goal is to generate a simple class declaration with one field, like that in Listing 1-9.

Listing 1-9. Generated Code

```
//------------------------------------------------------------------------------
// <auto-generated>
//     This code was generated by a tool.
//     Runtime Version:2.0.50727.1433
//
```

```
//      Changes to this file may cause incorrect behavior and will be lost if
//      the code is regenerated.
// </auto-generated>
//------------------------------------------------------------------------------

namespace CodeDOM
{
    using System.Data;

    public abstract class MyClass
    {

        // Name of the customer
        private string _szCustomerName;
    }
}
```

To output this code, you use the class in Listing 1-10. This CodeCreate class allows you to name a class, add as many fields as you wish, and output the code in the supported language of your choice. The header comments are automatically generated along with the code—you don't need to program them.

Listing 1-10. CodeCreate Class

```
class CodeCreate
{
    CodeCompileUnit oCodeCompileUnit;
    CodeTypeDeclaration oCodeTypeDeclaration;

    public CodeCreate()
    {
        oCodeCompileUnit = new CodeCompileUnit();
    }

    public void CreateNamespaceAndClass(string szNamespace,
                                        string szClassName,
                                        TypeAttributes sTypeAttributes)
    {
        //Create a new instance of the CodeNamespace object
        CodeNamespace oCodeNamespace = new CodeNamespace(szNamespace);

        //Make namespaces available to the code, the equivalent
        //of the "using" statement
        oCodeNamespace.Imports.Add(new CodeNamespaceImport("System.Data"));

        //Declare a CodeTypeDeclaration to create the class template, assign
        //it a name, indicate that it is indeed a class and set the attributes
        //as public and abstract. This is added to the CodeNamespace object which
```

```
        //in turn is added to the CodeCompileUnit object
        oCodeTypeDeclaration = new CodeTypeDeclaration();
        oCodeTypeDeclaration.Name = szClassName;
        oCodeTypeDeclaration.IsClass = true;
        oCodeTypeDeclaration.TypeAttributes = sTypeAttributes;
        oCodeNamespace.Types.Add(oCodeTypeDeclaration);
        oCodeCompileUnit.Namespaces.Add(oCodeNamespace);
    }

    public void AddField(MemberAttributes sMemberAttributes,
                         string szName,
                         string szComments,
                         string szType)
    {
        // Declare the field.
        CodeMemberField oCodeMemberField = new CodeMemberField();
        oCodeMemberField.Attributes = sMemberAttributes;
        oCodeMemberField.Name = szName;
        oCodeMemberField.Type = new CodeTypeReference(szType);
        oCodeMemberField.Comments.Add(new CodeCommentStatement(szComments));
        oCodeTypeDeclaration.Members.Add(oCodeMemberField);

    }

    public void GenerateCode(string szFileName, string szLanguage)
    {
        CodeDomProvider oCodeDomProvider =
            CodeDomProvider.CreateProvider(szLanguage);
        CodeGeneratorOptions oCodeGeneratorOptions = new CodeGeneratorOptions();
        oCodeGeneratorOptions.BracingStyle = "C";

        using (StreamWriter oStreamWriter = new StreamWriter(szFileName))
        {
            oCodeDomProvider.GenerateCodeFromCompileUnit(oCodeCompileUnit,
oStreamWriter, oCodeGeneratorOptions);
        }
    }

}
```

The main object, CodeCompileUnit, represents a code graph. A *code graph* is a structure that contains the outline of classes, methods, properties, fields, assignments, iterators, arrays, statements, and any other code construct you can imagine. In the CodeCreate class, the CodeCompileUnit object is instantiated in the constructor.

All the code generated after this is ultimately added to the CodeCompileUnit object. To create the namespace, instantiate the CodeNamespace object and pass the namespace name via its constructor. Then, instantiate a CodeTypeDeclaration object, set the IsClass property to true, set the name property to "MyClass", and add this to the `CodeNamespace` object's `Types` collection. The `CodeNamespace` object, in turn, is added to the `NameSpaces` collection of the `CodeCompileUnit` object. Thus, you wind up with a code hierarchy of `CodeCompileUnit` ➤ `CodeNamespace` ➤ `CodeTypeDeclaration`. The `CodeTypeDeclaration` in turn holds all the various parts of a class, such as fields, properties, constructors, and methods.

Next, to create the single field, invoke the `AddFields()` method, which accepts as parameters the attributes (public, private, and so on), the field name, the data type, and any inline code comments.

Finally, the `GenerateCode()` method outputs the code in the language of your choice. Notice that in setting up the code graph, no language-specific syntax is used. This is handled by the `CodeDomProvider` object. By instantiating `CodeDomProvider` with your choice of language passed via the constructor, the `GenerateCodeFromCompileUnit()` method knows how to write the appropriate syntax.

The `BracingStyle` property determines how the braces—{ }—are aligned in the code. Setting the value to "C" begins the braces on the line after the declaration they're associated with. Leaving this value at its default places the opening brace on the same line as its associated statement, like this:

```
public abstract class MyClass {
    // Name of the customer
    private string _szCustomerName;
}
```

If the `CodeCreate` class looks like a lot of code just to generate such a small amount of output, rest assured that you're only getting started. To generate this code, you invoke the class shown in Listing 1-11.

Listing 1-11. *Invoking CodeCreate*

```
CodeCreate oCodeCreate = new CodeCreate();

oCodeCreate.CreateNamespaceAndClass("CodeDOM",
    "MyClass",
    TypeAttributes.Public | TypeAttributes.Abstract);

oCodeCreate.AddFields(MemberAttributes.Private,
    "_szCustomerName",
    "Name of the customer",
    "System.String");

oCodeCreate.GenerateCode(@"c:\temp\SampleCode.cs", "CSharp");
```

Because the `CodeCompileUnit` object creates a graph, or code template, it maintains syntax neutrality; any supported language—that is, any language for which you have the assemblies—can be generated. Rather than use language-specific syntax to generate, say, VB code, you can change the "CSharp" parameter passed to `GenerateCode()` to "VB". Doing so creates the code in Listing 1-12 (shown minus the standard header comments).

Listing 1-12. *Visual Basic .NET Output*

```
Option Strict Off
Option Explicit On
```

```
Imports System.Data

Namespace CodeDOM

    Public MustInherit Class [MyClass]
        'Name of the customer
        Private _szCustomerName As String
    End Class

End Namespace
```
If you pass in "C++", you get the code in Listing 1-13.

Listing 1-13. C++ Output

```
#pragma once

#using <mscorlib.dll>

using namespace System::Security::Permissions;
[assembly:SecurityPermissionAttribute(SecurityAction::RequestMinimum,
    SkipVerification=false)];
namespace CodeDOM {
using namespace System::Data;
using namespace System;
ref class MyClass;

    public ref class MyClass abstract {
// Name of the customer
private: System::String^  _szCustomerName;
    };
}
```

Support Methods

The CodeDomCompiler offers several support methods to facilitate the runtime compile process. To determine what languages are supported by your .NET installation, execute the code in Listing 1-14.

Listing 1-14. Determining Supported Languages

```
CompilerInfo[] aCompilerInfo = CodeDomProvider.GetAllCompilerInfo();

foreach (CompilerInfo oCompilerInfo in aCompilerInfo)
{
    foreach (string szLanguage in oCompilerInfo.GetLanguages())
    {
        Console.WriteLine(szLanguage );
```

```
    }
}
```

This code should give you output similar to that shown in Figure 1-8.

Figure 1-8. *Supported .NET languages*

The GetAllCompilerInfo() method returns the various supported compilers; and for each compiler, the GetLanguages() method enumerates the different descriptors for the supported language. C#, for example, can be passed as *C#*, *CS*, or *CSharp*. VB can be *vb*, *vbs*, *visualbasic*, or *vbscript*.

To determine whether the specified language is supported, check the IsDefinedLanguage() method of CodeDomProvider like this:

```
if (!CodeDomProvider.IsDefinedLanguage("GW-BASIC"))
    Console.WriteLine("GW-BASIC Not supported");

if (!CodeDomProvider.IsDefinedLanguage("CSharp"))
    Console.WriteLine ("CSharp Not supported");
```

You can also perform a similar language support check by using a combination of the IsDefinedExtension() and GetLanguageFromExtension() methods:

```
string szExtension = "cs";

if (CodeDomProvider.IsDefinedExtension(szExtension))
    MessageBox.Show(CodeDomProvider.
        GetLanguageFromExtension(szExtension));
```

```
else
    Console.WriteLine ("Extension not recognized");
```

If you invoke the `GetLanguageFromExtension()` method by passing an invalid extension, you trigger a `ConfigurationErrorsException`.

In addition to checking whether specific languages are supported, you can also determine whether specific language features are supported for a given language. The `Supports` property of the `CodeDomProvider` accepts a `GeneratorSupport` enumerator and returns a Boolean to indicate whether that feature is recognized. Table 1-1 lists the members of the `GeneratorSupport` enumerator.

Table 1-1. GeneratorSupport Enumerator Members

Member	Supports…
ArraysOfArrays	Arrays of arrays.
AssemblyAttributes	Assembly attributes.
ChainedConstructorArguments	Chained constructor arguments.
ComplexExpressions	Complex expressions.
DeclareDelegates	Delegate declarations.
DeclareEnums	Enumeration declarations.
DeclareEvents	Event declarations.
DeclareIndexerProperties	Indexer property declarations.
DeclareInterfaces	Interface declarations.
DeclareValueTypes	Value type declarations.
EntryPointMethod	Program entry-point method designation.
GenericTypeDeclaration	Generic type declarations.
GenericTypeReference	Generic type references.
GotoStatements	Goto statements.
MultidimensionalArrays	Multidimensional array references. Currently, the CodeDOM can't be used to instantiate multidimensional arrays.

MultipleInterfaceMembers	Declaration of members that implement multiple interfaces.
NestedTypes	Nested type declarations.
ParameterAttributes	Parameter attributes.
PartialTypes	Partial type declarations.
PublicStaticMembers	Public static members.
ReferenceParameters	Reference and out parameters.
Resources	Compilation with .NET framework resources. These can be default resources compiled directly into an assembly, or resources referenced in a satellite assembly.
ReturnTypeAttributes	Return-type attribute declarations.
StaticConstructors	Static constructors.
TryCatchStatements	try...catch statements.
Win32Resources	Compilation with Win32 resources.

For example, in Listing 1-15, the Supports property is used to determine whether enumerations are supported. If they aren't, constants are output instead.

Listing 1-15. *Supports Property in Action*

```
if (oCodeDomProvider.Supports(GeneratorSupport.DeclareEnums))
{
    //output enums
}
else
{
    //output constants
}
```

It's possible to hard-code specific syntax using the CodeSnippetExpression object; but if you do so, you get hard-coded and therefore language-specific syntax. For example, if you create a method with the following directive

```
oCodeMemberMethod.Statements.Add(new
    CodeSnippetExpression("Dim szSQL AS String"));
```

then you get this line of VB code regardless of what output language you choose:

```
Dim szSQL As String
```

▪ **Note** I cover `CodeMemberMethod` in the "Methods" section.

Constants

You can declare constant values by adding `CodeMemberField` objects to the `CodeTypeDeclaration` that represents the class. These are class-level constants. Rather than add them individually, you can pass a generic `List<string>` to the `AddConstant()` method and iterate the members. Listing 1-16 shows how this is done.

Listing 1-16. Adding Constants

```
List<string> oList = new List<string>();

oList.Add("Car");
oList.Add("Bus");
oList.Add("Limo");
oList.Add("Tank");

public void AddConstants(List<string> oConstant)
{
    int iCnt = 0;

    //Iterate through the generic list. Instantiate a CodeMemberField
    //object for each constant value. Assign a sequential number as a value,
    //and indicate that it is a public constant that we desire
    foreach (string szConstant in oConstant)
    {
        CodeMemberField oCodeMemberField =
            new CodeMemberField(typeof(int), szConstant);
        oCodeMemberField.InitExpression =
            new CodePrimitiveExpression(iCnt++);
        oCodeMemberField.Attributes =
            MemberAttributes.Public | MemberAttributes.Const;
        oCodeTypeDeclaration.Members.Add(oCodeMemberField);
    }

}
```

This outputs the following code:

```
public const int Car = 0;
```

```
public const int Bus = 1;
public const int Limo = 2;
public const int Tank = 3;
```

Enums

You can add Enums in a fashion similar to constants. Rather than declare a series of free-standing CodeMemberFields, you first instantiate and name a CodeTypeDeclaration object and set IsEnum to true. Then, you add individual enumerator members to this object as CodeMemberFields, as shown in Listing 1-17.

Listing 1-17. Adding Enums

```
public void AddEnum(string szName, List<string> oEnums)
{
    //Instantiate a CodeTypeDeclaration and indicate that it is
    //for the creation of an enumerator.
     CodeTypeDeclaration oCodeTypeDeclarationEnum =
         new CodeTypeDeclaration(szName);
     oCodeTypeDeclarationEnum.IsEnum = true;

     int iCnt = 0;

     //Iterate through the generic list. Instantiate a CodeMemberField
     //object for each enum value. Assign a sequential number as a value,
     //and add the new enum value to the CodeTypeDeclaration Members collection

     foreach (string szEnum in oEnums)
     {
         CodeMemberField oCodeMemberField = new CodeMemberField();
         oCodeMemberField.Name = szEnum;
         oCodeMemberField.InitExpression =
             new CodePrimitiveExpression(iCnt++);
         oCodeTypeDeclarationEnum.Members.Add(oCodeMemberField);
     }

     oCodeNamespace.Types.Add(oCodeTypeDeclarationEnum);

}
```

Note that in this example, the CodeTypeDeclaration is being added to the CodeNamespace object. Doing so places the enum declaration within the namespace but before the class definition, as shown in Listing 1-18.

Listing 1-18. Generated Enumerations

```
namespace CodeDOM
```

```
{
   using System.Data;

   public enum Vehicle
   {
      Car = 0,
      Bus = 1,
      Limo = 2,
      Tank = 3,
   }
...
```

Properties

Having seen how to create a class stub and a single field, you now look at how to create a property. The code shown in Listing 1-19 shows the different options you can set when creating a property wrapper.

Listing 1-19. Creating Properties

```
public void AddPropertyMemberAttributes sMemberAttributes,
                      string szName,
                      string szComments,
                      string szType,
                      bool bHasGet,
                      bool bHasSet,
                      string szReturnField)
{
   //Instantiate a CodeMemberProperty object, indicate that this
   // is a public method, assign the name and indicate that it has
   //get and set accessors. Next, indicate the code that is associated
   //with these accessors.
   CodeMemberProperty oCodeMemberProperty = new CodeMemberProperty();
   oCodeMemberProperty.Attributes = sMemberAttributes;
   oCodeMemberProperty.Name = szName;
   oCodeMemberProperty.HasGet = bHasGet;
   oCodeMemberProperty.HasSet = bHasSet;
   oCodeMemberProperty.Type = new CodeTypeReference(szType);
   oCodeMemberProperty.Comments.Add(new CodeCommentStatement(szComments));
   oCodeMemberProperty.GetStatements.Add(new CodeMethodReturnStatement(
      new CodeFieldReferenceExpression(
      new CodeThisReferenceExpression(), szReturnField)));
   oCodeMemberProperty.SetStatements.Add(new CodeAssignStatement(
      new CodeFieldReferenceExpression(
      new CodeThisReferenceExpression(), szReturnField),
      new CodePropertySetValueReferenceExpression()));
   oCodeTypeDeclaration.Members.Add(oCodeMemberProperty);
```

```
}
```
This code produces the output in Listing 1-20.

Listing 1-20. Generated Property

```
// Comment goes here
public string CustomerName
{
    get
    {
        return this._szCustomerName;
    }
    set
    {
        this._szCustomerName = value;
    }
}
```

Setting the attributes, property name, data type, and comments are the same as for creating a field. Note that `CodeMemberProperty` has two Boolean properties called `HasGet` and `HasSet`. These determine whether the property is read-only, write-only, or read/write by generating the appropriate accessors. The hardest part is determining what goes on inside each of the accessors. The accessor code is managed by the `GetStatements` and `SetStatements` collections. In this case, you want to do the minimum you expect in a property. The `get` should return the value of the internal class field, and the `set` assigns the internal class field variable to `value`.

To set up the get accessor, you need to create a `CodeMethodReturnStatement` object that requires a `CodeFieldReferenceExpression` object as a parameter. This generates a `return` statement with a value following it. This object in turn requires an instance of a `CodeThisReferenceExpression` object as well as the name of the internal field. It assigns the name of the internal class equal to the value variable. After you set all this up, you output the following line:

```
return this._szCustomerName;
```

The `set` accessor is similar. You need to instantiate a `CodeAssignStatement` object because you're assigning one value to another. Then, create a `CodeFieldReferenceExpression` object, which takes as parameters a `CodeThisReferenceExpression` object instance and the name of the field. The second parameter of `CodeFieldReferenceExpression` is an instance of `CodePropertySetValueReferenceExpression`, which tells the `CodeDOM` to precede the field name with `this`. The output of these statements is

```
this._szCustomerName = value;
```

Methods

Creating a method is structurally similar to creating a property. Of course, methods are usually more complex than properties, and that complexity is reflected in the CodeDOM. Suppose you want to create a method called `DeleteCustomer()` that accepts a parameter called `iCustomerID`, which is then passed to a SQL statement that removes the customer's record from the database. The goal is to generate the code shown in Listing 1-21.

Listing 1-21. Generated DeleteCustomer Code

```
// Executes SQL that deletes a customer
public virtual void DeleteCustomer(int iCustomerID)
{
    string szSQL = "DELETE FROM";
    oDatabase.Parameters.Add(iCustomerID, "12345");
}
```

Obviously, this example is incomplete; this is necessary to keep it simple enough to show the features of the CodeDOM without exponentially increasing the amount of code. The AddMethod() method shown in Listing 1-22 shows how to output this code.

Listing 1-22. AddMethod Method

```
public void AddMethod(MemberAttributes sMemberAttributes,
                      string szName,
                      string szComments,
                      string szType)
{
    //Establish the structure of the method
    CodeMemberMethod oCodeMemberMethod = new CodeMemberMethod();
    oCodeMemberMethod.Attributes = sMemberAttributes;
    oCodeMemberMethod.Name = szName;
    oCodeMemberMethod.Comments.Add(new CodeCommentStatement(szComments));
    oCodeMemberMethod.ReturnType = new CodeTypeReference(szType);

    //Indicate the data type and name of the parameter
    oCodeMemberMethod.Parameters.Add(new
        CodeParameterDeclarationExpression("System.Int32", "iCustomerID"));

    //declare a variable within the body of the method that generates this line:
    //string szSQL = "DELETE FROM";
    CodeVariableDeclarationStatement oCodeVariableDeclarationStatement =
        new CodeVariableDeclarationStatement("System.String", "szSQL");
    CodeArgumentReferenceExpression oCodeArgumentReferenceExpression =
        new CodeArgumentReferenceExpression("\"DELETE FROM\"");
    oCodeVariableDeclarationStatement.InitExpression =
        oCodeArgumentReferenceExpression;
    oCodeMemberMethod.Statements.Add(oCodeVariableDeclarationStatement);


    //Generate code to add values to a collection. The result is this code;
    //oDatabase.Parameters.Add(iCustomerID, "12345");
    CodeVariableReferenceExpression oCodeVariableReferenceExpression =
```

```
        new CodeVariableReferenceExpression("oDatabase.Parameters");
    CodeMethodInvokeExpression oCodeMethodInvokeExpression =
        new CodeMethodInvokeExpression(oCodeVariableReferenceExpression, "Add");
    oCodeMethodInvokeExpression.Parameters.Add(
        new CodeVariableReferenceExpression("iCustomerID"));
    oCodeMethodInvokeExpression.Parameters.Add(
        new CodePrimitiveExpression("12345"));
    oCodeMemberMethod.Statements.Add(oCodeMethodInvokeExpression);

    oCodeTypeDeclaration.Members.Add(oCodeMemberMethod);
}
```

The `CodeMemberMethod` object encapsulates a method. Through its properties, you set the method's name, its return data type, and its attributes, and you write a brief source-code comment. Because the method requires a parameter, you can declare this by adding a `CodeParameterDeclarationExpression` object to its `Parameters` collection. Simply set the parameter's data type and name.

To write the code within the method, you need to declare a string variable called `szSQL` that is initialized to "DELETE FROM". To accomplish this, declare a `CodeVariableDeclarationStatement` object that receives the data type and the name of the variable as constructor parameters. Then, use the `CodeArgumentReferenceExpression` object to wrap the default value of "DELETE FROM". This is then set as the `InitExpression` on the `CodeVariableDeclarationStatement`. By adding this to the `Statements` collection of the `CodeMemberMethod`, the variable declaration is created with its default value.

The last section of the code passes values to a `Database` object. Here, you also need a `CodeVariableReferenceExpression` object to encapsulate the main object call of "oDatabase.Parameters". Because you need to invoke the `Add()` method of `oDatabase.Parameters`, you can do this via a `CodeMethodInvokeExpression` object and pass the text "Add". Because `CodeMethodInvokeExpression` is designed to wrap methods calls, it has a `Parameters` collection to receive the parameters passed to the method. In this case, you want to pass the `iCustomerID` value that is passed into the `DeleteCustomer()` method as well as a hard-coded string of "12345".

■ **Note** You may wonder why a simple piece of code like `oDatabase.Parameters.Add(iCustomerID, "12345");` needs to be wrapped in a series of nested objects, thereby increasing the complexity of the output line. The only difference between the generated code for this statement and most of the other supported languages is the addition of a semicolon at the end for C# and C++ support. Can't you use a `CodeSnippetExpression` object to output the entire line and then add a semicolon at the end if it's C#? The simple answer is yes, you can certainly do that, in this particular case. Because you probably use the CodeDOM to switch between VB and C# anyway, this is a viable option. Bear in mind, though, that some code changes internally, based on the output language. For example, `oDT.Rows(0).Fields("LName").ToString()` in VB becomes `oDT.Rows[0].Fields["LName"].ToString()` in C#. If you use `CodeSnippetExpression` to output such statements, you must have a well-tested method in place to handle the appropriate string-replacement logic. It's certainly possible, but be very careful.

Constructors

To add a custom constructor, use the `CodeConstructor` class. Because constructors are structurally very similar to methods, the code to generate them is similar as well. The code in Listing 1-23 shows how to create a constructor and pass an initialization parameter that is set to a field value of the class.

Listing 1-23. AddConstructor Method

```
public void AddConstructor()
{
   //Instantiate a CodeConstructor object
   CodeConstructor oCodeConstructor = new CodeConstructor();
   oCodeConstructor.Attributes =
       MemberAttributes.Public | MemberAttributes.Final;

  //Declare the constructor's parameter data type and name
   oCodeConstructor.Parameters.Add(new CodeParameterDeclarationExpression(
       typeof(System.Int32), "iInvoiceID"));

 //Set the field name
   CodeFieldReferenceExpression oCodeFieldReferenceExpression =
       new CodeFieldReferenceExpression(
       new CodeThisReferenceExpression(), "InvoiceID");

 //And set the variable containing the parameter to assign
 //to the Field.
   oCodeConstructor.Statements.Add(new
       CodeAssignStatement(oCodeFieldReferenceExpression,
       new CodeArgumentReferenceExpression("iInvoiceID")));

   oCodeTypeDeclaration.Members.Add(oCodeConstructor);
}
```

This method produces the code shown in Listing 1-24.

Listing 1-24. AddConstructor Method Output

```
public MyClass(int iInvoiceID)
{
   this.InvoiceID = iInvoiceID;
}
```

Source Code

Creating the structures of classes, fields, properties, methods, and constructors is straightforward. The code doesn't vary much, and it fits well in structured patterns so it can be wrapped in parameterized methods as shown previously. Things get complicated when you need to output the source code constructs that form the body of the methods. Because you have so many options, your CodeDOM structures become cumbersome. For example, suppose you want to create a simple `fornext` iteration with the goal of outputting the following code:

```
for (i = 1; (i < 5); i = (i + 1))
{
    MessageBox.Show(i.ToString());
}
```

This is how it appears in C#. If you choose VB as your language, you receive a `Do While` loop. To accomplish this, you must use the code in Listing 1-25.

Listing 1-25. Generating a Simple `fornext` Loop

```
CodeIterationStatement oCodeIterationStatement = new CodeIterationStatement(
    new CodeAssignStatement(new CodeVariableReferenceExpression("i"),
    new CodePrimitiveExpression(1)),
    new CodeBinaryOperatorExpression(new CodeVariableReferenceExpression("i"),
        CodeBinaryOperatorType.LessThan,
            new CodePrimitiveExpression(5)),
    new CodeAssignStatement(new CodeVariableReferenceExpression("i"),
        new CodeBinaryOperatorExpression(
            new CodeVariableReferenceExpression("i"),
                CodeBinaryOperatorType.Add,
                new CodePrimitiveExpression(1))),
    new CodeStatement[] { new CodeExpressionStatement(
        new CodeMethodInvokeExpression( new CodeMethodReferenceExpression(
    new CodeTypeReferenceExpression("MessageBox"), "Show" ),
        new CodeMethodInvokeExpression(
    new CodeVariableReferenceExpression("i"), "ToString" ) ) ) });
```

Crystal clear, right? Although you can simplify this code a bit by declaring some of the objects on separate lines, there's unfortunately no easy way to make it truly simple. Remember that you're creating a code graph that the `CodeDomProvider` can output into the syntax of your choice. Because you aren't marrying the template code to a particular syntax, you can only work with code structures. Every possible code construct has a method that wraps it. Because one code construct is often made up of other code constructs, each of which may be formed from still more code constructs, object references can be deeply nested. Imagine what the code would look like if this were a nested loop. Creating code templates of even moderate complexity is a difficult undertaking. You need to weigh the pros and cons of having code independence versus outputting language-specific code from a code generator.

Summary

This chapter discussed what data-driven programming is and why you use it. You examined how code generators work and how to use the metadata for SQL Server and Oracle to build your own. You also saw how to use the CodeDOM to create templates to output source code. The next chapter reviews the Reflection classes.

CHAPTER 2

Reflection

The .NET Reflection classes provide you with the ability to access the various types—classes, methods, properties, fields, attributes, events, and constructors—found within an assembly. Because dynamic programming often requires you to access code that won't be known to the application at compile time, knowledge of Reflection is vital to creating a data-driven application. This chapter explains how Reflection works and how you can use it in your data-driven projects. You review how to access the class structure of an application, instantiate classes and forms, set properties, and invoke methods—all at runtime.

Instantiating Classes

All managed code in a .NET application is compiled into assemblies, be they EXEs or DLLs. The key difference is that an EXE has an entry point from the operating system and a DLL doesn't. In all other respects, they're the same. You may need to access an assembly's internal structures at runtime, having had no knowledge of the names of the cases, properties, or methods available to you at compile time. Examine the `Invoice` class shown in Listing 2-1. This class would obviously have no real business value and is constructed solely to illustrate the various parts of Reflection.

Listing 2-1. Invoice Class

```
public interface IInvoice
{
    DateTime SaleDate {get; set;}
    double GetTotal();
}

public interface IMoreInvoice
{
    int SalesRepID { get; set;}
}

public delegate void UpdateEventHandler(object sender, EventArgs e);

public class Invoice : IInvoice, IMoreInvoice
{
```

```csharp
public int iInvoiceNumber;
public string szCustomerCode;

private DateTime _dSaleDate;
private int _iSalesRepID;

public DateTime SaleDate
{
    get { return _dSaleDate; }
    set { _dSaleDate = value; }
}

public int SalesRepID
{
    get { return _iSalesRepID; }
    set { _iSalesRepID = value; }
}

public Invoice()
{
}

public Invoice(DateTime dSaleDate, int iSalesRepID)
{
    dSaleDate = _dSaleDate;
    iSalesRepID = _iSalesRepID;
}

public event UpdateEventHandler Updated;

protected virtual void OnUpdated(EventArgs e)
{
    if (Updated != null)
        Updated(this, e);
}

public double GetTotal()
{
    return 150;
}

public double GetSalesTax()
{
    return 150 * .07;
}

public double ApplyDiscount(double dblDiscount)
```

```
    {
        return 150 * dblDiscount;
    }

}
```

If you had this class compiled in a .NET assembly and wanted to instantiate it at runtime, you could do so by loading the assembly and instantiating the string name of the class, as shown in Listing 2-2. Note that you can't strongly type the class as Invoice because you won't have access to this type definition at the time you write the code. The assumption is that this code will be compiled at runtime.

Listing 2-2 *Instantiating the Invoice Class at Runtime*

```
Assembly oAssembly;
Type oType;
object oInvoice;
oAssembly = Assembly.LoadFrom(@"C:\temp\Reflection.exe");
oInvoice= oAssembly.CreateInstance("ReflectionDemo.Invoice");
oType = oObject.GetType();
```

Here, you can use the LoadFrom() method of the Assembly class to load the assembly. The Assembly class, as its name suggests, represents a .NET assembly. The CreateInstance() method creates an instance of the class and returns it as type object. At this point, you can retrieve a Type object from this object instance; through this Type object, you can drill down into the class, as you see later in this chapter.

If the assembly were already loaded into your project, you could instantiate the Invoice object as follows:

```
Type oType;
object oInvoice;

oType = Type.GetType("ReflectionDemo.Invoice");
oInvoice = Activator.CreateInstance(oType);
```

The Activator class allows you to instantiate objects at runtime through its CreateInstance() method. Under normal circumstances, you strongly type an object reference as Invoice like this:

```
Invoice oInvoice = new Invoice();
```

But because you're building a data-driven application, you don't know the name of this object at compile time.

Loading Shared Assemblies

A *shared assembly* is one residing in the General Assembly Cache (GAC). You can locate these assemblies by browsing to c:\windows\assembly. There, you can see all the information needed to load any assembly you wish. Figure 2-1 shows some of the registered assemblies.

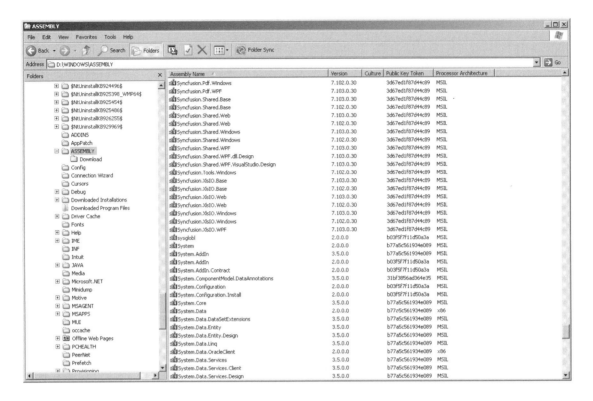

Figure 2-1. *Shared assemblies in the General Assembly Cache*

You can instantiate any one of these assemblies by using the Load() method of the Assembly object. In Listing 2-3, you obtain a Type reference to the Infragistics UltraListBar control.

Listing 2-3. *Referencing an Assembly in the GAC*

```
Assembly oAssembly =
                Assembly.Load(@"Infragistics2.Win.UltraWinListBar.v9.1,
                    Version=9.1.20091.1000,
                    PublicKeyToken=7dd5c3163f2cd0cb,
                    Culture = """);

Type oType = oAssembly.GetType("Infragistics.Win.UltraWinListBar.UltraListBar");
```

Examining Classes

When you have a Type object reference to your class, you can access its various components via the GetMethods(), GetFields(), GetProperties(), GetInterfaces(), GetConstructors(), and GetEvents() methods. Each of these methods is examined individually in the following sections.

Because the Reflection classes offer a rather labyrinthine layout of an assembly, this chapter focuses on the properties and methods you most use in dynamic programming.

Methods

The GetMethods() method returns an array of MethodInfo objects, each encapsulating a method of the class. The code in Listing 2-4 populates the tree view shown in Figure 2-2 with information about the class's methods.

Listing 2-4. *Retrieving Class Methods*

```
MethodInfo[] aMethodInfo = oType.GetMethods();

private void LoadMethods(MethodInfo[] aMethodInfo)
{
    TreeNode oTN;

    trvMethod.Nodes.Clear();

    foreach (MethodInfo oMI in aMethodInfo)
    {
        oTN = trvMethod.Nodes.Add(oMI.Name);

        oTN.Nodes.Add("IsAbstract: " + oMI.IsAbstract);
        oTN.Nodes.Add("IsGenericMethod: " + oMI.IsGenericMethod);
        oTN.Nodes.Add("IsPrivate: " + oMI.IsPrivate);
        oTN.Nodes.Add("IsPublic: " + oMI.IsPublic);
        oTN.Nodes.Add("IsStatic: " + oMI.IsStatic);
        oTN.Nodes.Add("IsVirtual: " + oMI.IsVirtual);
        oTN.Nodes.Add("ReturnType: " + oMI.ReturnType);

        if (oMI.GetParameters().Length > 0)
        {
            oTN = oTN.Nodes.Add("Parameters:");

        }

        foreach (ParameterInfo oPI in oMI.GetParameters())
        {
            oTN = oTN.Nodes.Add(oPI.Name);

            oTN.Nodes.Add("DefaultValue: " + oPI.DefaultValue);
            oTN.Nodes.Add("IsIn: " + oPI.IsIn);
            oTN.Nodes.Add("IsOut: " + oPI.IsOut);
            oTN.Nodes.Add("IsOptional: " + oPI.IsOptional);
            oTN.Nodes.Add("Position: " + oPI.Position.ToString());
```

33

```
        }

    }

    trvMethod.ExpandAll();
}
```

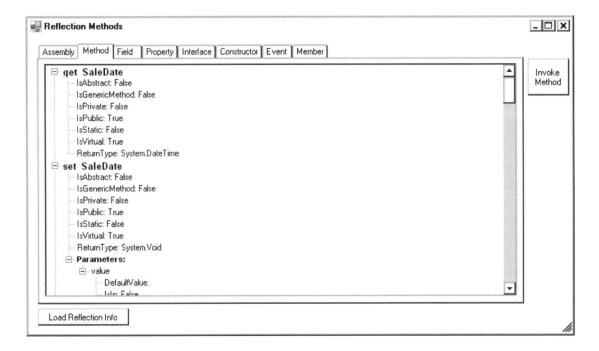

Figure 2-2. *Method information*

Note that several methods in the tree view weren't defined in the Invoice class. These methods—
GetType(), ToString(), Equals(), and GetHashCode()—are derived from System.Object, the base
class from which all classes, including Invoice, inherit by default. To restrict the method list to those
belonging to the Invoice class, pass the BindingFlags enumerators as follows:

```
MethodInfo[] aMethodInfo = oType.GetMethods(BindingFlags.Instance |
                                            BindingFlags.DeclaredOnly |
                                            BindingFlags.Public);
```

These enumerated values indicate that only public instance members declared at the level of the
supplied type's hierarchy should be considered. Inherited members aren't included. Further note that
there are get_ and set_ methods for each property. When you define a property, it's treated as a
method behind the scenes, and the compiler automatically creates get_ and set_ methods to
encapsulate the reading and writing of the associated field variable. You can execute class methods

accessed through Reflection via the Invoke() method. Suppose you wish to execute this simple parameterless method:

```
public double GetTotal()
{
    return 150;
}
```

The code in Listing 2-5 shows how to accomplish this.

Listing 2-5. Executing a Class Method

```
Type oType;
MethodInfo oMI;
object oInvoice;
object oResult;

oType = Type.GetType("ReflectionDemo.Invoice");
oInvoice = Activator.CreateInstance(oType);

oMI = oInvoice.GetType().GetMethod("GetTotal");
oResult = oMI.Invoke(oInvoice, null);
```

GetMethod() returns a MethodInfo object encapsulating the indicated method. Examining the contents of oResult, you see that it contains the hard-coded value 150. Suppose you need to pass a parameter value to a method. You do so via an argument array, as shown here:

```
object[] aParams = new object[1];
aParams[0] = .05;

oMI = oInvoice.GetType().GetMethod("ApplyDiscount");
oResult = oMI.Invoke(oInvoice, aParams);
```

When you execute this code, oResult contains 7.5. The Invoke() method returns values of type object because it has no knowledge of the type-specific values returned by the method.

Each method may accept multiple parameters. You can access these parameters via the GetProperties() method of the individual method object. This returns the structure of the method's parameter signature by enumerating each property, indicating its data type, whether it's an *in* or *out* parameter, whether the parameter is optional, and its ordinal position in the signature.

Fields

Fields are class-wide variables that, if declared public, can be accessed directly through an instance of the class. As a general rule, you should wrap such data access in properties. Normally, fields are declared private and serve as the internal storage mechanism for data within a class. Reflection gives you access to fields through the GetFields() method. Listing 2-6 shows how to extract them.

Listing 2-6. *Retrieving Class Fields*

```
FieldInfo[] aFieldInfo = oType.GetFields();
LoadFields(aFieldInfo);

private void LoadFields(FieldInfo[] aFieldInfo)
{
    TreeNode oTN;

    trvField.Nodes.Clear();

    foreach (FieldInfo oFI in aFieldInfo)
    {
        oTN = trvField.Nodes.Add(oFI.Name);


        oTN.Nodes.Add("IsPrivate: " + oFI.IsPrivate);
        oTN.Nodes.Add("IsPublic: " + oFI.IsPublic);
        oTN.Nodes.Add("IsStatic: " + oFI.IsStatic);
    }

    trvField.ExpandAll();
}
```

The output of this code is shown in Figure 2-3.

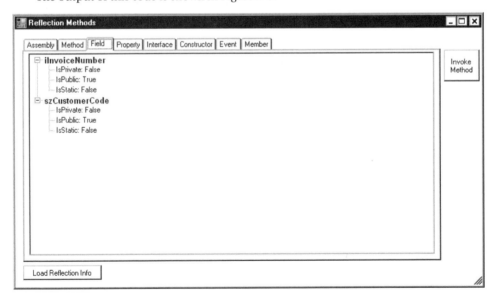

Figure 2-3. *Field information*

Properties

Properties are actually methods that allow access to internal data variables within a class. At compile time, .NET prepends get_ and set_ to the names of the properties and creates method wrappers for them. These accessor methods appear when you return the list of methods in an assembly. Listing 2-7 shows how you can display the properties in a class.

Listing 2-7. *Retrieving Class Properties*

```
PropertyInfo[] aPropertyInfo = oType.GetProperties();
LoadProperties(aPropertyInfo);

private void LoadProperties(PropertyInfo[] aPropertyInfo)
{
    TreeNode oTN;

    trvProperty.Nodes.Clear();

    foreach (PropertyInfo oPI in aPropertyInfo)
    {
        oTN = trvProperty.Nodes.Add(oPI.Name);

        oTN.Nodes.Add("CanRead: " + oPI.CanRead);
        oTN.Nodes.Add("CanWrite: " + oPI.CanWrite);
    }

    trvProperty.ExpandAll();
}
```

This example uses the GetProperties() method to display whether the properties are read/write, read only, or write only, depending on whether they have get only, set only, or get/set accessors defined. Figure 2-4 shows the results of this query.

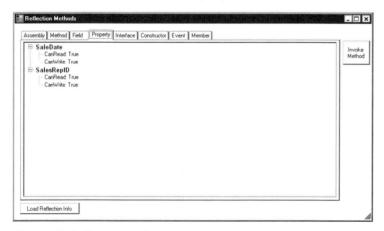

Figure 2-4. *Property information*

Interfaces

The GetInterfaces() method returns the interfaces used by the class. The code in Listing 2-8 returns the names of every associated interface.

Listing 2-8. *Retrieving Class Interfaces*

```
Type[] aInterfaces = oType.GetInterfaces();
LoadInterfaces(aInterfaces);

private void LoadInterfaces(Type[] aInterfaces)
{
    TreeNode oTN;

    trvInterfaces.Nodes.Clear();

    foreach (Type oType in aInterfaces)
    {
        oTN = trvInterfaces.Nodes.Add(oType.FullName);

    }

    trvInterfaces.ExpandAll();
}
```

Figure 2-5 shows the results of this query.

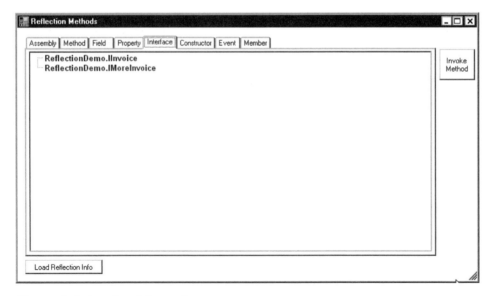

Figure 2-5. *Interface information*

Constructors

You can obtain a list of a class's constructors via the `GetConstructors()` method. There is no need to return the name of the constructor because in C# and VB, all constructors default to the name of their class. They only differ by their signatures. Even if you don't explicitly create a class constructor, a default parameterless constructor is created for you at compile time, so you'll always see at least one. Listing 2-9 shows how you can display the constructors in a class as well as their parameters.

Listing 2-9. Retrieving Class Constructors

```
ConstructorInfo[] aConstructorInfo = oType.GetConstructors();
LoadConstructors(aConstructorInfo);

private void LoadConstructors(ConstructorInfo[] aConstructorInfo)
{
    TreeNode oTN;
    TreeNode oSubTN;

    trvConstructors.Nodes.Clear();

    foreach (ConstructorInfo oCI in aConstructorInfo)
    {
        oTN = trvConstructors.Nodes.Add(oCI.Name);


        foreach (ParameterInfo oPI in oCI.GetParameters())
        {
            oSubTN = oTN.Nodes.Add(oPI.Name);

            oSubTN.Nodes.Add("DefaultValue: " + oPI.DefaultValue);
            oSubTN.Nodes.Add("IsIn: " + oPI.IsIn);
            oSubTN.Nodes.Add("IsOut: " + oPI.IsOut);
            oSubTN.Nodes.Add("IsOptional: " + oPI.IsOptional);
            oSubTN.Nodes.Add("Position: " + oPI.Position);
        }
    }

    trvConstructors.ExpandAll();
}
```

Figure 2-6 shows the results of this query.

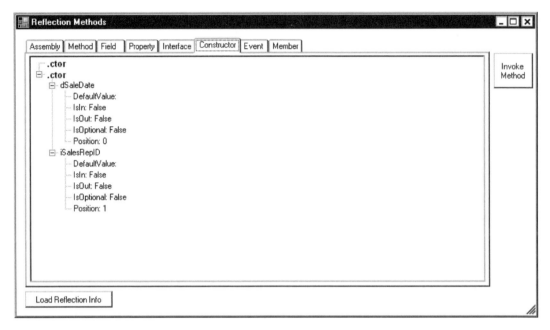

Figure 2-6. Constructor information

Events

GetEventInfo() returns a list of events exposed by the class. The code in Listing 2-10 displays the names of every associated event.

Listing 2-10. Retrieving Class Events

```
EventInfo[] aEventInfo = oType.GetEvents();
LoadEvents(aEventInfo);

private void LoadEvents(EventInfo[] aEventInfo)
{
    TreeNode oTN;

    trvEvents.Nodes.Clear();

    foreach (EventInfo oEI in aEventInfo)
    {
        oTN = trvEvents.Nodes.Add(oEI.Name);


        oTN = oTN.Nodes.Add(oEI.EventHandlerType.Name);
    }
```

```
    trvEvents.ExpandAll();
}
```

Figure 2-7 shows the results of this query.

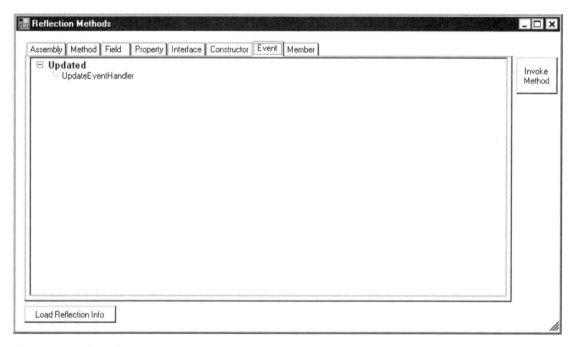

Figure 2-7. *Event information*

Drilling Down into Assembly Objects

Now that you've seen the types of data available through Reflection, you begin to understand the various uses to which it can be put. You can use Reflection to drill down into your assemblies and extract the entire object model. Without opening the source files of an application, Reflection shows you exactly what's inside it.

Building an Object Hierarchy

Suppose you want to display all the forms and controls in a given application. The goal is to produce a tree view like the one shown in Figure 2-8.

Figure 2-8. Hierarchy of objects within an assembly.

By using the Assembly object's GetTypes() method, you can iterate through all the objects and extract the different Forms. Then, you can instantiate these forms and iterate their Controls collections. The code is shown in Listing 2-11.

Listing 2-11. Building an Object Hierarchy

```
private void LoadObjects()
{
```

```csharp
        Assembly oAssembly = Assembly. LoadFrom(Application.ExecutablePath);
        Form oForm;
        TreeNode oTreeNode;
        string szName;
        string szBaseType;

        trvObjects.Nodes.Clear();

        try
        {
            foreach (Type oType in oAssembly.GetTypes())
            {
                szName = oType.FullName;

                if (oType.BaseType != null)
                {
                    szBaseType = oType.BaseType.Name;

                    if (szBaseType == "Form")
                    {
                        //Cast the object returned from CreateInstance
                        // to a Form in order to access the Controls collection
                        oForm = (Form)Activator.
CreateInstance(oAssembly.GetType(szName));

                        oTreeNode = trvObjects.Nodes.Add(oForm.Name);
                        DrillControls(oForm.Controls, oTreeNode);

                        oForm.Dispose();
                    }
                }

            }
        }
        catch (ReflectionTypeLoadException ex)
        {
            StringBuilder oExceptionSB = new StringBuilder();
            Exception[] aException = ex.LoaderExceptions;

            foreach (Exception oException in aException)
            {
                oExceptionSB.Append(oException.Message);
                oExceptionSB.Append("\n");
            }

            MessageBox.Show(oExceptionSB.ToString());
        }
```

```
        trvObjects.ExpandAll();
}
```

The `DrillControls` method, shown in Listing 2-12, recursively iterates through the `Controls` collection and adds each `Control` object's information to the tree view.

Listing 2-12. DrillControls Method

```
private void DrillControls(Control.ControlCollection oControls,
    TreeNode oTreeNode)
{
    TreeNode oSubTreeNode = null;
    string szControlType;

    foreach (Control oControl in oControls)
    {
        szControlType = oControl.GetType().Name;

        oSubTreeNode = oTreeNode.Nodes.Add(oControl.Name);

        if (oControl.HasChildren)
            DrillControls(oControl.Controls, oSubTreeNode);

    }
}
```

The `ReflectionTypeLoadException` object traps any errors associated with loading the assembly. Suppose there are a number of DLL dependencies for the EXE, and these DLLs are nowhere to be found. In this case, a `ReflectionTypeLoadException` error is thrown and the error object queried to determine which DLLs are missing in action.

This code is generic and won't work with many applications without modification for two reasons. First, the `BaseType.Name` property only returns *Form* if the object inherits from `Form` directly and not from some base form. You need to iterate through the `BaseType` ancestry to determine whether a `Form` object is found, because even a custom base `Form` eventually needs to inherit from a `Form` object. The code to perform this iteration is shown in Listing 2-13.

Listing 2-13. Determine an Object's Ultimate BaseType

```
private string GetBaseType(Type oType)
{
    Type oTypeInfo = oType.BaseType;
    string szResult = string.Empty;

    while (szResult != "Form" && szResult != "UserControl")
    {
```

```
        oTypeInfo = oType.BaseType;

        oType = oTypeInfo;

        if (oTypeInfo == null)
            break;

        if (oType.Name == "Form" || oType.Name == "UserControl")
        {
            szResult = oType.Name;
            break;
        }
    }

    return szResult;
}
```

The second problem is the instantiation of the Form itself. This code doesn't take into account any constructor parameters. If these are required, then you need to know what they are and supply them, or the code will throw an error. Ideally, each Form object has a parameterless constructor to allow the Reflection to function. The only reason you need to instantiate the Form is to obtain access to its Controls collection.

Importing Control Definitions

You may have an existing application that you wish to make data driven. You can accomplish this in one of two ways. You can set up the XML tags node (or database entries) form by form and control by control by entering their property settings individually. Clearly, this is a tedious and time-consuming process, and in a larger project it might trigger a nervous breakdown. Alternatively, you can use Reflection to iterate through the various Forms and their Controls collections programmatically, extracting the properties you need and storing them in a data source.

Suppose you have an application that has multiple forms, and you want to pick and choose which ones should be migrated to the data source. You can use Reflection to extract all the Form objects in the application and present them in a CheckedListBox, as shown in Figure 2-9.

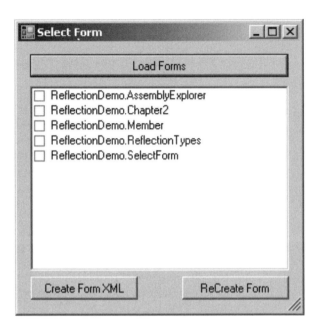

Figure 2-9. *Form objects within an assembly.*

The code to accomplish this is shown in Listing 2-14.

Listing 2-14. *Extract All Form Objects*

```
private void LoadForms()
{
    Assembly oAssembly = Assembly.LoadFrom(Application.ExecutablePath);
    string szName;

    foreach (Type oType in oAssembly.GetTypes())
    {
        szName = oType.FullName;

        if (oType.BaseType != null)
        {
            if (oType.BaseType.Name == "Form")
                lstForms.Items.Add(szName);
        }
    }
}
```

Next, you can select which forms you wish to migrate. Chapter 8 discusses the various ways you can store your control definitions, but here you use the most flexible way: XML. Because controls exist in a hierarchy, their definitions must be extracted using a recursive method. The goal is to produce XML for a selected form with the form's properties and each control definition nested underneath. The final output looks like Listing 2-15.

Listing 2-15. XML Form Object Representation

```
<Forms>
  <Form name="Members" text="Member Information" width="387"
      height="420" top="0" left="0">
    <Controls>
        <Control name="chkActive" type="CheckBox" width="56"
            height="17" top="9" left="295" text="Active" />
        <Control name="groupBox1" type="GroupBox" width="274"
            height="94" top="32" left="5" text="Address">
        <Control name="cmbState" type="ComboBox" width="209"
            height="21" top="70" left="59" dropdownstyle="DropDown" />
        <Control name="label6" type="Label" width="35"
            height="13" top="73" left="10" text="State:" />
        <Control name="txtCity" type="TextBox" width="209"
            height="20" top="45" left="59" />
        <Control name="label5" type="Label" width="27"
            height="13" top="48" left="10" text="City:" />
        <Control name="txtAddress" type="TextBox" width="209"
            height="20" top="19" left="59" />
        <Control name="label4" type="Label" width="48"
            height="13" top="22" left="10" text="Address:" />
      </Control>
      <Control name="txtMember" type="TextBox" width="199"
          height="20" top="6" left="80" />
      <Control name="label1" type="Label" width="79"
          height="13" top="9" left="2" text="Member Name:" />
      <Control name="cmdSave" type="Button" width="75"
          height="23" top="41" left="295" text="Save" />
      <Control name="cmdClose" type="Button" width="75"
          height="23" top="70" left="295" text="Close" />
      <Control name="tabControl1" type="TabControl" width="374"
          height="258" top="132" left="5">
        <Control name="tabPage1" type="TabPage" width="366"
            height="232" top="22" left="4" text="Contracts">
        <Control name="lstOptions" type="CheckedListBox" width="218"
            height="169" top="58" left="7" />
        <Control name="cmbVendor" type="ComboBox" width="166"
            height="21" top="16" left="59" dropdownstyle="DropDown" />
        <Control name="label2" type="Label" width="44"
            height="13" top="17" left="13" text="Vendor:" />
      </Control>
      <Control name="tabPage2" type="TabPage" width="366"
```

```
            height="232" top="22" left="4" text="Orders">
          <Control name="label3" type="Label" width="62"
            height="13" top="13" left="10" text="Order Date:" />
          <Control name="txtOrderDate" type="DateTimePicker" width="126"
            height="20" top="9" left="78" />
        </Control>
      </Control>
    </Controls>
  </Form>
</Forms>
```

The code to extract this XML is shown in Listing 2-16, which extracts the first Form selected on the list box and exports its structure to XML. Here, though, each form is instantiated to gain access to its Controls collection. In this example, you're interested in saving the name, title bar text, and dimensions of each form.

Listing 2-16. *Extracting Form Properties*

```
private void Form2XML()
{
    Assembly oAssembly = Assembly.LoadFrom(Application.ExecutablePath);
    Form oForm;
    XmlDocument oXmlDocument = new XmlDocument();
    XmlNode oXMLFormsNode;
    XmlNode oXMLControlsNode;
    XmlAttribute oXmlAttribute;
    XmlDeclaration oXmlDeclaration;
    string szBaseType;

    oXmlDeclaration = oXmlDocument.CreateXmlDeclaration("1.0", "UTF-8", null);

    oXmlDocument.AppendChild(oXmlDeclaration);

    oXMLFormsNode = oXmlDocument.CreateNode(XmlNodeType.Element,
        "Forms", string.Empty);
    oXmlDocument.AppendChild(oXMLFormsNode);

    foreach (object oItem in lstForms.CheckedItems)
    {
        string szName = oItem.ToString();

        foreach (Type oType in oAssembly.GetTypes())
        {
            if (oType.BaseType != null && oType.FullName == szName)
            {
                szBaseType = oType.BaseType.Name;
```

```
                if (szBaseType == "Form")
                {
                    XmlNode oXMLFormNode =
oXmlDocument.CreateNode(XmlNodeType.Element,
                        "Form", string.Empty);
                    oXMLFormsNode.AppendChild(oXMLFormNode);

                    oForm = (Form)Activator.
CreateInstance(oAssembly.GetType(szName));

                    oXmlAttribute = oXmlDocument.CreateAttribute("name");
                    oXmlAttribute.Value = oForm.Name;
                    oXMLFormNode.Attributes.Append(oXmlAttribute);

                    oXmlAttribute = oXmlDocument.CreateAttribute("text");
                    oXmlAttribute.Value = oForm.Text;
                    oXMLFormNode.Attributes.Append(oXmlAttribute);

                    oXmlAttribute = oXmlDocument.CreateAttribute("width");
                    oXmlAttribute.Value = oForm.Width.ToString();
                    oXMLFormNode.Attributes.Append(oXmlAttribute);

                    oXmlAttribute = oXmlDocument.CreateAttribute("height");
                    oXmlAttribute.Value = oForm.Height.ToString();
                    oXMLFormNode.Attributes.Append(oXmlAttribute);

                    oXmlAttribute = oXmlDocument.CreateAttribute("top");
                    oXmlAttribute.Value = oForm.Top.ToString();
                    oXMLFormNode.Attributes.Append(oXmlAttribute);

                    oXmlAttribute = oXmlDocument.CreateAttribute("left");
                    oXmlAttribute.Value = oForm.Left.ToString();
                    oXMLFormNode.Attributes.Append(oXmlAttribute);

                    oXMLControlsNode = oXmlDocument.CreateNode(XmlNodeType.Element,
                        "Controls", string.Empty);
                    oXMLFormNode.AppendChild(oXMLControlsNode);

                    DrillControls(oForm.Controls, oXmlDocument, oXMLControlsNode);

                    oForm.Dispose();
                }
            }
        }
    }
    oXmlDocument.Save(Application.StartupPath + @"\forms.xml");
}
```

Because this code instantiates a Form to obtain its properties, you may need to make some adjustments to the original source. If the Form's constructor requires parameters, you must supply them; or, if possible, you can modify the source application to provide each Form with a parameterless constructor. Moreover, you need to consider whether there are any dynamically instantiated controls on the Form. When you instantiate a Form object, you fire its constructor but not its Load event. There is no need to load the forms. Rather, you need instances of them in order to obtain their information. Ideally, dynamically instantiated controls on the form should be defined in its constructor and created along with those generated by Visual Studio in the InitializeComponent() method. However, the original developer may be instantiating dynamic controls in the Load event. If this is the case, these controls don't exist when the Form object is created.

After you have a Form object, access to its Controls collection is simply a matter of referencing the Form.Controls property. Listing 2-17 shows how to accomplish this.

Listing 2-17. Extracting the Controls Collection

```
private void DrillControls(Control.ControlCollection oControls,
    XmlDocument oXmlDocument, XmlNode oXMLControlsNode)
{
    XmlAttribute oXmlAttribute;
    XmlNode oXMLControlNode;
    string szControlType;

    foreach (Control oControl in oControls)
    {
        szControlType = oControl.GetType().Name;

        oXMLControlNode = oXmlDocument.CreateNode(XmlNodeType.Element,
            "Control", string.Empty);
        oXMLControlsNode.AppendChild(oXMLControlNode);

        oXmlAttribute = oXmlDocument.CreateAttribute("name");
        oXmlAttribute.Value = oControl.Name;
        oXMLControlNode.Attributes.Append(oXmlAttribute);

        oXmlAttribute = oXmlDocument.CreateAttribute("type");
        oXmlAttribute.Value = oControl.GetType().Name;
        oXMLControlNode.Attributes.Append(oXmlAttribute);

        oXmlAttribute = oXmlDocument.CreateAttribute("width");
        oXmlAttribute.Value = oControl.Width.ToString();
        oXMLControlNode.Attributes.Append(oXmlAttribute);

        oXmlAttribute = oXmlDocument.CreateAttribute("height");
        oXmlAttribute.Value = oControl.Height.ToString();
        oXMLControlNode.Attributes.Append(oXmlAttribute);
```

```
oXmlAttribute = oXmlDocument.CreateAttribute("top");
oXmlAttribute.Value = oControl.Top.ToString();
oXMLControlNode.Attributes.Append(oXmlAttribute);

oXmlAttribute = oXmlDocument.CreateAttribute("left");
oXmlAttribute.Value = oControl.Left.ToString();
oXMLControlNode.Attributes.Append(oXmlAttribute);

if (szControlType == "CheckBox" ||
    szControlType == "Button" ||
    szControlType == "Label" ||
    szControlType == "GroupBox" ||
    szControlType == "TabPage")
{
    oXmlAttribute = oXmlDocument.CreateAttribute("text");
    oXmlAttribute.Value = oControl.Text.ToString();
    oXMLControlNode.Attributes.Append(oXmlAttribute);
}

if (szControlType == "ComboBox")
{
    oXmlAttribute = oXmlDocument.CreateAttribute("dropdownstyle");
    oXmlAttribute.Value = ((ComboBox) oControl).DropDownStyle.ToString();
    oXMLControlNode.Attributes.Append(oXmlAttribute);
}

if (oControl.HasChildren)
    DrillControls(oControl.Controls, oXmlDocument, oXMLControlNode);

    }
}
```

Here, you recursively navigate the controls. Because each control has a name, a type, and width, height, top, and left dimensions, these attributes can be assigned to all of them. Certain properties, however, are only appropriate for certain controls, and you must handle them separately. The Text property only pertains to the CheckBox, Button, Label, GroupBox, and TabPage controls, so these are singled out for that property. The DropDownStyle property is specific to the ComboBox, so it's extracted only from that control.

▓ **Note** Because Reflection is used to extract form and control definitions into a data source, this process is covered here. Re-creating a user interface from these definitions is covered in Chapters 4, 5, and 6, depending on the type of interface you're building.

Decompiling Source Code

Although Reflection allows you to drill down into the structure of your assemblies, it doesn't take you as far as the source-code level. When a .NET program is compiled, the source code you write is compiled to Intermediate Language (IL) code. This IL is executed by the Common Language Runtime (CLR) when the application is run. Microsoft directly provides a way for you to see this IL code in the form of the Intermediate Language Disassembler (ILDASM) that ships with the .NET Framework SDK. You can find `ildasm.exe` at `\Program Files\Microsoft SDKs\Windows\v7.0A\bin`. If you run this utility and open the `reflection.exe` application in which the source code from this chapter is stored, your screen should look like Figure 2-10.

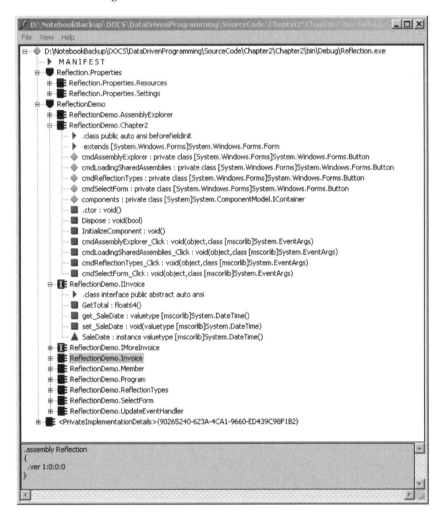

Figure 2-10. ILDASM.exe

From here, you can drill down into the individual properties and methods of your classes. If you open the Invoice class, you can double-click the ApplyDiscount() method and see the IL code it consists of. That code is shown in Listing 2-18.

Listing 2-18. *Retrieving Class Events*

```
.method public hidebysig instance float64
        ApplyDiscount(float64 dblDiscount) cil managed
{
  // Code size       17 (0x11)
  .maxstack  2
  .locals init ([0] float64 CS$1$0000)
  IL_0000:  nop
  IL_0001:  ldc.r8        150.
  IL_000a:  ldarg.1
  IL_000b:  mul
  IL_000c:  stloc.0
  IL_000d:  br.s          IL_000f
  IL_000f:  ldloc.0
  IL_0010:  ret
} // end of method Invoice::ApplyDiscount
```

It's all well and good that you can see the IL code; but if you're like most developers (myself included), you can't make much sense of it. The trick is to translate this back to .NET source. You could accomplish this by mastering the IL syntax and performing the translation manually. Microsoft provides documentation for the IL syntax, and you could write a converter tool to do this. This, however, isn't a task for the faint of heart and probably not worth your while unless you're developing programmer's tools. A better approach is to use a third-party tool like Red Gate Software's .NET Reflector. Reflector is a free tool, originally developed by Lutz Roeder of Microsoft, that has been enhanced by Red Gate. You can download it at http://www.red-gate.com/products/reflector/. After it's loaded, navigate to your assembly just as you did with ILDASM, and select the ApplyDiscount() method; you see the source code for it as shown in Figure 2-11.

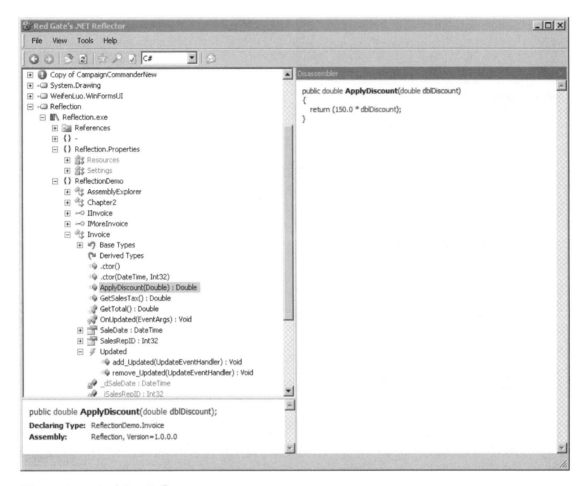

Figure 2-11. Red Gate Reflector

At this point, you may wonder how your production code can be kept safe from prying eyes. Unfortunately, there is no perfect answer to this. Tools called *obfuscators* can make the IL code many orders of magnitude more difficult to decompile than that produced by the compiler directly. Still, these tools aren't foolproof. If a hacker is determined enough, your source code can still be compromised.

An obfuscator performs a series of tasks that make the source code nearly impossible for a human to understand but perfectly acceptable to .NET's just-in-time compiler. (Of course, I've seen many an application where the developers created their own unreadable code, but that's a topic for another book. See www.thedailywtf.com for some fun examples.) One obfuscation approach is to rename methods and variables. Names like X2Er and uyer23iutgi make much less sense than ComputeDiscount and ApplyCommission.

The biggest drawback to obfuscation is that it can break code that depends on Reflection and remoting. It can also make runtime errors more difficult to debug. Just to confuse things further, multiple unrelated methods with different parameter signatures may be given the same name so as to take advantage of method overloading. Thus, ComputeDiscount and ApplyCommission(int iEmployeeID) may be both be renamed gad8f8j. Some obfuscators alter the code itself. Visual Basic code may have goto statements added instead of method calls, to make the code messier. Strings are encrypted, because they're easy clues for hackers. If you have a "Password" string embedded in your code, for example, the obfuscator transforms it into an unreadable mess that makes no sense to a human reader.

Several obfuscator tools are on the market, both commercial and freeware. I've used Eazfuscator.NET on some projects with success. You can download this tool here: http://www.foss.kharkov.ua/g1/projects/eazfuscator/dotnet/Default.aspx. .NET 4.0 will ship with Dotfuscator software services from Preemptive Solutions. The shipping version—the Community Edition—performs the basics of obfuscation and isn't aimed at professional developers. You must register to obtain the Enhanced Edition, which provides commercial-grade obfuscation.

To get an idea of what an obfuscator does, examine the code in Listing 2-19. Then, compare it to its obfuscated counterpart in Listing 2-20.

Listing 2-19. Before Obfuscation

```
private void cmdGo_Click(object sender, EventArgs e)
{
    int limit = 1000;
    int num = 2;
    int div;
    // first prime is 2 (1 is not a prime)
    lstPrimes.Items.Add(num.ToString());

    // only odd numbers need to be checked
    for (num = 3; num <= limit; num += 2)
    {
        // prime test loop
        for (div = 3; num % div != 0; div += 2) ;
        {
            if (div == num)
                // add prime to listbox
                lstPrimes.Items.Add(num.ToString());
        }
    }
}
```

Listing 2-20. After Obfuscation, Showing Basic Obfuscation Features

```
private void a(object A_0, EventArgs A_1)
{
    int num = 0x3e8;
    int num2 = 2;
    this.c.Items.Add(num2.ToString());
    for (num2 = 3; num2 <= num; num2 += 2)
    {
```

```
            int num3 = 3;
            while ((num2 % num3) != 0)
            {
                num3 += 2;
            }
            if (num3 == num2)
            {
                this.c.Items.Add(num2.ToString());
            }
        }
    }
}
```

One of the `for` loops was changed to a `while` loop, and the variables were renamed. In addition, the `limit` variable value was changed to a hexadecimal representation.

Listing 2-21 shows an example of obfuscated code generated by Eazfuscator.NET. Here, the code is far more scrambled. You can accomplish this by running the Eazfuscator.NET Assistant and dragging the project from the Solution Explorer. Then, reference `System.Reflection`, and add the following line after the using statements:

```
[assembly: Obfuscation(Feature =
"encrypt symbol names with password MyPass", Exclude = false)]
```

Listing 2-21. *Code Obfuscated by Eazfuscator.NET*

```
private void #=qLSjLAAKaI8XuRkwa3qkaoA==
(object #=qxmXifN7uOrHluI3KRCXsbQ==,
EventArgs #=qkvuzTWdDsZgFg8edzs4qoA==)
{
    int num = 0x3e8;
    int num2 = 2;
    this.#=qnaRFEoB6dZK3rOFvQy_ybg==
.Items.Add(num2.ToString());
    for (num2 = 3; num2 <= num; num2 += 2)
    {
        int num3 = 3;
        while ((num2 % num3) != 0)
        {
            num3 += 2;
        }
        if (num3 == num2)
        {
            this.#=qnaRFEoB6dZK3rOFvQy_ybg==
.Items.Add(num2.ToString());
        }
    }
}
```

Summary

This chapter covered the Reflection classes and how to use them to determine the composition of an assembly. You specifically examined how to extract the structure of a Form into an XML structure for later reassembly. In addition, you reviewed how to decompile .NET source code and what tools are available to prevent others from doing the same to your code. The next chapter covers runtime source code compilation.

CHAPTER 3

■ ■ ■

Runtime Code Compilation

One of the most powerful tools offered by .NET is the ability to compile and execute source code at runtime. The .NET Framework comes with C# and VB.NET compiler classes that expose the functionality of the .NET compiler and allow you to retrieve source code as a string from, say, an XML file or a database, compile it into an assembly, and execute it at runtime. This power lets you make your application as flexible as possible by applying changes to its functionality at runtime.

This chapter focuses largely on the `System.CodeDom.Compiler` namespace, which encapsulates the runtime compilers for the .NET languages. You examine how to references external DLLs, identify controls on a form, and perform proper testing.

System.CodeDom.Compiler Namespace

The `System.CodeDom.Compiler` namespace contains all the functionality you need to compile source code dynamically. There are several reasons you may wish to do this. In systems where users can define their own data-entry fields, you may also wish to let them define their own validation logic. You can accomplish this by building a user interface to a rules-based engine that checks for a predetermined number of scenarios. This can be presented as a wizard that prompts the user for, say, a range of values between x and y or perhaps greater than/less than a certain value. If the rule is violated during data entry, a message box appears. Such a wizard is shown in Figure 3-1.

Figure 3-1. Validation Rules Wizard

Although a wizard can be a powerful tool, its fixed interface doesn't allow coverage of every validation possibility. This is where you can allow the user to enter .NET source code to check the entered data. Then, you have the unlimited power of source code available to you. You can call a stored procedure that performs extensive server-side data validation, or perhaps write a series of steps that can never be defined with a wizard. Of course, you only allow such a privilege to specially trained power users. Many bright end users, although not professional developers, can handle this with minimal training. Given that Basic is still taught in high school and college programming classes, and given that many people learn VBA to write Excel, Word, and Outlook macros, your users will likely be far more comfortable with VB syntax than with C#. Given this situation, it's probably best to support VB.NET syntax in your custom validation screens. Even if the users have no programming background, VB.NET syntax is less formidable and far more user friendly than C#. True, VB is a more verbose language and most developers prefer C#, but the novice will feel more comfortable with VB.

Fortunately, Microsoft has a very simple version of the VB language called Small Basic, designed for the .NET compiler. You can download it from MSDN at `http://msdn.microsoft.com/en-you/devlabs/cc950524.aspx`. Small Basic is a subset of Visual Basic and is designed for amateur and beginner developers. Its simple syntax is excellent for creating the validation logic needed for a data-driven system. You can still plug in external assemblies so the user can take advantage of common routines in your libraries. The Small Basic IDE with some sample code is shown in Figure 3-2.

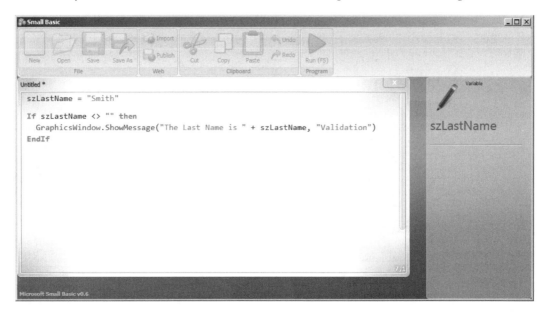

Figure 3-2. Small Basic IDE

Giving your users the power to write source code doesn't mean they need to do everything associated with common programming tasks. You can make their lives easier by shielding them from many low-level development tasks like connecting to a database. Suppose the user needs to write some complex validation code that takes the value entered and passes it to a stored procedure that contains the business rules. Rather than require the user to set up a connection to the database and deal with `SqlDataAdapter` and `SqlCommand` objects, you can create a class wrapper that handles all that behind the scenes. For example, the user can do this

```
oDT = ExecuteDBProc "spc_sel_IsDataValid",  iUserEnteredValue);
```

where `ExecuteDBProc()` is your wrapper method to all the messy code behind a stored procedure call. It pulls the connection string from the `app.config` file and performs the needed object cleanup. Even a power user shouldn't be required to worry about dealing with this overhead.

Another attractive feature of runtime code compilation is the avoidance of many of the stumbling blocks involved in change control. If all your code is compiled into assemblies, you need to navigate a change-control process to deploy a new version. Moreover, you may have these assemblies distributed on multiple machines, so deploying new versions isn't something you want to do frequently (although ClickOnce technology makes this easier than it was in the past). You may also work in an industry (like pharmaceuticals) where a change to the compiled code requires a redo of the validation process—a lengthy, boring, and expensive task that involves a lot of paperwork. Using runtime compiled code, you can update rows in a database table or XML file and avoid much of this overhead.

Compiling the Code

Compiling .NET code at runtime requires a number of steps. After you master this architecture, you can compile almost any code imaginable. Suppose you wish to compile the code shown in Listing 3-1.

Listing 3-1. Simple Code Sample

```
string szCode =
@"using System;
  using System.Windows.Forms;

  namespace RunTimeCompile
  {
      public class MyClass
      {
          public void DisplayMessage()
          {
              MessageBox.Show(""Hello World"");
          }
      }
  }";
```

This code is a simple class that references a few assemblies and declares a class with one method that, when invoked, displays a message. To compile this code and display the message, you first need an instance of `CodeDomProvider` to which you pass the language of your choice:

```
oCodeDomProvider = CodeDomProvider.CreateProvider("CSharp");
```

Next, you need to tell the compiler a few things via the `CompilerParameters` object. Even though the code references the `System` and `System.Windows.Forms` namespaces via the `using` statement, you still need to make the compiler aware of these assemblies by adding them to the `ReferencedAssemblies` collection, as shown in Listing 3-2.

Listing 3-2. *Referencing Assemblies*

```
CompilerParameters oCompilerParameters = new CompilerParameters();
oCompilerParameters.ReferencedAssemblies.Add("system.dll");
oCompilerParameters.ReferencedAssemblies.Add("system.windows.forms.dll");
```

This is the programmatic equivalent of adding assemblies to the References node in the Solution Explorer. If you can't anticipate what assemblies the users will need, you can require them to enter `using` statements and then parse the code to retrieve the appropriate assembly names.

Next, the compiler needs to know how the output will be generated. Do you want an EXE or a DLL? In this case, you need a DLL, so the `GenerateExecutable` property should be set to false:

```
oCompilerParameters.GenerateExecutable = false;
```

■ **Note** If you want an EXE, you need to set up a `Main()` method in Listing 3-1 to serve as a point of entry. This is the only difference between and EXE and a DLL.

Likewise, this assembly shouldn't be written to disk, because it won't be used outside of the runtime of the host application. Therefore, set the `GenerateInMemory` property to true:

```
oCompilerParameters.GenerateInMemory = true;
```

Then, pass the `CompilerParameters` object to the `CodeDomProvider`'s `CompileAssemblyFromSource()` method to produce a `CompilerResults` object like this:

```
oCompilerResults =
  oCodeDomProvider.CompileAssemblyFromSource(oCompilerParameters, szCode);
```

Of course, you aren't restricted to compiling only a text-string representation of source code. You can use the `CompileAssemblyFromFile()` method to compile a series of files on disk, as shown in Listing 3-3.

Listing 3-3. *Setting the Compiler Options*

```
CompilerParameters oCompilerParameters = new CompilerParameters();
oCompilerParameters.GenerateInMemory = true;
oCompilerParameters.GenerateExecutable = false;
oCompilerParameters.IncludeDebugInformation = true;
oCompilerParameters.ReferencedAssemblies.Add("system.dll");
oCompilerParameters.ReferencedAssemblies.Add("system.windows.forms.dll");

string[] aFiles = new string[1];

aFiles[0] = @"c:\temp\source.cs";

oCompilerResults = oCodeDomProvider.
    CompileAssemblyFromFile(oCompilerParameters, aFiles);
```

You can also use the CompileAssemblyFromDom() method to compile a code graph created using the CodeCompileUnit class, described in Chapter 1.

Error Handling

At this point in the process, you know if there are any errors in the code. If any do arise, they're contained in the CompilerResults.Errors collection. The code in Listing 3-4 shows the first error found.

Listing 3-4. *Code-Compilation Errors*

```
if (oCompilerResults.Errors.Count > 0)
{
    MessageBox.Show(oCompilerResults.Errors[0].ToString(), "Errors found");
}
```

If the compiler finds an error in your source code, it creates a CompilerError object and adds that to the collection. If, in the source code in Listing 3-1 you tried to compile the invalid DessageBox instead of MessageBox, you would get a CompilerError object containing the information shown in Table 3-1.

Table 3-1. CompilerError Object Properties

CompilerError property	Value	Explanation
ErrorText	The name 'DessageBox' does not exist in the current context	Description of the error.
Line	10	The error was thrown ten lines of code from the top
Column	26	Error was thrown on the twenty-sixth column, in this case the end of the word "*DessageBox*"
IsWarning	false	No, its not a warning, it's an actual error
FileName	c:\\Documents and Settings\\Owner\\Local Settings\\Temp\\2gz9umxi.0.cs	The name of the temporary work file where the compiler found the error
ErrorNumber	CS0103	The Microsoft error reference number which you can use to look up more information

Compiling code through the `CodeDomProvider` doesn't mean you sacrifice the feedback you'd get from doing the same in the Visual Studio IDE. The Output window information is still available to you via the `CompilerResults.Output` property. After you compile the code with the error, you can find the line-by-line results of the Output window in the individual elements of the `Output` string collection. The code in Listing 3-5 shows how to access this data.

Listing 3-5. Checking for Compile Errors

```
StringCollection oOutput = oCompilerResults.Output;
StringBuilder oOutputSB = new StringBuilder();

foreach (string szOutput in oOutput)
{
    oOutputSB.Append(szOutput);
}
```

You should get output similar to the following:

```
D:\\NotebookBackup\\DOCS\\DataDrivenProgramming\\
SourceCode\\Chapter3\\Chapter3\\bin\\Debug>
\"c:\\WINDOWS\\Microsoft.NET\\Framework\\v2.0.50727\\csc.exe\"
/t:library /utf8output /R:\"system.dll\" /R:\"system.windows.forms.dll\" /out:
\"C:\\Documents and Settings\\Owner\\Local Settings\\Temp\\j6v3quz6.dll\"
/debug- /optimize+  \"C:\\Documents and Settings\\Owner\\Local Settings\\
Temp\\j6v3quz6.0.cs\

Microsoft (R) Visual C# 2005 Compiler version 8.00.50727.3053for
Microsoft (R) Windows (R) 2005 Framework version 2.0.50727Copyright (C)
Microsoft Corporation 2001-2005. All rights reserved.c:\\Documents and Settings\\
Owner\\Local Settings\\Temp\\j6v3quz6.0.cs(10,26): error CS0103:
The name 'DessageBox' does not exist in the current context"
```

Compiling this code in the IDE yields the output shown in Figure 3-3.

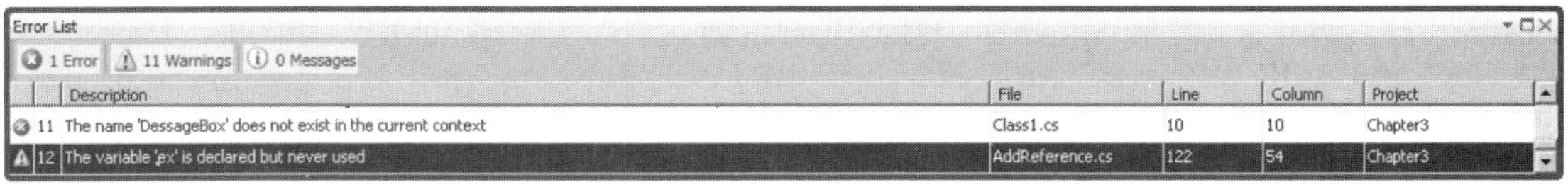

Figure 3-3. Error window

Of course, you should always try to prevent foreseeable errors. If you're generating code, for example, you can't always assume that a column name in a database table is a valid name in the language you're outputting. Suppose you have a column named `public`. If you try to create a property with this name, you wind up with something like this:

```
public string public {get; set;}
```

Because `public` is a reserved word in C#, this code won't compile. You can avoid these problems via the `IsValidIdentifier()` method, which checks your proposed name for a property, method, class, variable, and so on to determine its validity for the language you select. Examining the return value of the method in the Immediate window looks like this:

```
?oCodeDomProvider.IsValidIdentifier("public")
false
```

```
?oCodeDomProvider.IsValidIdentifier("3")
false
```

This is the case because no entity in C# can be named after a reserved word, nor can the name begin with a number. Knowing this, you can substitute accordingly:

```
?oCodeDomProvider.IsValidIdentifier("public1")
true

?oCodeDomProvider.IsValidIdentifier("_3")
true
```

Executing the Code

If your code compiles properly, the assembly is encapsulated in an Assembly object that you can retrieve like this:

```
oAssembly = oCompilerResults.CompiledAssembly;
```

The Assembly object is the result of compiling the code and can reside either in memory or physically on disk. To execute the code, create an instance of the RunTimeCompile.MyClass class, as illustrated in Listing 3-6. Then, create a MethodInfo object to hold a reference to the method. Use Invoke() to execute the method and display the message box shown in Figure 3-4. These methods are part of the System.Reflection namespace and are covered in Chapter 2.

Listing 3-6. *Executing Runtime Compiled Code*

```
oObject = oAssembly.CreateInstance("RunTimeCompile.MyClass");
oType = oObject.GetType();

oMethodInfo = oType.GetMethod("DisplayMessage");

oReturnValue = oMethodInfo.Invoke(oObject, null);
```

Figure 3-4. *Message box from runtime compiled code*

You can also generate an EXE at runtime (if you have a Main() method). To do so, you need to instruct the compiler to generate an executable, but not in memory only. This file goes to disk. The code in Listing 3-7 shows how to accomplish this.

Listing 3-7. Generating an EXE on Disk

```
oCompilerParameters.GenerateExecutable = true;
oCompilerParameters.GenerateInMemory = false;

//Set the name and location of the output assembly
oCompilerParameters.OutputAssembly = @"c:\temp\HelloWorld.exe";

//Create a PDB file to allow debugging
oCompilerParameters.IncludeDebugInformation = true;

//Name the main class of the EXE
oCompilerParameters.MainClass = "RunTimeCompile.MyClass";

//Treat warnings like errors, thereby terminating compilation
oCompilerParameters.TreatWarningsAsErrors = true;

//Any warning level 2 or above will count as an error
oCompilerParameters.WarningLevel = 2;
```

You can even set the command-line parameters to the compiler by assigning them to the `CompilerOptions` property. For example, you can set the name of the output assembly like this

```
oCompilerParameters.CompilerOptions = @"/out:c:\temp\HelloWorld.exe";
```

which is the equivalent of executing this at the command prompt:

```
csc.exe /out:c:\temp\HelloWorld.exe
```

Because you're creating an EXE and declaring the main class, you need an entry point to the application. This is the `Main()` method. Change the sample code to look like Listing 3-8.

Listing 3-8. Code with a Main Method

```
string szCode =
@"using System;
  using System.Windows.Forms;

  namespace RunTimeCompile
  {
      public class MyClass
      {
          static void Main()
          {
```

```
            MessageBox.Show(""Hello World"");
        }
    }
}";
```

Now, when you run the EXE, the message box immediately displays.

Referencing Controls on Forms

Creating code to run at compile time is a powerful feature, but that code probably needs to reference controls that aren't instantiated until runtime. Examine the code in Listing 3-9. It's very similar to the example shown in Listing 3-1; but instead of displaying a text string in the message box, you display the contents of a user control.

Listing 3-9. *Referencing a User Control*

```
string szCode =
@"using System;
  using System.Windows.Forms;

  namespace RunTimeCompile
  {
      public class MyClass
      {
          private void DisplayMessage()
          {
              MessageBox.Show(txtFirstName.Text);
          }
      }
  }";
```

But when you compile this code, the following error is thrown:

```
error CS0103: The name 'txtFirstName' does not exist in the current context
```

The reason is that txtFirstName doesn't yet exist to the compiler because the form that hosts it hasn't been instantiated. To handle this scenario, you pass the name of the control to a method that looks it up by name in the Controls collection of the host form. This method recursively iterates through the Controls collection and returns a match on the name. The code to accomplish this is shown in Listing 3-10.

Listing 3-10. *FindControl Method*

```
public static T FindControl<T>(string formName,
                               string controlName) where T : Control
```

```
{
    T control = default(T);
    Control parent = Application.OpenForms[formName];
    if (parent != null)
    {
        control = FindControlObject(parent, controlName) as T;
    }
    return control;
}

public static Control FindControlObject(Control oParentControl,
    string szControlName)
{
    Control oTargetControl;

    if (oParentControl.Name == szControlName)
        return oParentControl;

    foreach (Control oControl in oParentControl.Controls)
    {
        oTargetControl = FindControlObject(oControl, szControlName);

        if (oTargetControl != null)
            return oTargetControl;
    }

    return null;
}
```

You can compile this code into a separate support assembly that is linked into your application like this:

```
oCompilerParameters.ReferencedAssemblies.Add("DataDriven.dll");
```

Assuming your FindControl() method is located in a namespace called Common, you can reference it in your code like this:

```
using Common;
```

If, for example, you want to write code for an event that toggles a check box on and off, you can add the following code to the CheckChanged event:

```
FindControlByType<CheckBox>("Form1", "chkTest").Enabled =
  ! FindControlByType<CheckBox>("Form1", "chkTest").Enabled;
```

SIMPLIFYING THINGS FOR THE USER

If you're planning to allow users to write their own routines, you may wish to make it easier for them to do so by creating a class that holds the current values of the various controls. Thus, if a user wishes to see if the last name `TextBox` is blank, they shouldn't need to write this:

```
if (FindControl("txtLastName").Text == string.Empty)
```

Rather, they should be able to refer to it through an object wrapper that you provide:

```
if (Data.LastName == string.Empty)
```

Adding References

When you provide a code window for your users, you may wish to allow them to add references to their project much as developers do in the Visual Studio IDE. Figure 3-5 shows the Add Reference dialog.

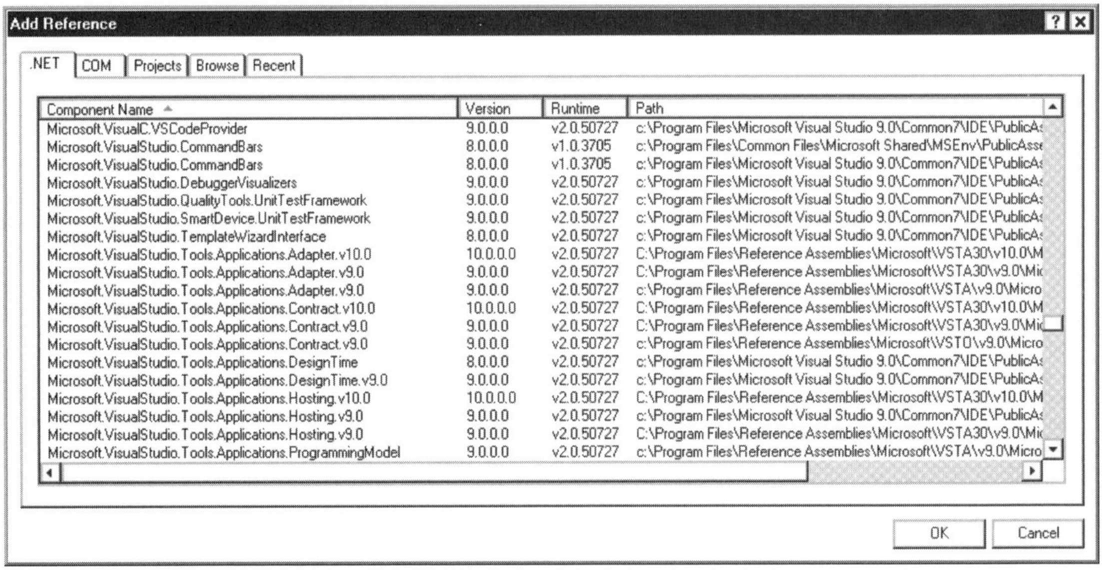

Figure 3-5. Add Reference dialog

Creating a similar dialog requires a few steps. You need to iterate through the directories specified in two registry keys:

```
HKEY_LOCAL_MACHINE\SOFTWARE\Microsoft\.NETFramework\AssemblyFolders
HKEY_LOCAL_MACHINE\SOFTWARE\Microsoft\.NETFramework\v4.0.20506\AssemblyFoldersEx
```

The version number of the second directory should pertain to the version of Visual Studio you're using. A sample of the contents of these registry keys is shown in Figure 3-6.

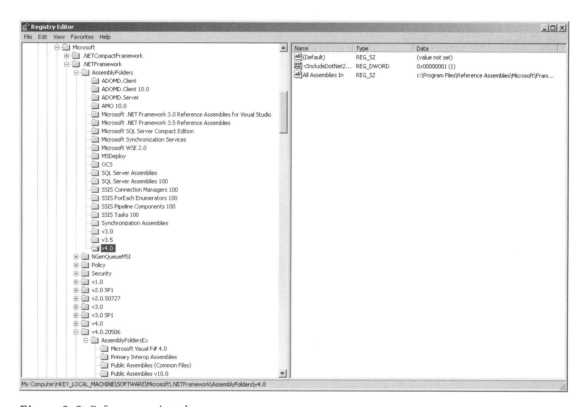

Figure 3-6. *Reference registry keys*

These registry entries are the locations that contain the assemblies known to Visual Studio for inclusion in your projects. The code in Listing 3-11 illustrates how to access the full list of assemblies.

Listing 3-11. *Extracting List of Assemblies*

```
List<string> oKeyList = new List<string>();
List<string> oFileList = new List<string>();
RegistryKey oRegistryKey;
```

71

```
RegistryKey oSubKey;
DataTable oDT = new DataTable();
string szDirectory = string.Empty;

oDT.Columns.Add(new DataColumn("Name"));
oDT.Columns.Add(new DataColumn("Version"));
oDT.Columns.Add(new DataColumn("RunTime"));
oDT.Columns.Add(new DataColumn("Path"));

oKeyList.Add(@"SOFTWARE\Microsoft\.NETFramework\AssemblyFolders\");
oKeyList.Add(@"SOFTWARE\Microsoft\.NETFramework\v4.0.20506\AssemblyFoldersEx\");

//begin iterating through the two main registry entries
foreach (string szRegistryKey in oKeyList)
{
    //Get a reference to the registry entry
    oRegistryKey = Registry.LocalMachine.OpenSubKey(szRegistryKey);

    //for each entry in this registry entry
    foreach (string szKey in oRegistryKey.GetSubKeyNames())
    {
        oSubKey = oRegistryKey.OpenSubKey(szKey);

        //iterate through every subkey contained within it.
        foreach (string szValueName in oSubKey.GetValueNames())
        {
            //if that subkey has a value...
            if (oRegistryKey.OpenSubKey(szKey).GetValue(szValueName) != null)
            {
                //it will be a reference to a directory on disk
                szDirectory =
oRegistryKey.OpenSubKey(szKey).GetValue(szValueName).ToString();

                //if that directory exists...
                if (Directory.Exists(szDirectory))
                {
                    //iterate through the files contained within it.
                    foreach (string szFile in Directory.
                        GetFiles(szDirectory, "*.dll"))
                    {

                        try
                        {
                            //if that file has not already been counted
                            if (!oFileList.Contains(szFile))
                            {
```

```
                            oFileList.Add(szFile);

                            oDT = LoadAssemblyInformation(oDT, szFile);
                        }

                    }
                    catch (Exception ex)
                    {
                    }

                }

            }

        }
    }
}

FormatGrid(dgAvailable, oDT);

dgAvailable.Columns[0].AutoSizeMode =
    DataGridViewAutoSizeColumnMode.AllCells;
dgAvailable.Columns[1].AutoSizeMode =
    DataGridViewAutoSizeColumnMode.AllCells;
```

The LoadAssemblyInformation() method instantiates the assembly at the specified path and loads its metadata information into a DataRow. This code is shown in Listing 3-12.

Listing 3-12. *LoadAssemblyInformation() Method*

```
private DataTable LoadAssemblyInformation(DataTable oDT, string szFile)
{
    Assembly oAssembly;
    DataRow oDR;

    //...load it into an Assembly object
    oAssembly = Assembly.LoadFrom(szFile);

    //...and extract the version information
    //which is added to the DataTable for
    //binding to the DataGridView
    oDR = oDT.NewRow();

    oDR["Name"] = oAssembly.GetName().Name;
    oDR["Version"] = oAssembly.GetName().Version;
```

```
        oDR["RunTime"] = oAssembly.ImageRuntimeVersion;
        oDR["Path"] = szFile;

        oDT.Rows.Add(oDR);

        return oDT;
}
```

The result is shown in Figure 3-7.

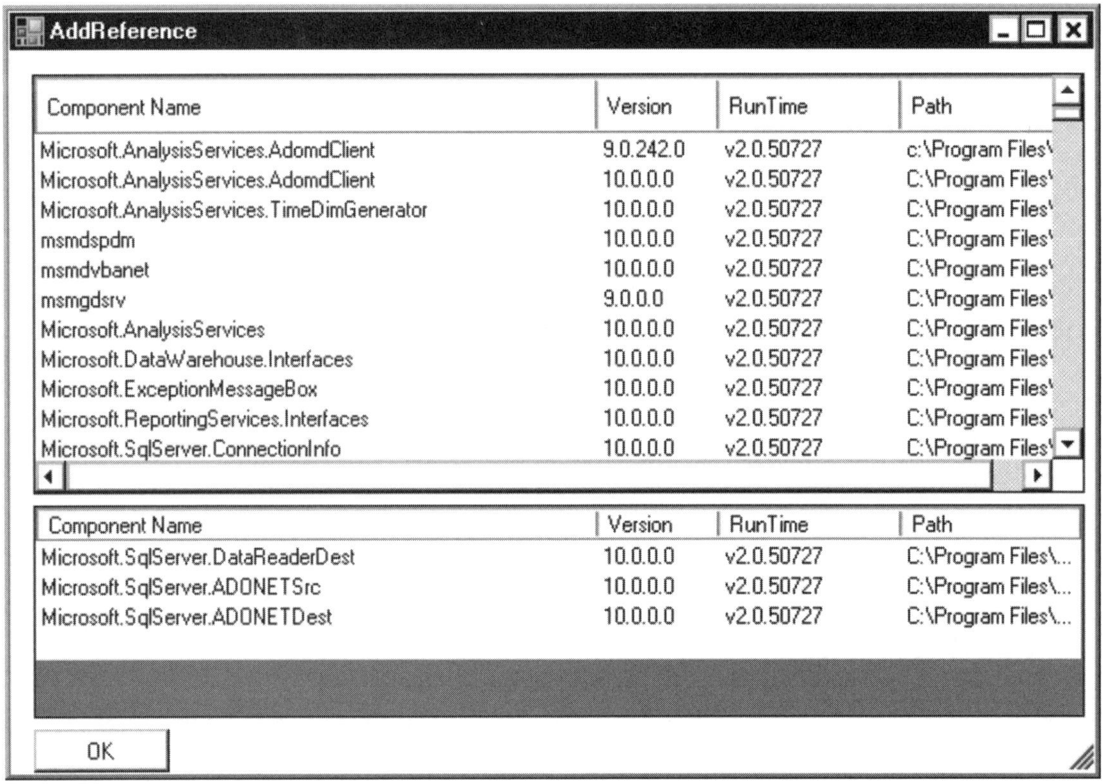

Figure 3-7. Custom Add Reference dialog

User selections can easily be persisted to an XML file and then loaded into the ReferencedAssemblies collection of the CompilerParameters object.

Testing

When testing your data-driven code, you need to consider that you won't have the runtime error-checking that comes with declaring all your objects ahead of time. You receive some runtime checking in that syntax errors are caught by the compiler. However, object reference errors aren't. Because you reference controls by their text name, and some methods and properties by their text names as well, it isn't possible to catch misnamed controls, methods, and properties at compile time. These object references are essentially late-bound, and you need to perform the same rigorous testing that late-bound coding requires.

Summary

This chapter covered one of .NET's most powerful features: runtime code compilation. Anything that you can accomplish with source code in the IDE, you can accomplish at runtime. Next, you looked at how to gather the list of available assemblies and present them to the user in a custom equivalent of the Add Reference dialog. Then, the chapter reviewed the issues you need to consider in testing runtime compiled code. Chapter 4 looks at how to dynamically instantiate controls and tie them to this runtime compiled code via event handlers.

CHAPTER 4

■ ■ ■

Dynamic WinForms

In this chapter, you look at how to create data-driven WinForms applications. This chapter is longer than those for web and WPF applications because most of the principles of data-driven development are the same for all three, and these principles are covered in detail here. You learn how to dynamically instantiate forms and controls, wire events, and link them to runtime compiled code to validate the input. Then, you examine a number of practical examples of how data-driven WinForms development can work for you.

Instantiating Forms

When you lay out a form in the Visual Studio IDE, the code for the form and all its composite controls is automatically generated and executed in a data-driven fashion. Look at the code behind any form and its associated designer file, and you'll see this to be true. Examine the form in Figure 4-1.

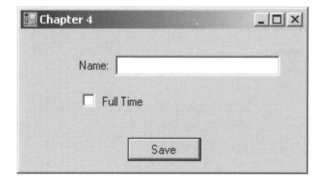

Figure 4-1. *A (very) simple data-entry form*

Here is a simple screen that has a group box with two child controls—a `Label` and a `TextBox`. In addition, there is a `Button` owned directly by the form itself. Merely doing this, with no further coding, outputs the necessary code to instantiate these controls at runtime.

All the controls that display on the form are instantiated at runtime. Listing 4-1 shows how this is accomplished.

Listing 4-1. *Autogenerated Code*

```
private System.Windows.Forms.Button cmdSave;
private System.Windows.Forms.Label label1;
private System.Windows.Forms.TextBox txtName;
private System.Windows.Forms.CheckBox chkFullTime;

private void InitializeComponent()
{
    this.cmdSave = new System.Windows.Forms.Button();
    this.label1 = new System.Windows.Forms.Label();
    this.txtName = new System.Windows.Forms.TextBox();
    this.chkFullTime = new System.Windows.Forms.CheckBox();
    this.SuspendLayout();
    //
    // cmdSave
    //
    this.cmdSave.Location = new System.Drawing.Point(111, 108);
    this.cmdSave.Name = "cmdSave";
    this.cmdSave.Size = new System.Drawing.Size(75, 23);
    this.cmdSave.TabIndex = 0;
    this.cmdSave.Text = "Save";
    this.cmdSave.UseVisualStyleBackColor = true;
    //
    // label1
    //
    this.label1.AutoSize = true;
    this.label1.Location = new System.Drawing.Point(57, 29);
    this.label1.Name = "label1";
    this.label1.Size = new System.Drawing.Size(38, 13);
    this.label1.TabIndex = 1;
    this.label1.Text = "Name:";
    //
    // txtName
    //
    this.txtName.Location = new System.Drawing.Point(98, 26);
    this.txtName.Name = "txtName";
    this.txtName.Size = new System.Drawing.Size(169, 20);
    this.txtName.TabIndex = 2;
    //
    // chkFullTime
    //
    this.chkFullTime.AutoSize = true;
    this.chkFullTime.Location = new System.Drawing.Point(64, 63);
    this.chkFullTime.Name = "chkFullTime";
    this.chkFullTime.Size = new System.Drawing.Size(68, 17);
    this.chkFullTime.TabIndex = 3;
```

```
            this.chkFullTime.Text = "Full Time";
            this.chkFullTime.UseVisualStyleBackColor = true;
            //
            // Form1
            //
            this.AutoScaleDimensions = new System.Drawing.SizeF(6F, 13F);
            this.AutoScaleMode = System.Windows.Forms.AutoScaleMode.Font;
            this.ClientSize = new System.Drawing.Size(292, 140);
            this.Controls.Add(this.chkFullTime);
            this.Controls.Add(this.txtName);
            this.Controls.Add(this.label1);
            this.Controls.Add(this.cmdSave);
            this.Name = "Form1";
            this.Text = "Chapter 4";
            this.ResumeLayout(false);
            this.PerformLayout();
}
```

The fundamental idea behind data-driven programming is to store these settings in a database rather than hard-code them into the assembly. Otherwise, the idea of instantiating the controls at runtime is the same. To accomplish this properly, you must first understand how the controls relate to both the owner form and one another.

A form and its controls are part of an object ownership hierarchy. In this example, the form owns two controls directly—a Button and a TextBox. This relationship is set through the Add() method of the form's Controls collection like this:

```
Form oForm = new Form();
TextBox oTextBox = new TextBox();
oForm.Controls.Add(oTextBox);
```

Controls can own other controls through their Controls collection, and this nesting can go on and on. Examine the code in Listing 4-2.

Listing 4-2. *Hierarchy of Controls*

```
Form oForm = new Form();
GroupBox oGroupBox1 = new GroupBox();
GroupBox oGroupBox2 = new GroupBox();
GroupBox oGroupBox3 = new GroupBox();
TextBox oTextBox = new TextBox();

oGroupBox1.Size = new Size(250, 250);
oGroupBox1.Text = "Box 1 owned by Form";

oGroupBox2.Size = new Size(200, 200);
oGroupBox2.Location = new Point(20, 20);
oGroupBox2.Text = "Box 2 owned by Box 1";
```

```
oGroupBox3.Size = new Size(150, 150);
oGroupBox3.Location = new Point(20, 20);
oGroupBox3.Text = "Box 3 owned by Box 2";

oTextBox.Location = new Point(20, 20);
oTextBox.Text = "Owned by Box 3";

oGroupBox3.Controls.Add(oTextBox);
oGroupBox2.Controls.Add(oGroupBox3);
oGroupBox1.Controls.Add(oGroupBox2);
oForm.Controls.Add(oGroupBox1);

oForm.Show();
```

This code produces the form shown in Figure 4-2.

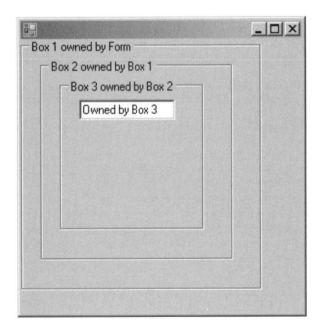

Figure 4-2. *A simple data-entry form*

In this example, the form owns a GroupBox, which owns another GroupBox, which owns still another GroupBox, which owns a TextBox. I've tested this hierarchy to a dozen levels deep, and it works fine. The maximum level, if there is one, goes deeper than that, but I doubt you'll ever need to go that far. Because of this nesting, any methods that deal with controls need to be recursive.

Using Third-Party Controls?

Many developers have settled on a set of third-party controls that they've used for years. I'm a long-time user of Infragistics for both web and Windows development and like their controls very much. Dynamically instantiating a third-party control is programmatically no different from instantiating a control that ships with .NET. The following code shows how to instantiate an Infragistics `UltraMaskedEdit` control and add it to the owner form:

```
Infragistics.Win.UltraWinMaskedEdit.UltraMaskedEdit oUltraMaskedEdit =
    new Infragistics.Win.UltraWinMaskedEdit.UltraMaskedEdit();
oUltraMaskedEdit.Name = "txtPhoneNumber";
oUltraMaskedEdit.Location = new Point(200, 20);
oUltraMaskedEdit.Size = new Size(100, 24);
oUltraMaskedEdit.InputMask = "(999) 999-Insert 9999";
this.Controls.Add(oUltraMaskedEdit);
```

Wiring Events

Creating a user interface at runtime provides you with a visual interface, but this interface won't do anything truly useful until the controls are wired to events. Listing 4-3 illustrates how to create a form with a single `Button` object on it. This `Button` is then wired to an event that displays a message box.

Listing 4-3. *Wiring Events*

```
private void DisplayForm()
{
    Form oForm = new Form();
    Button oButton = new Button();

    oButton.Text = "Press Me";
    oButton.Click += new EventHandler(Button_Click);
    oForm.Controls.Add(oButton);

    oForm.Show();
}

private void Button_Click(object sender, EventArgs e)
{
    MessageBox.Show("Do something");
}
```

In the example in Listing 4-4, you instantiate a `Form` and two `Button` objects. Each `Button` is wired to the same event.

Listing 4-4. *Wiring Two Controls to the Same Event*

```
Form oForm = new Form();
Button oButton1 = new Button();
Button oButton2 = new Button();

oButton1.Text = "Press This";
oButton1.Click += new EventHandler(Button_Click);

oButton2.Text = "Press That";
oButton2.Click += new EventHandler(Button_Click);
oButton2.Top = oButton1.Top + oButton1.Height + 10;

oForm.Controls.Add(oButton1);
oForm.Controls.Add(oButton2);

oForm.Show();

private void Button_Click(object sender, EventArgs e)
{
    Button oButton = sender as Button;
    MessageBox.Show("Do something with " + oButton.Text);
}
```

The signature for the Click event receives a sender object that represents the object that fired the event. By casting the sender object to an object of type Button, you can retrieve the properties of the individual button and determine which one triggered the event. You could create one Button_Click event that contains the code for every Button on your form. In a data-driven application, this is easier to manage than dealing with individual Button events. After the button is identified, you know which block of runtime-compiled code to execute.

SuspendLayout and ResumeLayout

Although they aren't shown in the preceding examples of control instantiation, you may wish to employ the SuspendLayout() and ResumeLayout() methods. The designer-generated code uses these methods. Their purpose is to suspend the execution of layout methods while the controls are being sized and positioned, or while child controls are being added to their Controls collections. Suspending the layout methods reduces any screen flicker, speeds up loading, and avoids any unintended consequences associated with events that aren't intended to fire at this point. In the following code sample, the form constructor is instantiating a TextBox. TextChanged and Layout events are also being assigned. Setting the Text to "Hello World" triggers the TextChanged event, and setting the Size property triggers the Layout event. In this example, the SuspendLayout() and ResumeLayout() methods are commented, so the events fire as soon as the Text and Size properties receive their values. When you uncomment these methods, the TextChanged event is unaffected but the Layout event fires only when the `SuspendLayout()` method is invoked. You can best see the effect of this by stepping through the sample code:

```
public Form1()
{
    InitializeComponent();

    TextBox oTextBox = new TextBox();
    //oTextBox.SuspendLayout();

    oTextBox.TextChanged += new EventHandler(this.Text_Changed);
    oTextBox.Layout += new LayoutEventHandler(this.Text_Layout);

    oTextBox.Text = "Hello World";
    oTextBox.Size = new Size(20, 100);

    this.Controls.Add(oTextBox);
    //oTextBox.ResumeLayout();
}

private void Text_Changed(object sender, EventArgs e)
{
    MessageBox.Show("Text_Changed fired");
}

private void Text_Layout(object sender, LayoutEventArgs e)
{
    MessageBox.Show("Text_Layout fired");
}
```

Loading Control Definitions

After the control definitions are stored in their data source, you need a way to load them on the form. As the controls are loaded, you need to check for any event code and wire each event appropriately. Each type of control must be dealt with individually, so you first need to determine what controls you wish to support and then create an enumeration to refer to them. See Listing 4-5 for an example.

Listing 4-5. ControlType Enumeration

```
public enum ControlType
{
    TabControl = 0,
    TabPage = 1,
    GroupBox = 2,
```

```
        CheckBox = 3,
        ComboBox = 4,
        CheckedListBox = 5,
        RadioButton = 6,
        TextBox = 7,
        Label = 8,
        Button = 9,
        DateTimePicker = 10,
        MaskedTextBox = 11
}
```

You can see a hierarchy developing just within this enumeration. A `TabControl` owns `TabPages`. A `TabPage` may own `GroupBoxes`. `GroupBoxes` may own controls of the remaining types.

Loading from XML

Examine the code in Listing 4-6. This code re-creates a `Form` object from a `<Form>` element with the same format as shown in the XML in Listing 2-15 from Chapter 2. The `LoadControls()` method creates the controls on that form before it's displayed to the user.

Listing 4-6. *Dynamically Instantiating a Form*

```
XmlDocument oXmlDocument = new XmlDocument();
XmlElement oXmlElement;
Form oForm = new Form();

oXmlDocument.Load(Application.StartupPath + @"\form.xml");

oXmlElement = oXmlDocument.DocumentElement;

oForm.Name = oXmlElement.Attributes["name"].Value;
oForm.Text = oXmlElement.Attributes["text"].Value;
oForm.Width = int.Parse(oXmlElement.Attributes["width"].Value);
oForm.Height = int.Parse(oXmlElement.Attributes["height"].Value);
oForm.Top = int.Parse(oXmlElement.Attributes["top"].Value);
oForm.Left = int.Parse(oXmlElement.Attributes["left"].Value);

LoadControls(oForm.Controls, oXmlElement.ChildNodes[0].ChildNodes);

oForm.ShowDialog();
```

This process is straightforward: it instantiates a `Form` object and sets its properties from the XML attributes. After the `Form` object is instantiated, the individual controls need to be added to it. This process is shown in Listing 4-7. For the sake of brevity, it's a simplified example showing only `GroupBoxes`, `ComboBoxes`, and `Buttons`.

Listing 4-7. *Dynamically Instantiating Controls on a Form from XML*

```
private void LoadControls(Control.ControlCollection oControls,
   XmlNodeList oXmlNodeList)
{
    Button oButton = null;
    GroupBox oGroupBox = null;
    ComboBox oComboBox = null;
    string szControlType;
    string szName;
    int iTop = 0;
    int iLeft = 0;
    int iWidth = 0;
    int iHeight = 0;

    foreach (XmlNode oXmlNode in oXmlNodeList)
    {
        szControlType = oXmlNode.Attributes["type"].Value;
        szName = oXmlNode.Attributes["name"].Value;
        iWidth = int.Parse(oXmlNode.Attributes["width"].Value);
        iHeight = int.Parse(oXmlNode.Attributes["height"].Value);
        iTop = int.Parse(oXmlNode.Attributes["top"].Value);
        iLeft = int.Parse(oXmlNode.Attributes["left"].Value);

        switch (szControlType)
        {
            case "Button":
                oButton = new Button();
                oButton.Name = szName;
                oButton.Text = oXmlNode.Attributes["text"].Value;
                oButton.Width = iWidth;
                oButton.Height = iHeight;
                oButton.Top = iTop;
                oButton.Left = iLeft;
                oControls.Add(oButton);
                break;

            case "GroupBox":
                oGroupBox = new GroupBox();
                oGroupBox.Name = szName;
                oGroupBox.Text = oXmlNode.Attributes["text"].Value;
                oGroupBox.Width = iWidth;
                oGroupBox.Height = iHeight;
                oGroupBox.Top = iTop;
                oGroupBox.Left = iLeft;
                oControls.Add(oGroupBox);
```

```
                    if (oXmlNode.HasChildNodes)
                        LoadControls(oGroupBox.Controls, oXmlNode.ChildNodes);

                    break;

                case "ComboBox":
                    oComboBox = new ComboBox();
                    oComboBox.Name = szName;
                    oComboBox.Width = iWidth;
                    oComboBox.Height = iHeight;
                    oComboBox.Top = iTop;
                    oComboBox.Left = iLeft;

                    oComboBox.DropDownStyle =
        (ComboBoxStyle)Enum.Parse(typeof(ComboBoxStyle),
    oXmlNode.Attributes["dropdownstyle"].Value, true);

                    oControls.Add(oComboBox);
                    break;

            }
        }
}
```

The bulk of the XML contains the definitions for the various controls on the form. Each control is nested under its owner control in the hierarchy. Because all controls have a name, a type, and size/position coordinates, these values are set to variables at the beginning of the `foreach` loop. The control is instantiated, its properties are set, and it's added to the `Controls` collection of the parent. The parent could be the form itself, and in many cases it is. Even if you present your user controls in a `TabForm`, the `TabForm` is owned by the `Form` object.

Loading from a Table

Although you aren't required to store form/control definitions in XML, its hierarchical nature makes it a natural and highly recommended data source. If you wish, you can use a table-based solution, at which point you need to consider other options in maintaining the control hierarchy. Because the structure of a data table doesn't lend itself to recursion, you must maintain a reference to the control's owner and make sure that control is instantiated first. The table relationships for such a database are shown in Figure 4-3.

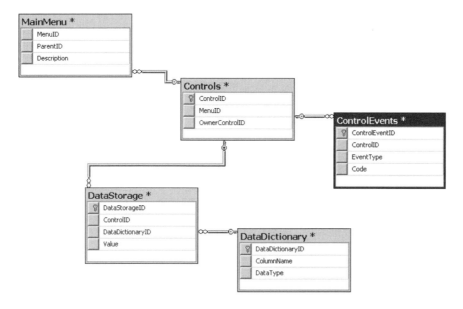

Figure 4-3. *Entity relationships for data-driven storage*

By loading the control ID and object reference in the `Dictionary` object, you can be assured of establishing the correct ownership of all controls loaded. Listing 4-8 shows how to load the controls from a table.

Listing 4-8. *Dynamically Instantiating Controls on a Form from a Data Table*

```
private string AddControls(int iFormID)
{
    SqlDatabase oSqlDatabase;
    DataTable oDT;
    Dictionary<int, Control> oControlDict = new Dictionary<int, Control>();
    Control oParent;
    GroupBox oGroupBox = null;
    Button oButton;
    StringBuilder oCodeSB = new StringBuilder();
    int iOwnerControlID;
    int iControlID;
    string szCode;
    string szName;
    int iTop = 0;
    int iLeft = 0;
    int iWidth = 0;
```

```
int iHeight = 0;

oSqlDatabase = new SqlDatabase(Common.ConnectString);

using (DbCommand oDBCommand =
    oSqlDatabase.GetStoredProcCommand("spc_sel_Controls"))
{
    oSqlDatabase.AddInParameter(oDBCommand, "@FormID", SqlDbType.Int, iFormID);
    oDT = oSqlDatabase.ExecuteDataSet(oDBCommand).Tables[0];
}

this.Controls.Clear();

foreach (DataRow oDR in oDT.Rows)
{
    iOwnerControlID = int.Parse(oDR["OwnerControlID"].ToString());
    iControlID = int.Parse(oDR["ControlID"].ToString());
    szName = oDR["Name"].ToString().Trim();
    iTop = int.Parse(oDR["TopPosition"].ToString());
    iLeft = int.Parse(oDR["LeftPosition"].ToString());
    iWidth = int.Parse(oDR["Width"].ToString());
    iHeight = int.Parse(oDR["Height"].ToString());

    switch (int.Parse(oDR["Type"].ToString()))
    {

        case (int)Common.ControlType.GroupBox:
            oGroupBox = new GroupBox();
            oGroupBox.Text = oDR["Caption"].ToString();
            oGroupBox.Name = szName;
            oGroupBox.Top = iTop;
            oGroupBox.Left = iLeft;
            oGroupBox.Width = iWidth;
            oGroupBox.Height = iHeight;

            oControlDict.Add(iControlID, oGroupBox);

            oParent = GetParent(oControlDict, iOwnerControlID);

            oParent.Controls.Add(oGroupBox);
            break;

        case (int)Common.ControlType.Button:
            oButton = new Button();
            oButton.Name = szName;
            oButton.Text = oDR["Caption"].ToString();
            oButton.Top = iTop;
```

```
                oButton.Left = iLeft;
                oButton.Width = iWidth;
                oButton.Height = iHeight;

                szCode = GetCode(iControlID, Common.ControlEvent.Click);

                if (szCode != string.Empty)
                {
                    oButton.Click += new EventHandler(Button_Click);

                    oCodeSB.Append("public void " + oButton.Name + "_Click()\r");
                    oCodeSB.Append("{\r");
                    oCodeSB.Append(szCode);
                    oCodeSB.Append("}\r");
                }

                oControlDict.Add(iControlID, oButton);

                oParent = GetParent(oControlDict, iOwnerControlID);

                oParent.Controls.Add(oButton);
                break;

        }

    }

    return oCodeSB.ToString();

}
```

As each control is instantiated and added to its owner's Controls collection, the code associated with it is collected into a StringBuilder object. The contents of this object are returned from the AddControls() method for compilation at runtime.

First, declare a generic Dictionary object to hold a reference to each control. Because controls exist in an ownership hierarchy, you need to know the parent when creating a new control. Next, retrieve your control definitions into a DataTable. Then, iterate through the DataRows and examine each control definition. As each control is processed, add the control to the generic Dictionary, using the control's ID as the key. Each control must be checked to see if its parent object is in this Dictionary via the GetParent() method. This method is shown in Listing 4-9.

Listing 4-9. *GetParent() Method*

```
private Control GetParent(Dictionary<int, Control> oControlDict,
    int iOwnerControlID)
{
    Control oResult = this;
```

```
    Control oParent;

    oControlDict.TryGetValue(iOwnerControlID, out oParent);

    if (oParent != null)
        oResult = oParent;

    return oResult;

}
```

By loading the control ID and object reference in the `Dictionary`, you can be assured of establishing the correct ownership of all controls loaded.

Connecting Event Code

Note that the `Button` object in Listing 4-8 is checking for the presence of code for the event specified by the enumeration reference. You need to determine which events you plan to support for your controls. Then, create an enumeration hat defines them, as shown in Listing 4-10.

Listing 4-10. ControlEvent Enumeration

```
public enum ControlEvent
{
    SelectedIndexChanged = 0,
    CheckStateChanged = 1,
    Click = 2,
    Enter = 3,
    Leave = 4,
    ItemCheck = 5,
    TextChanged = 6
}
```

If you find code associated with a particular event, then you can associate it with a common event handler. The code in Listing 4-11 shows how to retrieve the event code and name a handler.

Listing 4-11. Retrieving the Event Code

```
szCode = GetCode(iControlID, Common.ControlEvent.Click);

if (szCode != string.Empty)
{
    oButton.Click += new EventHandler(Button_Click);

    oCodeSB.Append("public void " + oButton.Name + "_Click()\r");
    oCodeSB.Append("{\r");
    oCodeSB.Append(szCode);
```

```
        oCodeSB.Append("}\r");
}
```

The `Button_Click` event handler processes the `Click` event for every `Button` on your form. To create unique method names for specific controls, the specific event method is named after the control. For a `Button` named `cmdSave`, the event is called `cmdSave_Click`. When the event is triggered, the event in Listing 4-12 fires.

Listing 4-12. *Button_Click() Event Handler Method*

```
private void Button_Click(object sender, EventArgs e)
{
    string szButtonName = ((Button)sender).Name;

    RunMethod(szButtonName + "_Click", this, sender, e);
}
```

All `Button_Click` events are wired to this one event handler. When one fires, the name of the `Button` is obtained, concatenated to "_Click", and passed to the `RunMethod()` method as shown in Listing 4-13. The `RunTimeCompile.EventHandler` class is a wrapper class stored in the database that acts as a container for all the event handling code. This class needs a reference to the host form, the sender object, and any event arguments encapsulated in an `EventArgs` object. These values are passed using Reflection. Then, the method reference is retrieved and invoked.

Listing 4-13. *RunMethod() method*

```
private void RunMethod(string szMethodName,
                Form oForm,
                object sender,
                EventArgs e)
{
    MethodInfo oMethodInfo;
    FieldInfo oFieldInfo;
    Type oType;
    object oObject;
    object oReturnValue;

    //Instantiate the data validation class and
    //obtain a Type object reference to it
    oObject = oAssembly.CreateInstance("RunTimeCompile.EventHandler");
    oType = oObject.GetType();

    //Obtain a reference to the indicated property,
    //and set the value of this property to the value you entered on the form.
    oFieldInfo = oType.GetField("Form");
    oFieldInfo.SetValue(oObject, oForm);

    oFieldInfo = oType.GetField("sender");
```

```
    oFieldInfo.SetValue(oObject, sender);

    oFieldInfo = oType.GetField("e");
    oFieldInfo.SetValue(oObject, e);

    //Obtain a reference to the event handler
    oMethodInfo = oType.GetMethod(szMethodName);

    //Now that the property is set invoke the method
    oReturnValue = oMethodInfo.Invoke(oObject, null);
}
```

Practical Solutions

By way of example, let's examine some practical examples of where data-driven techniques can be particularly useful. This section looks at how to persist the user selections on filter screens and how to create a menu that displays the last files used by the user.

Building a Filter Screen

One of the most useful, data-driven applications you can create is a filter screen. These can be used to filter data on a grid control or pass parameters to a report. Suppose you wish to present the user with a screen that offers a myriad of controls to allow filtering of data. When the user makes their selections, these choices should be persisted to a data source and then restored the next time the form is loaded. Examine the filter screen in Figure 4-4.

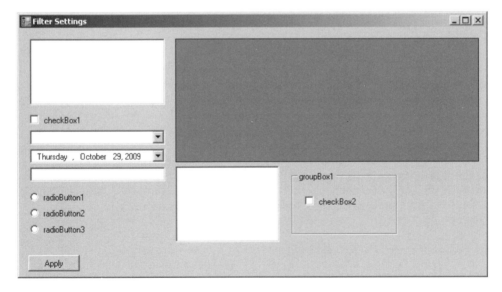

Figure 4-4. Filter screen

XML is an ideal storage medium for this data. You can build whatever data-storage structure you need without modifying the database. By creating a table that stores the user ID, the filter name, and the settings, you can easily retrieve this information and repopulate the form. It doesn't matter if the filter controls are created dynamically or not. The approach is the same either way.

In order to distinguish between those controls that belong to your filter and other controls that may be on the form, it's best to use a `Panel` control as the container for all things related to the filter. Then, by iterating through the `Controls` collection of the `Panel`, you only access controls you're interested in and collect the various settings. By using this dynamic approach, you have code that is completely independent of the layout of your controls and even of the structure of the database. Any collection of filters in any application can use this approach.

The goal is to produce XML that looks like Listing 4-14.

Listing 4-14. Controls Collection XML Mapping

```xml
<Controls>
  <Control type="CheckBox" name="checkBox2" value="False" />
  <Control type="TextBox" name="textBox1" value="Fred" />
  <Control type="ListBox" name="listBox1">
    <value>302</value>
    <value>303</value>
  </Control>
  <Control type="RadioButton" name="radioButton3" value="False" />
  <Control type="RadioButton" name="radioButton2" value="False" />
  <Control type="RadioButton" name="radioButton1" value="True" />
  <Control type="DateTimePicker" name="dateTimePicker1"
      value="Tuesday, October 14, 2008" />
  <Control type="ComboBox" name="comboBox1" value="103" />
  <Control type="CheckedListBox" name="checkedListBox1">
    <value>201</value>
  </Control>
  <Control type="CheckBox" name="checkBox1" value="True" />
</Controls>
```

Because SQL Server 2005 introduced the XML data type, this makes it the perfect storage medium. You can create a table containing columns for the user ID, the form name, the filter name, and finally the filter settings themselves as an `xml` type. This way, these settings are available to users no matter what machine they're working on.

Saving the User Selections

The structure in Listing 4-14 stores the control type, name, and value as attributes for those controls that have only single values associated with them. For controls such as `ListBoxes`, `CheckedListBoxes`, and `DataGridViews`, multiple values are stored as elements of the control elements. You can create this XML via the code in Listing 4-15.

Listing 4-15. Preparing the XmlDocument Object

```
XmlDocument oXmlDocument = new XmlDocument();
XmlNode oXMLMainNode;

oXmlDeclaration = oXmlDocument.CreateXmlDeclaration("1.0", "UTF-8", null);

oXmlDocument.AppendChild(oXmlDeclaration);

oXMLMainNode = oXmlDocument.CreateNode(XmlNodeType.Element,
    "Controls", string.Empty);
oXmlDocument.AppendChild(oXMLMainNode);

oXmlDocument = SaveFilter(panel1, oXmlDocument, oXMLMainNode);
```

The SaveFilter() method shown in Listing 4-16 receives the owner control as a parameter along with the XmlDocument object. This code shows how to handle both single-value and multiple-value controls. You can find the full source in the download file.

Listing 4-16. SaveFilter() Method

```
private XmlDocument SaveFilter(Control oControl,
                              XmlDocument oXmlDocument,
                              XmlNode oXMLMainNode)
{
    string szControlType;
    string szName;


    foreach (Control oSubControl in oControl.Controls)
    {
        //Get the name of the control type - ListBox, CheckBox, etc.
        szControlType = oSubControl.GetType().Name;

        //Get the name of the control to serve as a unique identifier
        szName = oSubControl.Name;

        switch (szControlType)
        {
            case "CheckBox":
                oXmlDocument = AddNode(oXmlDocument, oXMLMainNode, szControlType,
                    szName, ((CheckBox)oSubControl).Checked.ToString());
                break;

            case "CheckedListBox":
                oXmlDocument = AddCheckedListBoxItems(oXmlDocument, oXMLMainNode,
```

```
                    szControlType,  szName,
                    ((CheckedListBox)oSubControl).CheckedItems);
                break;
        }

        //Perform recursion to handle child controls
        if (oSubControl.HasChildren)
            oXmlDocument = SaveFilter(oSubControl, oXmlDocument, oXMLMainNode);

    }

    return oXmlDocument;
}
```

By recursively iterating through the Controls collection of the Panel, you can identify those controls that can hold data. Then, based on the type of control, the contents are extracted and written to XML nodes. Listing 4-17 shows how this is accomplished for single-value controls like the CheckBox shown in the example.

Listing 4-17. Saving Properties for Single-Value Controls

```
private XmlDocument AddNode(XmlDocument oXmlDocument,
                            XmlNode oXMLMainNode,
                            string szControlType,
                            string szName,
                            string szValue)
{
    XmlNode oXMLNode;
    XmlAttribute oXmlAttribute;

    oXMLNode = oXmlDocument.CreateNode(XmlNodeType.Element,
        "Control", string.Empty);
    oXMLMainNode.AppendChild(oXMLNode);

    oXmlAttribute = oXmlDocument.CreateAttribute("type");
    oXmlAttribute.Value = szControlType;
    oXMLNode.Attributes.Append(oXmlAttribute);

    oXmlAttribute = oXmlDocument.CreateAttribute("name");
    oXmlAttribute.Value = szName;
    oXMLNode.Attributes.Append(oXmlAttribute);

    oXmlAttribute = oXmlDocument.CreateAttribute("value");
    oXmlAttribute.Value = szValue;
    oXMLNode.Attributes.Append(oXmlAttribute);

    return oXmlDocument;
```

```
}
```

The `AddNode()` method simply creates a node with three attributes, one each for the control type, name, and value. The final result looks like this:

```
<Control type="CheckBox" name="checkBox2" value="False" />
```

Multiple-value controls like the `CheckedListBox` must be handled a bit differently. In the code shown in Listing 4-18, the type and name attributes are handled in the same fashion, but the selected items are stored in a child node called `value`.

Listing 4-18. *Saving Properties for Multivalue Controls*

```
private XmlDocument AddCheckedListBoxItems(XmlDocument oXmlDocument,
                      XmlNode oXMLMainNode,
                      string szControlType,
                      string szName,
                      CheckedListBox.CheckedItemCollection oItems)
{
    XmlNode oXMLNode;
    XmlNode oXMLItemNode;
    XmlAttribute oXmlAttribute;

    oXMLNode =
      oXmlDocument.CreateNode(XmlNodeType.Element, "Control", string.Empty);
    oXMLMainNode.AppendChild(oXMLNode);

    oXmlAttribute = oXmlDocument.CreateAttribute("type");
    oXmlAttribute.Value = szControlType;
    oXMLNode.Attributes.Append(oXmlAttribute);

    oXmlAttribute = oXmlDocument.CreateAttribute("name");
    oXmlAttribute.Value = szName;
    oXMLNode.Attributes.Append(oXmlAttribute);

    foreach (ListItem oItem in oItems)
    {
        oXMLItemNode =
            oXmlDocument.CreateNode(XmlNodeType.Element, "value", string.Empty);
        oXMLItemNode.InnerText = oItem.Value.ToString();
        oXMLNode.AppendChild(oXMLItemNode);
    }

    return oXmlDocument;
}
```

ListItem is a custom object that provides properties for a value and description (you can find it in the code download). The end result of this operations looks like this:

```
<Control type="CheckedListBox" name="checkedListBox1">
  <value>201</value>
  <value>202</value>
</Control>
```

Restoring the User Selections

To repopulate the filter, you need to retrieve the persisted values from the XML. Listing 4-19 shows how to extract the XML string and reference the root element.

Listing 4-19. *Extracting Filter Settings into an XmlDocument*

```
XmlDocument oXmlDocument = new XmlDocument();
XmlElement oXmlElement;

//Pull from database here into DataTable

//Load this XML into an XmlDocument object
oXmlDocument.LoadXml(oDT.Rows[0]["FilterData"].ToString());

//Obtain a reference to the root element
oXmlElement = oXmlDocument.DocumentElement;

LoadFilter(panel1, oXmlElement);
```

Then, by passing the root element to the LoadFilter() method, shown in Listing 4-20, you can look up each control reference via SelectNodes() and, if it's found, populate the control as appropriate.

Listing 4-20. *LoadFilter() Method*

```
private void LoadFilter(Control oControl, XmlElement oXmlElement)
{
    XmlNodeList oXmlNodeList;
    string szControlType;
    string szNodeQuery;

    //iterate through every control in the control
    //collection of the owner object
    foreach (Control oSubControl in oControl.Controls)
    {
        //Get the name of the control type - ListBox, CheckBox, etc.
        szControlType = oSubControl.GetType().Name;
```

```
        //Find the control's saved data in the XML
        szNodeQuery = "Control[@name='" + oSubControl.Name + "']";

        //Obtain a reference to that control's information
        oXmlNodeList = oXmlElement.SelectNodes(szNodeQuery);

        if (oXmlNodeList.Count > 0)
        {
            switch (szControlType)
            {
                case "CheckBox":
                    ((CheckBox)oSubControl).Checked =
                        bool.Parse(oXmlNodeList[0].Attributes["value"].Value);
                    break;

                case "CheckedListBox":
                    foreach (XmlNode oXmlNode in oXmlNodeList[0].ChildNodes)
                    {
                        CheckItem(((CheckedListBox)oSubControl),
oXmlNode.InnerXml);
                    }
                    break;
            }
        }

        //Perform recursion to handle child controls
        if (oSubControl.HasChildren)
            LoadFilter(oSubControl, oXmlElement);
    }
}
```

A single-value control like CheckBox reads the value from its XML attribute. For a multivalue control like the CheckedListBox, you need to iterate through the ChildNodes of its XML entry and match each value to the Items collection, using the method shown in Listing 4-21.

Listing 4-21. CheckItem() Method

```
private void CheckItem(CheckedListBox oCheckedListBox, string szValue)
{
    int iCnt = 0;

    foreach (ListItem oItem in oCheckedListBox.Items)
    {
        if (oItem.Value.ToString() == szValue)
        {
            oCheckedListBox.SetItemChecked(iCnt, true);
```

```
        }

    iCnt++;
    }
}
```

Saving Grid Settings

One complaint users often have about applications is the inability to persist their data-grid adjustments. Users have different needs, even for the same screen. You may have a grid on a screen that shows customer information arranged as company name, address, city, state, zip, phone number, terms, CEO name, and accounts payable contact. This much information likely requires left/right scrolling, because it's too much to fit in the grid's visible display area. The sales manager may need to know only the state, company name, CEO name, and phone number, sorted by state. The shipping department may only need to see the company name, address, city, state, and zip, sorted by company name. Each user may wish to adjust the width and ordinal positions of these columns as their needs dictate. Fortunately, you can use data-driven techniques to accomplish this.

Just like for controls, you can store these settings in your database in XML format. You're interested in saving the sort column of the grid as well as the ordinal position, visible flag, and width of each column. The XML to store this looks like Listing 4-22.

Listing 4-22. *Grid Settings XML Mapping*

```
<DataGridView name="dataGridView1" sortedcolumn="" sortorder="Ascending">
  <Column name="LastName" displayindex="0" width="64" visible="True" />
  <Column name="FirstName" displayindex="2" width="267" visible="True" />
  <Column name="DOB" displayindex="1" width="77" visible="True" />
</DataGridView>
```

Then, when the user opens the screen in question, their grid is re-created exactly the way they left it. You can do this with one set of grid methods that can handle all grids across all applications. Listing 4-23 shows how to iterate through a DataGridView and extract its information into custom GridInfo and GridColumn objects that are then persisted to XML.

Listing 4-23. GridInfo() *Method*

```
public GridInfo(DataGridView oDataGridView)
{
    GridColumn oGridColumn;

    _oList = new List<GridColumn>();

    this.Name = oDataGridView.Name;

    if (oDataGridView.SortedColumn == null)
        this.SortedColumn = string.Empty;
    else
```

```
        this.SortedColumn = oDataGridView.SortedColumn.Name;

    if (oDataGridView.SortOrder == SortOrder.Descending)
        this.ListSortDirection = ListSortDirection.Descending;
    else
        this.ListSortDirection = ListSortDirection.Ascending;

    foreach (DataGridViewColumn oDataGridViewColumn in oDataGridView.Columns)
    {
        oGridColumn = new GridColumn();

        oGridColumn.Name = oDataGridViewColumn.Name;
        oGridColumn.DisplayIndex = oDataGridViewColumn.DisplayIndex;
        oGridColumn.Width = oDataGridViewColumn.Width;
        oGridColumn.Visible = oDataGridViewColumn.Visible;

        this.AddColumn(oGridColumn);
    }
}
```

The structures of the GridInfo and GridColumn objects are shown in Figure 4-5.

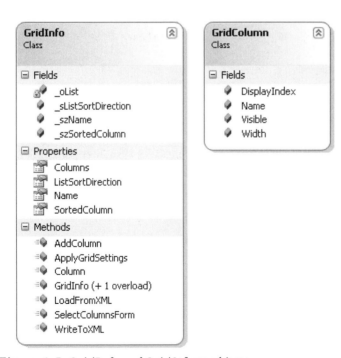

Figure 4-5. GridInfo and GridColumn objects

This class constructor receives a `DataGridView` as a parameter, although you can easily adjust it to handle the third-party grid of your choosing. Each grid's name, sort column, and sort direction are assigned to the corresponding `GridInfo` class properties. Then, the column collection is iterated to retrieve the name, ordinal position, width, and visible flag of each one. After this class is built, it can be persisted to XML through the method shown in Listing 4-24.

Listing 4-24. *WriteToXML() Method*

```
public XmlDocument WriteToXML()
{
    XmlDocument oXmlDocument = new XmlDocument();
    XmlDeclaration oXmlDeclaration;
    XmlNode oXMLMainNode;
    XmlNode oXMLNode;


    oXmlDeclaration = oXmlDocument.CreateXmlDeclaration("1.0",
                "UTF-8", null);

    oXmlDocument.AppendChild(oXmlDeclaration);
    oXMLMainNode = oXmlDocument.CreateNode(XmlNodeType.Element,
        "DataGridView", string.Empty);
    oXmlDocument.AppendChild(oXMLMainNode);

    Common.AddXmlAttribute(oXmlDocument, oXMLMainNode,
        "name", this.Name);
    Common.AddXmlAttribute (oXmlDocument, oXMLMainNode,
        "sortedcolumn", this.SortedColumn);
    Common.AddXmlAttribute (oXmlDocument, oXMLMainNode,
        "sortorder", this.ListSortDirection.ToString());

    foreach (GridColumn oGridColumn in this.Columns)
    {
        oXMLNode = oXmlDocument.CreateNode(XmlNodeType.Element,
            "Column", string.Empty);
        oXMLMainNode.AppendChild(oXMLNode);

        Common.AddXmlAttribute (oXmlDocument, oXMLNode,
            "name", oGridColumn.Name);
        Common.AddXmlAttribute (oXmlDocument, oXMLNode,
            "displayindex", oGridColumn.DisplayIndex.ToString());
        Common.AddXmlAttribute (oXmlDocument, oXMLNode,
            "width", oGridColumn.Width.ToString());
        Common.AddXmlAttribute (oXmlDocument, oXMLNode,
            "visible", oGridColumn.Visible.ToString());
    }
```

```
    return oXmlDocument;
}
```

Restoring the grid layout requires a simple reversal of the preceding code. This process is shown in Listing 4-25.

Listing 4-25. *LoadFromXML() Method*

```
public void LoadFromXML(XmlDocument oXmlDocument)
{
    XmlNode oXmlMainNode;

    if (oXmlDocument.ChildNodes.Count == 0)
        return;

    oXmlMainNode = oXmlDocument.ChildNodes[0];

    this.Name = oXmlMainNode.Attributes["name"].Value;
    this.SortedColumn = oXmlMainNode.Attributes["sortedcolumn"].Value;

    if (oXmlMainNode.Attributes["sortorder"].Value != string.Empty)
        this.ListSortDirection =
            (ListSortDirection)Enum.Parse(typeof(ListSortDirection),
            oXmlDocument.ChildNodes[0].Attributes["sortorder"].Value, true);
    else
        this.ListSortDirection = ListSortDirection.Ascending;

    foreach (XmlNode oXmlNode in oXmlDocument.ChildNodes[0].ChildNodes)
    {
        GridColumn oGridColumn = new GridColumn();

        oGridColumn.Name = oXmlNode.Attributes["name"].Value;
        oGridColumn.Visible = bool.Parse(oXmlNode.Attributes["visible"].Value);
        oGridColumn.DisplayIndex =
            int.Parse(oXmlNode.Attributes["displayindex"].Value);
        oGridColumn.Width = int.Parse(oXmlNode.Attributes["width"].Value);

        this.Columns.Add(oGridColumn);
    }
}
```

Here, the XML data is written to the GridInfo object, which acts as an intermediate layer between the XML and the grid control. This object allows you to support the column-selection screen shown in Figure 4-6.

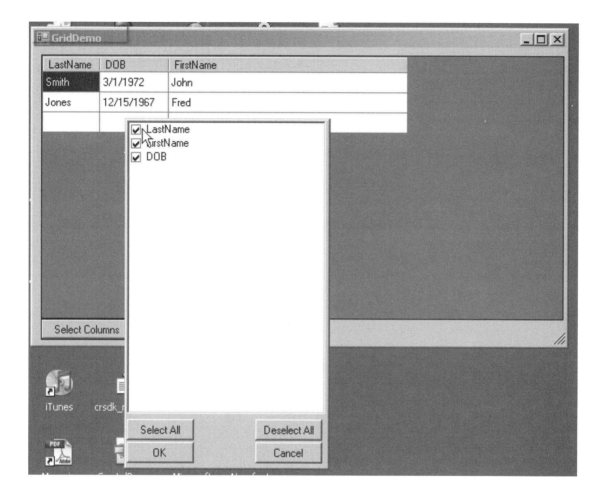

Figure 4-6. Column-selection dialog

Now you can let your users customize any grid in your application. This is intended as a one-size-fits-all solution. You can find the remainder of the code in the download file on the Apress web site.

Data-Driven Menus

Menus have labyrinthine hierarchies that map perfectly to XML. You can store an application's menu structure in XML, much like a *sitemap* file in ASP.NET. You may wish to build a menu that is fully or partially data-driven to allow add-on features for an application. Suppose you wish to allow your users to write their own assemblies and link this functionality into the application. The assembly may be an entire subsystem that needs to be made an option on the menu. Or, you may wish to let users store the most recently opened files and offer them as menu options. The following sections illustrate how to create dynamic menus.

Application Menus

Examine the code in Listing 4-26. Here, you're storing the entire structure of a menu. Each element has

- A text label
- The menu object name
- Indicators of whether the options should be enabled or checked
- The name of the method that ties to the Click event

Listing 4-26. XML Menu Mapping

```
<MainMenu>
   <MainMenuItem Text="Accounts" Name="mnuAccounts" Enabled="true"
        Checked="false">
     <MenuItem Text="Receivable" Name="mnuReceivable" Click="Receivables"
        Enabled="true" Checked="false"/>
     <MenuItem Text="Payable" Name="mnuPayable" Click ="Payables"
        Enabled="true" Checked="false">
       <MenuItem Text="Overdue Report" Name="mnuOverdueReport" Click ="Overdue"
        Enabled="true" Checked="false"/>
       <MenuItem Text="Aging Schedule" Name="mnuAgingSchedule" Click ="Aging"
        Enabled="true" Checked="false"/>
     </MenuItem>
</MainMenuItem>
   <MainMenuItem Text="Employees" Name="mnuEmployees" Enabled="true"
        Checked="false">
     <MenuItem Text="Personnel" Name="mnuPersonnel" Click ="PersonnelMgt"
        Enabled="true" Checked="false"/>
     <MenuItem Text="Print Roster" Name="mnuPrintRoster" Click ="Roster"
        Enabled="true" Checked="false"/>
   </MainMenuItem>
</MainMenu>
```

The goal is to produce a menu structure that looks like Figure 4-7.

Figure 4-7. XML-generated menu structure

To achieve this result, the code in Listing 4-27, specifically the BuildMenuStrip() method, first creates a MenuStrip object and adds to it the menu options that appear across the top of the menu—in this example, Accounts and Employees. Then, for each of these menu options, the BuildMenu() method is invoked recursively to build the drop-down portion of the menu.

Listing 4-27. Generating a Menu from XML

```
private void BuildMenuStrip()
{
    XmlDocument oXmlDocument = new XmlDocument();
    MenuStrip oMenuStrip = new MenuStrip();
    ToolStripMenuItem oToolStripMenuItem;

    oXmlDocument.Load(Application.StartupPath + @"\menu.xml");
    foreach (XmlNode oXmlNode in oXmlDocument.FirstChild)
    {
        oToolStripMenuItem = new ToolStripMenuItem();
        oToolStripMenuItem.Text = oXmlNode.Attributes["Text"].Value;
        oToolStripMenuItem.Name = oXmlNode.Attributes["Name"].Value;
        oToolStripMenuItem.Enabled =
            bool.Parse(oXmlNode.Attributes["Enabled"].Value);
        oToolStripMenuItem.Checked =
            bool.Parse(oXmlNode.Attributes["Checked"].Value);
```

```
            if (oXmlNode.HasChildNodes)
                BuildMenu(oXmlNode, oToolStripMenuItem);

            oMenuStrip.Items.Add(oToolStripMenuItem);

        }

        this.Controls.Add(oMenuStrip);
    }

    private void BuildMenu(XmlNode oXmlNode, ToolStripMenuItem oTopMenuItem)
    {
        ToolStripMenuItem oToolStripMenuItem;

        foreach (XmlNode oXmlMenuNode in oXmlNode.ChildNodes)
        {
            oToolStripMenuItem = new ToolStripMenuItem();
            oToolStripMenuItem.Text = oXmlMenuNode.Attributes["Text"].Value;
            oToolStripMenuItem.Name = oXmlMenuNode.Attributes["Name"].Value;
            oToolStripMenuItem.Enabled =
                bool.Parse(oXmlMenuNode.Attributes["Enabled"].Value);
            oToolStripMenuItem.Checked =
                bool.Parse(oXmlMenuNode.Attributes["Checked"].Value);
            oToolStripMenuItem.Click += Menu_Click;

            oTopMenuItem.DropDownItems.Add(oToolStripMenuItem);

            if (oXmlMenuNode.HasChildNodes)
                BuildMenu(oXmlMenuNode, oToolStripMenuItem);
        }
    }
}
```

Overall, building the menus dynamically is relatively easy. Logically, it's not much different from building hierarchies of controls as explained earlier in the chapter. The harder part is hooking the event methods to the individual menu items. Note that the XML contains a Click attribute that includes the name of the method to be fired when this event is triggered. Rather than assign the Click event to a predefined Menu_Click event handler, you can specify the name of the method like this, taking it from the XML file:

```
WireEvent(oToolStripMenuItem, this, "Click",
    oXmlMenuNode.Attributes["Click"].Value);
```

Listing 4-28 shows how to connect the menu object to the method.

Listing 4-28. Wiring a Click Event to a Method

```
private void WireEvent(ToolStripMenuItem oToolStripMenuItem,
                       Form oForm,
                       string szEventName,
                       string szMethodName)
{
    MethodInfo oMethodInfo;
    Delegate oDelegate;
    EventInfo oEventInfo = oToolStripMenuItem.GetType().GetEvent(szEventName);
    Type oType = oForm.GetType();

    oMethodInfo = oType.GetMethod(
                  szMethodName,
                  System.Reflection.BindingFlags.IgnoreCase |
                  System.Reflection.BindingFlags.Instance |
                  System.Reflection.BindingFlags.NonPublic);

    if (oMethodInfo != null)
    {
        oDelegate = Delegate.CreateDelegate(oEventInfo.EventHandlerType,
            oForm, oMethodInfo.Name);

        oEventInfo.AddEventHandler(oToolStripMenuItem, oDelegate);
    }

}
```

You pass in the object references to the menu item and the owner form, along with the name of the event (here, Click) and the name of the event method to attach it to. Then, you can use Reflection to obtain a reference to the Event method of the menu item and the method of the owner form that contains that method. By creating a Delegate object referencing the target method, you can assign that to the AddEventHandler method of the Event object to link the two together. An example of an event method is shown here:

```
private void Receivables(object sender, EventArgs e)
{
    MessageBox.Show("Receivables");
}
```

Provided the method has the expected signature—in this case two parameters, one object and one EventArgs—you can use it validly for a Click event. Of course, different events require methods with different signatures.

Most Recently Used File Menu

Another common, and much simpler, menu practice is the most recently used file menu. Here, the latest files opened by the user are stored in the Registry, as shown in Figure 4-8.

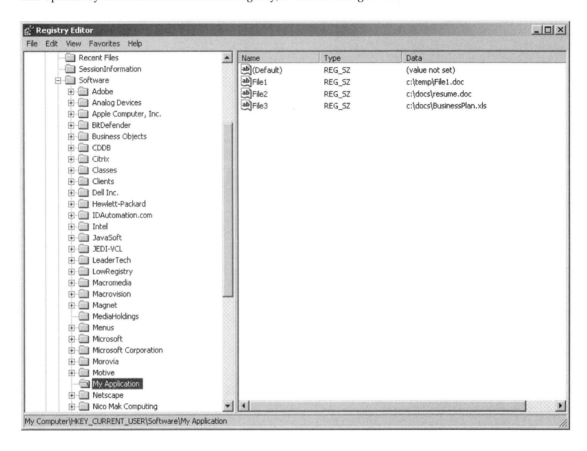

Figure 4-8. Registry showing last files opened

Extracting them requires accessing the registry using the RegistryKey class of the System.Diagnostics namespace. The code shown in Listing 4-29 adds a separator menu item to the File menu; the names of the most recently opened files are added after that.

Listing 4-29. Accessing the Most Recently Used Files

```
private void LoadFromRegistry()
{
    MenuStrip oMenuStrip = new MenuStrip();
    ToolStripMenuItem oToolStripMainMenuItem;
```

```
ToolStripMenuItem oToolStripMenuItem;
RegistryKey oRegistryKey =
    Registry.CurrentUser.OpenSubKey("Software\\My Application", true);

oToolStripMainMenuItem = new ToolStripMenuItem();
oToolStripMainMenuItem.Text = "Last Used Files";

oMenuStrip.Items.Add(oToolStripMainMenuItem);

foreach (string szValue in oRegistryKey.GetValueNames())
{
    oToolStripMenuItem = new ToolStripMenuItem();
    oToolStripMenuItem.Text = oRegistryKey.GetValue(szValue).ToString();

    oToolStripMainMenuItem.DropDownItems.Add(oToolStripMenuItem);
}

this.Controls.Add(oMenuStrip);
}
```

The result is shown in Figure 4-9.

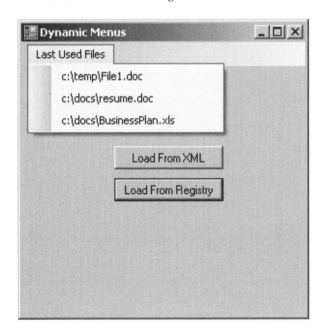

Figure 4-9. *Dynamically generated menu*

Creating Criteria Screens

Report criteria screens are prime candidates for data-driven development because the payoff for doing so is substantial. Regardless of how many reports you have, you can feed them criteria through one criteria-collection form. The controls typically required for criteria screens in any desktop or web applications are text/numeric input boxes, date controls, check boxes, list boxes, and combo boxes. Radio buttons aren't necessary because combo boxes handle these choices just as well. Radio buttons are also more difficult to work with when you're using data-driven programming techniques, because they need to be grouped within an owner object and positioned relative to one another. Moreover, the general rule for radio buttons is to stop using them when more than six options are involved. After that, its time to use a combo box.

Using the classes described in this section, you can dynamically create a WinForms interface for your reports with just a few lines of code. You can extract the user selections with a few lines of code as well.

Dynamic Criteria Controls

Because criteria screens repeat the same controls and use them in relatively the same fashion, it's possible to build a library that creates them for you dynamically with a few simple method calls. In this section you examine how to dynamically create a list box control, populate it with data, and extract the selections made by the user. The approach for the other types of controls is very similar; you can find the code in the download.

Suppose you want the user to select any number of departments, or none at all, from a list box. You can reduce the creation of the interface to these two lines of code:

```
oDT = GetDepartments();

ShowListBox(Criteria.Department, oDT, "DictionaryID",
    "Description", 20, 420, 125, 25, "Department:");
```

To accomplish this feat, you must create a report criteria form—and this form should be the only one you need to display the criteria for every report. You need customized forms only for those reports whose criteria are very unique and/or that interact with one another in very specific ways. It's a maintenance nightmare to have a different criteria form for every report in your application.

In this new form, you declare an ArrayList with form-wide scope:

```
ArrayList aControlList = new ArrayList();
```

The purpose of this ArrayList is to manage the various controls that will be dynamically instantiated. Then, you need a class to maintain the collection of controls required to create a list box display. These controls include a CheckedListBox control, a Label control to display the caption above it, and a Button control below to allow the user to clear the selections made. The display looks like screen shown in Figure 4-10.

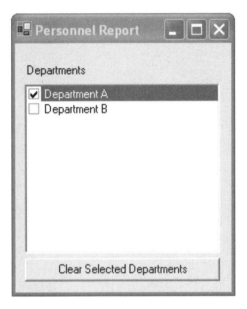

Figure 4-10. *CheckedListBox filter*

The class that maintains this three-control grouping is shown in Listing 4-30. Because every set of controls comes with multiple elements—a textbox and a label, a combo box and a label, and so on—they can more easily be managed by storing references to the related component objects in classes designed to hold each set. Every control has a label and an index, so you can store these properties in a ControlManager base class from which the individual control classes inherit.

Listing 4-30. *ControlManager and ListBoxManager Classes*

```
abstract class ControlManager
{
   private Criteria iIndex;
   private Label oLabelControl;

   public Criteria Index
   {
      get { return iIndex; }
      set { iIndex = value; }
   }

   public Label LabelControl
   {
      get { return oLabelControl; }
      set { oLabelControl = value; }
   }
```

```
}

class ListBoxManager : ControlManager
{
   private CheckedListBox oListBoxControl;
   private Button oButtonControl;

   public CheckedListBox ListBoxControl
   {
      get { return oListBoxControl; }
      set { oListBoxControl = value; }
   }

   public Button ButtonControl
   {
      get { return oButtonControl; }
      set { oButtonControl = value; }
   }
}
```

You need to pass the Criteria enumeration to the ShowListBox() method (Listing 4-31) along with the data source information, the dimensions of the list box, and the caption. ShowListBox() instantiates an object of type ListBoxManager, which receives the instantiated objects of the Label, CheckedListBox, and Button types. These controls are added to the properties of the ListBoxManager objects, which in turn are added to the ArrayList object that contains all the different criteria collections and allows their form-wide management.

Listing 4-31. ShowListBox() Method

```
private void ShowListBox(Criteria iIndex,
   DataTable oDT,
   string szID,
   string szDescription,
   int iLeft,
   int iTop,
   int iWidth,
   int iHeight,
   string szCaption)
{
   ListBoxManager oListBoxManager = new ListBoxManager();


   oListBoxManager.Index = iIndex;
   oListBoxManager.LabelControl =  AddDynamicLabel(iIndex, iLeft, iTop, szCaption);

   iTop = oListBoxManager.LabelControl.Top +
      oListBoxManager.LabelControl.Height + 5;
```

```
oListBoxManager.ListBoxControl =
    AddDynamicListBox(iIndex, iLeft, iTop, iWidth, iHeight);

iTop = oListBoxManager.ListBoxControl.Top +
    oListBoxManager.ListBoxControl.Height + 5;

oListBoxManager.ButtonControl =
    AddDynamicListBoxButton(iIndex, iLeft, iTop, iWidth, 23, szCaption);

LoadCheckedListBox(oListBoxManager.ListBoxControl,
    oDT, "DictionaryID", "Description", false);

aControlList.Add(oListBoxManager);
}
```

The `LoadCheckedListBox()` method populates the `Items` collection of the `ListBox` with data. The code is in the source file for the book.

The `AddDynamicLabel()` method (Listing 4-32) instantiates a `Label` object and assigns its location via a `Point` object. The `AutoSize` property is set to `true` so the control sets its width to the size necessary to display the text contained within it. This new `Label` object is then added to the `Controls` collection of the owner form. When you display a `Label` control on a form using the visual designer, the IDE generates code very similar to what you see here.

Listing 4-32. *AddDynamicLabel() Method*

```
private Label AddDynamicLabel(Criteria iIndex,
    int iLeft,
    int iTop,
    string szCaption)
{
    Label oLabel = new Label();

    oLabel.AutoSize = true;
    oLabel.Name = "Label" + iIndex.ToString();
    oLabel.Location = new Point(iLeft, iTop);
    oLabel.Text = szCaption;

    this.Controls.Add(oLabel);

    return oLabel;
}
```

The `CheckedListBox` control is displayed in a similar fashion, as illustrated in the `AddDynamicListBox()` method shown in Listing 4-33. Other than the type of control object, the only major difference here is that the size is explicitly set via a `Size` object.

Listing 4-33. AddDynamicListBox() Method

```
private CheckedListBox AddDynamicListBox(Criteria iIndex,
    int iLeft,
    int iTop,
    int iWidth,
    int iHeight)
{
    CheckedListBox oCheckedListBox;

    oCheckedListBox = new CheckedListBox();

    oCheckedListBox.Name = "ListBox" + iIndex.ToString();
    oCheckedListBox.Size = new Size(iWidth, iHeight);
    oCheckedListBox.Location = new Point(iLeft, iTop);

    this.Controls.Add(oCheckedListBox);

    return oCheckedListBox;
}
```

You create and display the `Button` control in a fashion similar to the `Label` and `CheckedListBox`, as shown in Listing 4-34. The `Button` control triggers an event—that is, when clicked, it must clear the selections in the list box to which it's associated. You do this using the `System.EventHandler()` method, just as it is in the code generated by the IDE.

Listing 4-34. AddDynamicListBoxButton() Method

```
private Button AddDynamicListBoxButton(Criteria iIndex,
    int iLeft,
    int iTop,
    int iWidth,
    int iHeight,
    string szCaption)
{
    Button oButton;

    oButton = new Button();

    oButton.Name = "ListBoxButton" + iIndex.ToString();
    oButton.Size = new Size(iWidth, iHeight);
    oButton.Location = new Point(iLeft, iTop);
    oButton.Text = "Clear Selected " + szCaption;

    oButton.Click += new System.EventHandler(this.Button_Click);
```

```
    this.Controls.Add(oButton);

    return oButton;
}
```

This event handler, shown in Listing 4-35, needs to identify what button was clicked. It does this by iterating through the aControlList ArrayList object until it finds an entry of type ListBoxManager. When it finds one, it extracts a reference to the button associated with it and determines if that is the button that was clicked. If so, then you've found the right CheckedListBox, and this object can be referenced and the selections cleared.

Listing 4-35. Button Event Handler

```
private void Button_Click(object sender, System.EventArgs e)
{
    ListBoxManager oListBoxManager = null;
    CheckedListBox oListbox;
    int iIndex;

    foreach(object oItem in aControlList)
    {
        if (oItem is ListBoxManager)
        {
            oListBoxManager = ((ListBoxManager) oItem);

            if (oListBoxManager.ButtonControl == sender)
                break;
        }

    }

    oListbox = oListBoxManager.ListBoxControl;

    for(iIndex = 0; iIndex <= oListbox.Items.Count - 1; iIndex++)
        oListbox.SetItemChecked(iIndex, false);

}
```

Cascading Prompts

Cascading prompts are those where one control filters the data in another. For example, you may have a combo box filled with departments and adjacent to it a list box filled with the names of employees who work in those departments. When you select a department in the combo box, the list box refreshes with the employees for that department. To accomplish this in the framework of the data-driven controls just examined, use the `SelectedIndexChanged()` event handler of the generic `ComboBox` control. The code for this is shown here:

```
ComboBoxManager oComboBoxManager = null;
ListBoxManager oListBoxManager = null;
ComboBox oComboBox;
ListBox oListBox;
DataTable oDT;
ListItem oListItem;
string szData = string.Empty;

//Walk through each control set
foreach(object oSourceItem in aControlList)
{
   //If you find a combo box let's see if
   //its really the one you want
   if (oSourceItem is ComboBoxManager)
   {
      //Cast to a ComboBoxManager
      oComboBoxManager = ((ComboBoxManager) oSourceItem);

      //Is it the combo box collection you want?
      if (oComboBoxManager.Index == Criteria.Department)
      {
         //If so, extract the combo box control
         oComboBox = ((ComboBox) oComboBoxManager.ComboBoxControl);

         //Get the ListItem object...
         oListItem = ((ListItem) oComboBox.SelectedItem);

         //...and retrieve the unique key for the department
         szData = oListItem.Value;

         //Loop through the control set again
         foreach(object oTargetItem in aControlList)
         {
            //If this is a list box collection
            if (oTargetItem is ListBoxManager)
            {
               //Cast to a ListBoxManager
               oListBoxManager = ((ListBoxManager) oTargetItem);

               //Is it the list box collection you want?
               if (oListBoxManager.Index == Criteria.Employee)
               {
                  //If so, extract the list box control and populate
                  //with the employees belonging to the selected department
```

```
                    oListBox = ((ListBox) oListBoxManager.ListBoxControl);

                    oDT = GetDeptEmployees(szData);

                    LoadCheckedListBox(oListBoxManager.ListBoxControl, oDT,
                        "DictionaryID", "Description", false);

                    break;
                }
            }
        }

        break;
    }
  }
}
```

Extracting the User Selections

After the user has made their selections, you need to extract the information selected and pass it to your data source. Because all the controls are managed via classes, you can accomplish this easily and generically using one function call. Just as the list box was displayed with two lines of code, each of the selected values can be retrieved with one. For example

```
string szDepartments = GetCriteria(Criteria.Department);
```

assigns a value to the szDepartments variable that looks like this: "(12,45,23)". This is a comma-delimited string that can be used in a SQL IN clause to restrict the departments that are extracted from the database. The GetCriteria() method is partially shown in Listing 4-36. This section shows how the ListBoxManager is handled. Each element in the ArrayList is checked for its class type and then cast to that type. If the Index property, which identifies the control to which it's associated, matches the enumerated value passed to it, then you extract the selected data in a fashion appropriate to the control. All the other control collection types are handled similarly.

Listing 4-36. GetCriteria() Method

```
ListBoxManager oListBoxManager = null;
CheckedListBox oListBox = null;
string szData = string.Empty;

foreach(object oItem in aControlList)
{
   if (oItem is ListBoxManager)
   {
      oListBoxManager = ((ListBoxManager) oItem);
```

```
        if (oListBoxManager.Index == iIndex)
        {
            oListBoxManager = ((ListBoxManager) oItem);

            oListBox = ((CheckedListBox) oListBoxManager.ListBoxControl);

            szData = ParseIt(oListBox, false, 0, true);
            break;
        }
    }

...

}

return szData;
```

The selection-extraction approach appropriate to a ListBox control is the ParseIt() method shown in Listing 4-37. This method receives a CheckedListBox control and a Boolean indicating whether quotes should surround each item, which column—0 (ID) or 1 (description)—to return, and another Boolean to indicate if all or only the checked items are returned.

Listing 4-37. ParseIt() Method

```
public static string ParseIt(CheckedListBox oList,
    bool bQuotes, int sCol, bool bCheckedOnly)
{
    string szResult = String.Empty;
    string szQuotes = String.Empty;
    string szData = String.Empty;
    System.Text.StringBuilder oResult = new System.Text.StringBuilder();

    //use quotes or not
    szQuotes = (bQuotes) ? "'" : String.Empty;

    //count all or just the checked items
    IList oListItems = (bCheckedOnly) ?
        (IList)oList.CheckedItems : (IList)oList.Items;

    foreach (object oItem in oListItems)
    {
        ListItem oCheckBoxItem = oItem as ListItem;

        if (oCheckBoxItem != null)
        {
```

```
        //depending on the column selected, extract the requested property
        switch (sCol)
        {
            case 0:
                szData = oCheckBoxItem.Value;
                break;

            case 1:
                szData = oCheckBoxItem.Text;
                break;

            case 2:
                szData = oCheckBoxItem.OtherText;
                break;
        }

        if (oResult.Length > 0)
            oResult.Append(",");

        oResult.AppendFormat("{0}{1}{2}", szQuotes, szData, szQuotes);
        }
    }

    szResult = (oResult.Length == 0) ? oResult.ToString() :
        string.Format("({0})", oResult.ToString());

    return szResult;
}
```

To allow the ParseIt() method to handle ListBox, instead of CheckedListBox, controls, you overload it so that the first parameter receives an object of type ListBox and, when iterating through the chosen options, refer to the SelectedItems collection instead of the CheckedItems collection. That's the only difference.

After the data as been extracted from the control, you can pass it to a stored procedure. There is a catch here, however. SQL Server, Sybase, and Oracle stored procedures, among others, don't allow you to pass a parameter to an IN clause as shown in Listing 4-38.

Listing 4-38. *Invalid Passing of a Parameter to an IN Clause*

```
DECLARE @Data Varchar(1000)

SET @Data = '1,2'

SELECT * FROM Employees WHERE EmployeeID IN @Data
```

Therefore, you need to parse the data using a SQL Server function. Avoid using dynamic SQL if at all possible; it's slow, and you're just asking for problems. The way to handle this situation in SQL Server is shown in Listing 4-39.

Listing 4-39. *SQL Server Function to Parse to a Virtual Table*

```
DECLARE @Data Varchar(1000)

SET @Data = '1,2'

SELECT *
FROM Employees
WHERE EmployeeID IN
  (SELECT data
   FROM dbo.fnc_NumericCodes(@Data, ','))
```

The function fnc_NumericCodes returns a virtual table containing the parsed values from the delimited string passed into it. You can see this by executing the code in Listing 4-40.

Listing 4-40. Extracting a Virtual Table

```
DECLARE @Data Varchar(1000)

SET @Data = '1,2'

SELECT data
    FROM dbo.fnc_NumericCodes(@Data, ',')
```

This produces the result set shown in Figure 4-11.

	data
1	1
2	2

Figure 4-11. *fnc_NumericCodes result set*

The IN clause performs a subquery on this result set, which returns the matching rows in the Employee table. The code for this stored procedure is shown in Listing 4-41.

Listing 4-41. *fnc_NumericCodes Function*

```
CREATE FUNCTION dbo.fnc_NumericCodes
```

```
(
@Items varchar(4000),
@Delimiter varchar(1)
)

    RETURNS @DataTable TABLE (data int) AS

BEGIN

    DECLARE @Pos int
    DECLARE @DataPos int
    DECLARE @DataLen smallint
    DECLARE @Temp varchar(4000)
    DECLARE @DataRemain varchar(4000)
    DECLARE @OneItem varchar(4000)

    SET @DataPos = 1
    SET @DataRemain = ''

    WHILE @DataPos <= DATALENGTH(@Items) / 2

        BEGIN

            SET @DataLen = 4000 - DATALENGTH(@DataRemain) / 2
            SET @Temp = @DataRemain + SUBSTRING(@Items, @DataPos, @DataLen)
            SET @DataPos = @DataPos + @DataLen
            SET @Pos = CHARINDEX(@Delimiter, @Temp)

            WHILE @Pos > 0

                BEGIN
                    SET @OneItem = LTRIM(RTRIM(LEFT(@Temp, @Pos - 1)))

                    INSERT @DataTable (data) VALUES(@OneItem)

                    SET @Temp = SUBSTRING(@Temp, @Pos + 1, LEN(@Temp))
                    SET @Pos = CHARINDEX(@Delimiter, @Temp)

            END

        SET @DataRemain = @Temp

    END

    IF LEN(@Items) = 1
        SET @DataRemain = @Items
```

```
    INSERT @DataTable(data) VALUES (LTRIM(RTRIM(@DataRemain)))

    RETURN

END
```

fnc_NumericCodes is a table-valued function that receives a string of delimited values and a delimiter character (usually a comma). By iterating through this string, it breaks off each distinct value and inserts it into a table variable. As the function name suggests, it only returns numeric values, because the table variable is defined with a column called data that is of type int. You may wish to perform an IN search on a list of string values also. The code for this is very similar and is included in the download code for the book.

You can accomplish the same results as an IN clause by using CHARINDEX (or INSTR in Oracle). Both examples are shown in Listing 4-42.

Listing 4-42. Using CHARINDEX and INSTR

```
'SQL Server
DECLARE @Data varchar(1000)

SET @Data = ',1,2,3,'

SELECT EmployeeID
FROM Employees
WHERE CHARINDEX(',' + CONVERT(varchar(10), EmployeeID)
    + ',', @Data) <> 0

'Oracle
SELECT EmployeeID
FROM Employees
WHERE INSTR(',1,2,3,',',',''||EmployeeID||',') <> 0
```

Each of these SQL statements returns the rows that match on the indicated column value. Because these approaches use string values and convert numeric table data to strings to perform the match, they aren't as efficient as subquerying numeric values against a numeric column in a temporary table. Test both approaches to see which one works best for you.

Summary

In this chapter, you went to the heart of data-driven development. You covered how to dynamically instantiate objects for display on a form and how to wire those objects to events. Then, you reviewed some practical examples of how to use data-driven techniques to persist and reload filter and grid settings and how to create menus. Coming up, you see how to apply these same techniques to ASP.NET web applications.

CHAPTER 5

Dynamic ASP.NET

Programmatically, generating a web interface at runtime is similar to generating one in WinForms. Controls are drawn on a web page either visually or directly in HTML. The code-behind file or inline code instantiates controls, and the result is output to the web page. The Web is a naturally data-driven environment because everything about a web application is designed to emit data-driven HTML. That is what a web page is, essentially. All the advances made in web development technology since classic ASP was introduced over a decade ago simply better facilitate the creation of HTML and JavaScript.

In this chapter, you examine data-driven web applications. You cover dynamic control instantiation, how to work with user controls, and dynamic HTML. Finally, you look at some practical examples of how this can be used in production applications.

Instantiating Web Controls

When you lay out your web pages at design time, the controls and all their settings are stored in the ASP.NET ASPX file. The ASPX files are the approximate web equivalent of a WinForms Designer file. The main difference is that the web page defines controls as a series of ASP.NET tags that translate into source code, which instantiates the objects. A WinForms application stores the generated source code itself.

Suppose you design the web page shown in Figure 5-1.

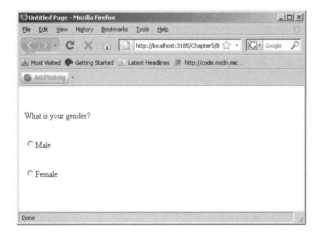

Figure 5-1. Basic web page

The ASPX file looks like that found in Listing 5-1.

Listing 5-1. ASPX File

```
<html xmlns="http://www.w3.org/1999/xhtml" >
<head runat="server">
    <title>Untitled Page</title>
</head>
<body>
    <form id="form1" runat="server">
    <div>
                <table>
            <tr>
                <td>
                    <asp:Label ID="lblGender" runat="server"
                        Text="What is your gender?"></asp:Label></td>
            </tr>
            <tr>
                <td>
                    <asp:RadioButton ID="rbMale" runat="server"
                        GroupName="Gender" Text="Male" /></td>
            </tr>
            <tr>
                <td>
                    <asp:RadioButton ID="rbFemale" runat="server"
                        GroupName="Gender" Text="Female" /></td>
            </tr>
        </table>
    </div>
    </form>
</body>
</html>
```

When you request the web page, this ASPX source file is converted to a .NET code file (*.cs or *.vb) and stored in a temporary subdirectory under C:\WINDOWS\Microsoft.NET\Framework\<*version*>\Temporary ASP.NET Files\<*AppName*>. A sample of this runtime generated code is shown in Listing 5-2.

Listing 5-2. .NET Code File Created from ASPX Source

```
[System.Diagnostics.DebuggerNonUserCodeAttribute()]
private global::System.Web.UI.WebControls.Label @__BuildControllblGender()
{
    global::System.Web.UI.WebControls.Label @__ctrl;

#line 16 "C:\Inetpub\wwwroot\Chapter5\Default.aspx"
    @__ctrl = new global::System.Web.UI.WebControls.Label();
```

```
#line default
#line hidden
    this.lblGender = @__ctrl;
    @__ctrl.ApplyStyleSheetSkin(this);

#line 16 "C:\Inetpub\wwwroot\Chapter5\Default.aspx"
    @__ctrl.ID = "lblGender";

#line default
#line hidden

#line 16 "C:\Inetpub\wwwroot\Chapter5\Default.aspx"
    @__ctrl.Text = "What is your gender?";

#line default
#line hidden
    return @__ctrl;
}

[System.Diagnostics.DebuggerNonUserCodeAttribute()]
private global::System.Web.UI.WebControls.RadioButton @__BuildControlrbMale()
{
    global::System.Web.UI.WebControls.RadioButton @__ctrl;

#line 20 "C:\Inetpub\wwwroot\Chapter5\Default.aspx"
    @__ctrl = new global::System.Web.UI.WebControls.RadioButton();

#line default
#line hidden
    this.rbMale = @__ctrl;
    @__ctrl.ApplyStyleSheetSkin(this);

#line 20 "C:\Inetpub\wwwroot\Chapter5\Default.aspx"
    @__ctrl.ID = "rbMale";

#line default
#line hidden

#line 20 "C:\Inetpub\wwwroot\Chapter5\Default.aspx"
    @__ctrl.GroupName = "Gender";

#line default
#line hidden

#line 20 "C:\Inetpub\wwwroot\Chapter5\Default.aspx"
    @__ctrl.Text = "Male";
```

125

```
#line default
#line hidden
    return @__ctrl;
}
```

As you can see, this code is rather verbose. This example shows the definitions for a Label and a RadioButton. The #line pragmas allow .NET to indicate the line number of errors found in the markup, not the generated code that you would normally never see. Obviously, this provides you with more useful feedback in case of an error. When you instantiate web controls at runtime, you're essentially doing exactly what .NET is doing to the markup. The key point to understand is that the markup control instantiation performed by .NET happens at a different time in the Page life cycle than controls instantiated in source code. In a similar fashion, the timing of the introduction of the ViewState is different as well. When .NET creates controls from the markup, they're created in their pristine format as defined in the markup. Only then are the ViewState settings applied. Therefore, dynamically created controls must be instantiated before the ViewState is applied so their state remains the same between postbacks.

■ **Note** ViewState is responsible for maintaining the state of the controls only—not the control tree itself. That is your responsibility as a developer. If your dynamic controls aren't appearing between postbacks, that isn't the fault of the ViewState. On postbacks, the control tree must be re-created. Only then can the ViewState be applied. Logically, state can't be restored to controls that don't exist yet.

If you call your runtime instantiation routine from within Page_Load, you've missed the window of opportunity to apply the ViewState. Most of the problems experienced using data-driven web controls result from not keeping this in mind. Therefore, web controls should be instantiated every time in the Page_Init or Page_PreInit method, and they must be instantiated again after every postback. The properties and settings must then be applied in Page_Load. This is the data-driven equivalent of applying the ViewState.

You need to add a PlaceHolder control to your form. Then, all instantiated controls are added to the PlaceHolder's Controls collection. Adding controls directly to the Page object's controls collection gets you an error like this:

```
this.Controls.Add(oTextBox);
```

Control 'txtLastName' of type 'TextBox' must be placed inside a form tag with runat=server.

Note the code in Listing 5-3.

Listing 5-3. Dynamic TextBox Control

```
public partial class _Default : System.Web.UI.Page
{
    TextBox oTextBox = new TextBox();
```

```
    protected void Page_Init(object sender, EventArgs e)
    {

        oTextBox.ID = "txtLastName";
        oTextBox.Text = "Smith";
        this.PlaceHolder1.Controls.Add(oTextBox);

    }
}
```

Here, a Page-wide variable of type TextBox is declared. This control is instantiated in Page_Init, assigned a default value, and added to the PlaceHolder's Controls collection. The result is the web page shown in Figure 5-2. If you want to set a default value that persists between postbacks, you need to do this in the Page_Load event as shown here:

```
protected void Page_Load(object sender, EventArgs e)
{
    oTextBox.Text = "Smith";
}
```

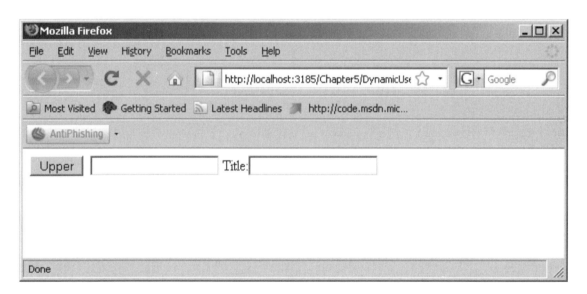

Figure 5-2. Dynamically instantiated TextBox

Understanding the Page Life Cycle

Before you can appreciate how dynamic and static controls work within the framework of a Page object, you must first understand the life cycle of a web page. When users post back a web page, they normally do so via a button or link object. This object may have JavaScript code attached to it which may contain some validation routines. There's no point in even attempting an expensive full-page postback unless the data being posted back is valid. Then, a series of postback events trigger, most of which you never need to worry about. The following list contains this series of postback events:

- PreInit: You can instantiate user controls in the PreInit method if you wish. You can also set properties of static controls. However, this only applies to pages that don't have master pages. If they do, the static controls aren't available at this stage. The reason is that all controls placed in the content page are within the master page's ContentPlaceholder. When the master page merges with the content pages, all events except Init and Unload are triggered from the outermost to the innermost control. Therefore, the PreInit event in the content page fires first. User controls and, by extension, a master page, which is itself is treated as a user control, don't possess a PreInit event. Therefore, in the Page_PreInit event, neither the master page nor any user control has been instantiated, and only the controls inside the content page are set to their default values. In general, you would do better to instantiate your dynamic controls in the Init event. But you must use PreInit to assign themes and skins.

- Init: At this point, every control has been instantiated. Each control has its own Init event that also fires. This (or the Load event) is the spot to set control properties.

- InitComplete: At this point, the controls are instantiated, but their attributes aren't yet populated from the ViewState.

- PreLoad

- Load

- LoadComplete. Here you can execute code that requires all controls on the Page object to be both instantiated and initialized, either by you or from the ViewState.

- PreRender

- PreRenderComplete

- Unload

When the Page is posted back to the server, it begins its process of rebirth anew. First, the Page object is instantiated; the controls defined with it are instantiated as well. After this is accomplished, the controls' properties are initialized from the ViewState to reset the values and attributes they held before the postback. Next, the postback data is restored. The Page_Init method fires at this point. Next, the Page_Load event fires. After this is completed, the web page is rendered—the PreRender event fires— and the page is returned to the web client.

It's important to understand the Page life cycle because the sequence of events directly affects your ability to use dynamic controls. First, it's important to understand that dynamic controls don't persist between postbacks and must be re-created every time the page posts back. This means your routine to instantiate these controls can't be invoked from with an if (!Page.IsPostback) construct.

The code in Listing 5-4 shows the firing sequence of the page and control events for a page that has one Button control on it.

Listing 5-4. Page and Control Events

```csharp
public partial class _Default : System.Web.UI.Page
{
    protected void Page_PreLoad(object sender, EventArgs e)
    {
        Response.Write("Fire Page_PreLoad" + "<BR>");
    }

    protected void Page_Load(object sender, EventArgs e)
    {
        Response.Write("Fire Page_Load" + "<BR>");
    }

    protected void Page_LoadComplete(object sender, EventArgs e)
    {
        Response.Write("Fire Page_LoadComplete" + "<BR>");
    }

    protected void Page_PreInit(object sender, EventArgs e)
    {
        Response.Write("Fire Page_PreInit" + "<BR>");

        Button1.Init += new EventHandler(this.Button1_Init);
        Button1.Load += new EventHandler(this.Button1_Load);
        Button1.PreRender += new EventHandler(this.Button1_PreRender);
        Button1.Unload += new EventHandler(this.Button1_Unload);
    }

    protected void Page_Init(object sender, EventArgs e)
    {
        Response.Write("Fire Page_Init" + "<BR>");
    }

    protected void Page_InitComplete(object sender, EventArgs e)
    {
        Response.Write("Fire Page_InitComplete" + "<BR>");
    }

    protected void Page_PreRender(object sender, EventArgs e)
    {
        Response.Write("Fire Page_PreRender" + "<BR>");
    }

    protected void Page_PreRenderComplete(object sender, EventArgs e)
    {
        Response.Write("Fire Page_PreRenderComplete" + "<BR>");
```

```
        }

        protected void Page_Unload(object sender, EventArgs e)
        {
            // Fires last after all other events;
        }



        protected void Button1_Unload(object sender, EventArgs e)
        {
            // Fires after all other events except Page_Unload;
        }

        protected void Button1_Load(object sender, EventArgs e)
        {
            Response.Write("Fire Button1_Load" + "<BR>");
        }

        protected void Button1_Init(object sender, EventArgs e)
        {
            Response.Write("Fire Button1_Init" + "<BR>");
        }

        protected void Button1_PreRender(object sender, EventArgs e)
        {
            Response.Write("Fire Button1_PreRender" + "<BR>");
        }

        protected void Button1_Click(object sender, EventArgs e)
        {
            Response.Write("Fire Button1_Click" + "<BR>");
        }
}
```

When this code is executed, you see the web page shown in Figure 5-3. The Unload events can't write to the page because by then it's too late to use Response.Write. These are the last events fired in the sequence.

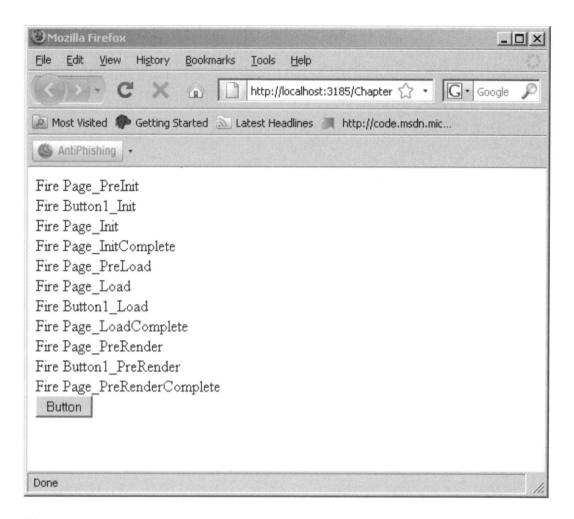

Figure 5-3. Firing page and static control events

If the static button control is dynamically instantiated as shown in Listing 5-5, you get the same results as shown in Figure 5-4. All the controls exist at the same time, and the events fire in the same sequence.

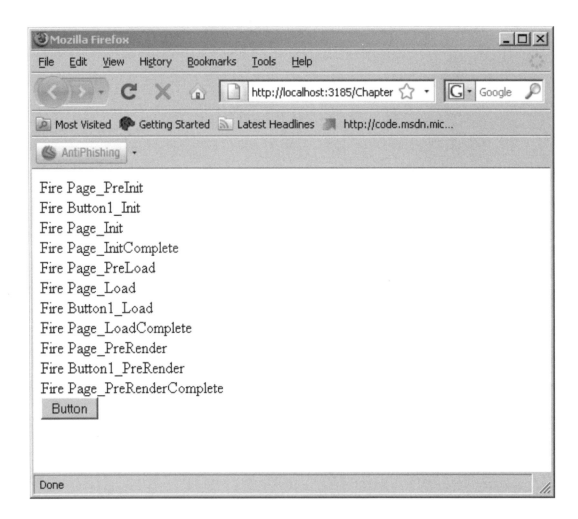

Figure 5-4. *Firing page and dynamically instantiated control events*

Listing 5-5. *Wiring Event Handlers*

```
protected void Page_Init(object sender, EventArgs e)
{
    Response.Write("Fire Page_PreInit" + "<BR>");

    Button oButton = new Button();
    oButton.Text = "Button";

    oButton.Init += new EventHandler(this.Button1_Init);
    oButton.Load += new EventHandler(this.Button1_Load);
```

```
    oButton.PreRender += new EventHandler(this.Button1_PreRender);
    oButton.Unload += new EventHandler(this.Button1_Unload);

    PlaceHolder1.Controls.Add(oButton);
}
```

Using HTML Tables

HTML tables are a popular way to position controls on a page, although many developers consider CSS the best way to accomplish this. You still have this option in a data-driven application. The `HtmlTable` object encapsulates this structure and manages its columns, rows, cells, and other settings. In the web page shown in Figure 5-5, users are presented with a survey from which they can select answers to questions by clicking radio buttons. These questions are stored in an XML format, as shown in Listing 5-6.

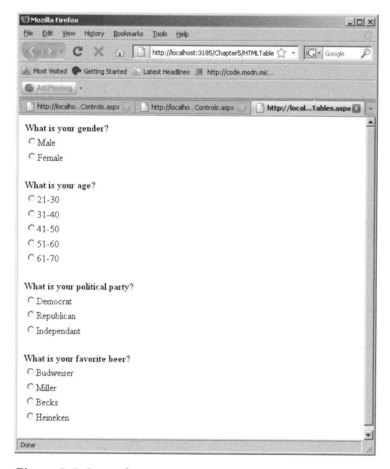

Figure 5-5. Survey form

Listing 5-6. XML-Based User Interface

```
<Survey ID="3">
    <Question group="Gender" text="What is your gender?">
        <Answer ID="1" text="Male"/>
        <Answer ID="2" text="Female"/>
    </Question>
    <Question group="Age" text="What is your age?">
        <Answer ID="1" text="21-30"/>
        <Answer ID="2" text="31-40"/>
        <Answer ID="3" text="41-50"/>
        <Answer ID="4" text="51-60"/>
        <Answer ID="5" text="61-70"/>
    </Question>
    <Question group="Party" text="What is your political party?">
        <Answer ID="1" text="Democrat"/>
        <Answer ID="2" text="Republican"/>
        <Answer ID="3" text="Independent"/>
    </Question>
    <Question group="Beer" text="What is your favorite beer?">
        <Answer ID="1" text="Budweiser"/>
        <Answer ID="2" text="Miller"/>
        <Answer ID="3" text="Becks"/>
        <Answer ID="4" text="Heineken"/>
    </Question>
</Survey>
```

Absolute vs. Static Positioning

Some of the code in this chapter uses absolute positioning. This can be a controversial topic with developers because many justifiably hate absolute positioning. *Absolute positioning* refers to setting specific coordinates for controls so they're placed at particular spots on the web page. The downfall of this technique is when users change the font size in their browsers. Suppose you've set the top of a control to 100px. It always appears 100px from the top. If you place a control above it, the first control remains 100px from the top. It may be covered by the control you just added, and it may end up covering something else. If you use absolute positioning, the controls no longer line up the same. Some developers use absolutely positioned div tags so the graphic design professionals can adjust later.

This code is easily modified by the survey administrator either through a user interface or by editing the XML directly. The code shown in Listing 5-7 reads this XML and creates a web survey from it. To position the questions and answers appropriately, you use an HTML table. Each question and answer is in its own row. When an HtmlTableRow is instantiated, an HtmlTableCell is instantiated as well. The question Label and answer RadioButton are then assigned to the cell.

Listing 5-7. Dynamic Survey

```
protected void BuildSurvey()
{
    XmlDocument oXmlDocument = new XmlDocument();
    XmlNode oQuestionNode;
    HtmlTable oHtmlTable = new HtmlTable();
    HtmlTableRow oHtmlTableRow;
    HtmlTableCell oHtmlTableCell;
    Label oLabel;
    RadioButton oRadioButton;
    string szGroup;

    oXmlDocument.Load(MapPath("survey.xml"));

    oQuestionNode = oXmlDocument.ChildNodes[0];

    foreach (XmlNode oXmlNode in oQuestionNode.ChildNodes)
    {
        szGroup = oXmlNode.Attributes["group"].Value;

        oHtmlTableRow = new HtmlTableRow();

        //Create a new question
        oHtmlTableCell = new HtmlTableCell();
        oLabel = new Label();
        oLabel.Text = oXmlNode.Attributes["text"].Value;
        oLabel.Font.Bold = true;
        oHtmlTableCell.Controls.Add(oLabel);
        oHtmlTableRow.Cells.Add(oHtmlTableCell);

        oHtmlTable.Rows.Add(oHtmlTableRow);

        //Output the answers
        foreach (XmlNode oAnswerNode in oXmlNode.ChildNodes)
        {
            oHtmlTableRow = new HtmlTableRow();

            oHtmlTableCell = new HtmlTableCell();
            oRadioButton = new RadioButton();
            oRadioButton.Text = oAnswerNode.Attributes["text"].Value;
            oRadioButton.GroupName = szGroup;
            oRadioButton.ID = szGroup + oAnswerNode.Attributes["ID"].Value;
            oHtmlTableCell.Controls.Add(oRadioButton);
            oHtmlTableRow.Cells.Add(oHtmlTableCell);

            oHtmlTable.Rows.Add(oHtmlTableRow);
```

```
        }

        //Put some space between each question
        oHtmlTableRow = new HtmlTableRow();
        oHtmlTableRow.Height = "20";
        oHtmlTable.Rows.Add(oHtmlTableRow);
    }

    this.PlaceHolder1.Controls.Add(oHtmlTable);
}
```

The survey has its own unique identifier, and passing this to the survey routine (although not shown for simplicity's sake) can filter the required survey from a collection of survey question sets. Each question has a unique group name assigned to it that identifies the question and serves as the GroupName property for the RadioButtons. This keeps the buttons independent of one another.

You can retrieve the answers two ways. One way is through recursion of the Controls collection. Because all RadioButton objects are answers to questions, you need to examine the Checked property of each button and derive its ID property to determine the answers. The code to accomplish this is shown in Listing 5-8.

Listing 5-8. *Retrieving Survey Responses*

```
private void GetAnswers(ControlCollection oControls)
{
    RadioButton oRadioButton;

    foreach (Control oControl in oControls)
    {
        if (oControl is RadioButton)
        {
            oRadioButton = ((RadioButton) oControl);

            if (oRadioButton.Checked)
                Response.Write(oRadioButton.ID + "<BR>");
        }
        else
            GetAnswers(oControl.Controls);
    }
}
```

This produces results that look something like this:

```
Gender1
Age2
Party3
Beer4
```

This method works well because most of the controls on the page are answer controls (RadioButtons) that need to be checked anyway. You're not wasting time wading through a huge collection of controls to find only the subset that you need.

One other approach is to start with the XML file that generated the survey screen to begin with and iterate through its nodes. Because the name of the RadioButton control is the unique combination of group name (Gender, Age, and so on) and the question ID, you have a unique name to pass to the FindControl() method of the PlaceHolder object. Listing 5-9 shows this approach in action. The results are the same as shown previously.

Listing 5-9. *Retrieving Survey Responses via XML Definition*

```
private void GetAnswers()
{
    XmlDocument oXmlDocument = new XmlDocument();
    XmlNode oQuestionNode;
    Control oControl;
    RadioButton oRadioButton;
    string szGroup;

    oXmlDocument.Load(MapPath("survey.xml"));

    oQuestionNode = oXmlDocument.ChildNodes[0];

    foreach (XmlNode oXmlNode in oQuestionNode.ChildNodes)
    {
        szGroup = oXmlNode.Attributes["group"].Value;

        foreach (XmlNode oAnswerNode in oXmlNode.ChildNodes)
        {
            oControl = PlaceHolder1.FindControl(szGroup +
                oAnswerNode.Attributes["ID"].Value);
            oRadioButton = ((RadioButton) oControl);

            if (oRadioButton.Checked)
                Response.Write(oRadioButton.ID + "<BR>");
        }
    }
}
```

ParseControl

Another option to dynamically instantiate controls is the Page object's ParseControl() method. This method receives a string that defines a control as you would see in the ASP.NET file. The method returns a Control object that is then added to the Controls collection of the PlaceHolder object, as shown in Listing 5-10.

Listing 5-10. *ParseControl() Method*

```
protected void Page_Init(object sender, EventArgs e)
{

    Control oLastNameControl;
    Control oFirstNameControl;
    Control oRealNameControl;

    oLastNameControl = this.ParseControl(@"Last Name:
        <asp:TextBox id='txtLastName' runat='server'/>");
    oFirstNameControl = this.ParseControl(@"First Name:
        <asp:TextBox id='txtFirstName' runat='server'/>");
    oRealNameControl = this.ParseControl(@"<asp:CheckBox id='chkRealName'
        Text='Real Name' runat='server' />");

    this.PlaceHolder1.Controls.Add(oLastNameControl);
    this.PlaceHolder1.Controls.Add(oFirstNameControl);
    this.PlaceHolder1.Controls.Add(oRealNameControl);

}
```

The disadvantage of using this approach is that you need to cast these `Control` objects to specific control object types (`TextBox`, `CheckBox`, and so on) before setting any properties specific to those objects. This code produces the page shown in Figure 5-6.

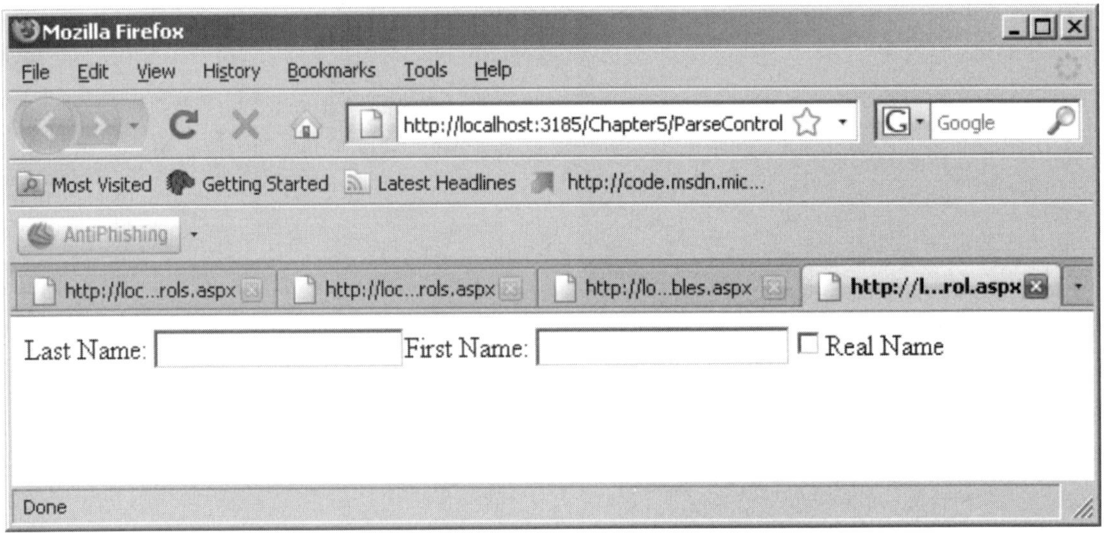

Figure 5-6 *ParseControl() method in action*

It would make for a cleaner user interface to place these controls within an `HtmlTable` object, but this wasn't done for the sake of brevity.

■ **Note** You take a bit of a performance hit when you use parsed controls, because they must be reinterpreted every time. The parsed results of pages can at least be cached.

Instantiating User Controls

User controls are essentially mini–web pages that are contained within other web pages. They contain one or more static controls and use an ASCX file to define their component controls. They're usually declared within an owner ASPX page. Examine the user control in Figure 5-7.

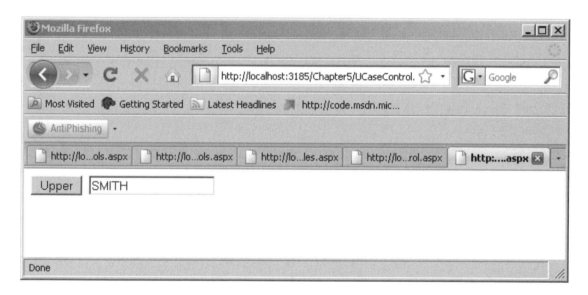

Figure 5-7. *User control*

This simple control consists of a `TextBox` and a `Button` and accepts a string of text that it converts to uppercase. Its definition is shown in Listing 5-11, and the code for the control class is shown in Listing 5-12.

Listing 5-11 *User Control Code*

```
<%@ Control Language="C#" AutoEventWireup="true" CodeFile="UCaseControl.ascx.cs"
Inherits="UCaseControl" %>
<asp:Button ID="cmdUpper" runat="server" OnClick="cmdUpper_Click"
```

```
Text="Upper" /> 
<asp:TextBox ID="txtData" runat="server"></asp:TextBox>
```

Listing 5-12 *User Control Class*

```
public partial class UCaseControl : System.Web.UI.UserControl
{
    protected void cmdUpper_Click(object sender, EventArgs e)
    {
        txtData.Text = txtData.Text.ToUpper();
    }
}
```

The user control is referenced by adding the following line to the owner:

```
<%@ Register Src="UCaseControl.ascx" TagName="UCaseControl" TagPrefix="uc1" %>
```

When you drag and drop the user control onto the owner page, Visual Studio adds this line for you. This line essentially tells the owner page the location of the user control, which in turn references its code file.

Logically, it would make sense that you could instantiate a user control like you would any other control—that is, like this:

```
UCaseControl oUCaseControl = new UCaseControl();

this.PlaceHolder1.Controls.Add(oUCaseControl);
```

Doing this won't throw an error but will cause you a lot of frustration when your control fails to appear in the web page. You won't even see any evidence of it if you choose View Source on the browser. Rather, you need to do this:

```
Control oControl = this.LoadControl("~/UCaseControl.ascx");
this.PlaceHolder1.Controls.Add(oControl);
```

Because a user control is simply an extension of the main page's control hierarchy, you can add to it dynamically after you instantiate a reference to it. Suppose this last name uppercase user control requires a title field added under certain circumstances. You can achieve this by adding a Label control to the Controls collection of the user control. Listing 5-13 shows how this is done.

Listing 5-13. *Dynamically Loading a User Control*

```
Control oControl = this.LoadControl("~/UCaseControl.ascx");
Label oLabel = new Label();
TextBox oTextBox = new TextBox();

oLabel.Text = "Title:";

oTextBox.ID = "txtTitle";
```

```
oControl.Controls.Add(oLabel);
oControl.Controls.Add(oTextBox);

this.PlaceHolder1.Controls.Add(oControl);
```

It's important to understand that a control can have only one parent. Suppose you had two user controls—the UCase control and its equally useless companion LCase—each of which needed a control dynamically added to it. If you tried to save a few lines of code by adding the same object to both controls, as shown in Listing 5-14, you'd find that the object was ultimately assigned to the LCase control.

Listing 5-14. Dynamically Loading Server Controls to a User Control (the Wrong Way)

```
Control oControl = this.LoadControl("~/UCaseControl.ascx");
Label oLabel = new Label();
TextBox oTextBox = new TextBox();

oLabel.Text = "Title:";

oTextBox.ID = "txtTitle";

//Assign to the UCase control
oControl.Controls.Add(oLabel);
oControl.Controls.Add(oTextBox);

this.PlaceHolder1.Controls.Add(oControl);

oControl = this.LoadControl("~/LCaseControl.ascx");

//No, wait! Assign to the LCase control
oControl.Controls.Add(oLabel);
oControl.Controls.Add(oTextBox);

this.PlaceHolder1.Controls.Add(oControl);
```

Executing this code produces the web pages shown in Figure 5-8.

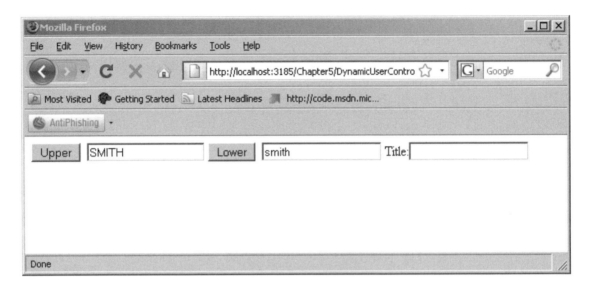

Figure 5-8. *Dynamic user control*

This code essentially transferred ownership of the title Label and TextBox from the UCase control to the LCase control. It didn't add them to both. To do this, you need to create two completely separate object references, as shown in Listing 5-15.

Listing 5-15. *Dynamically Loading Server Controls to a User Control (the Right Way)*

```
Control oControl = this.LoadControl("~/UCaseControl.ascx");
Label oLabelUCase = new Label();
TextBox oTextBoxUCase = new TextBox();

oLabelUCase.Text = "Title:";

oTextBoxUCase.ID = "txtTitle";

//Assign to the UCase control
oControl.Controls.Add(oLabelUCase);
oControl.Controls.Add(oTextBoxUCase);

this.PlaceHolder1.Controls.Add(oControl);

oControl = this.LoadControl("~/LCaseControl.ascx");

//Create a completely new set of objects
Label oLabelLCase = new Label();
TextBox oTextBoxLCase = new TextBox();
```

```
oLabelLCase.Text = "Title:";

oTextBoxLCase.ID = "txtTitle";

//Assign to the LCase control
oControl.Controls.Add(oLabelLCase);
oControl.Controls.Add(oTextBoxLCase);

this.PlaceHolder1.Controls.Add(oControl);
```

This code produces the web page shown in Figure 5-9.

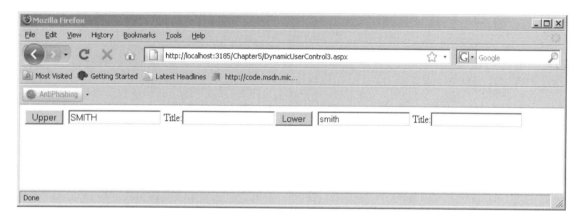

Figure 5-9. *Dynamic user and server controls*

Repeater Controls

A `Repeater` control is a data-bound list that repeats a customized template for every row in a data source. A `DataGrid` control is like a repeater control in that it displays a row of data for each row in its data source. Although you could build the functionality of a grid in a repeater control, it's best to take advantage of its data-driven nature to display a series of edit fields for each row of data.

Listing 5-16 shows the basics of a `Repeater` control.

Listing 5-16. *Repeater control*

```
<form id="form1" runat="server">
<div>
  <h3>Repeater Control</h3>

  <asp:repeater id="Repeater1" datasourceid="SqlDataSource1" runat="Server">
```

```
    <headertemplate>
      <table border="1">
        <tr>
          <td><b>Last Name</b></td>
          <td><b>First Name</b></td>
          <td><b>Hire Date</b></td>
        </tr>
    </headertemplate>

    <itemtemplate>
      <tr>
        <td> <%# Eval("LastName")%> </td>
        <td> <%# Eval("FirstName")%> </td>
        <td> <%# Eval("HireDate")%> </td>
      </tr>
    </itemtemplate>

    <footertemplate>
        <tr>
          <td><b>Last Name</b></td>
          <td><b>First Name</b></td>
          <td><b>Hire Date</b></td>
        </tr>
    </footertemplate>
  </asp:repeater>

  <asp:SqlDataSource
      ConnectionString="<%$ ConnectionStrings:NorthWind %>"
      ID="SqlDataSource1" runat="server"
      SelectCommand="SELECT LastName, FirstName, HireDate
                     FROM Employees
                     ORDER BY LastName, FirstName">
  </asp:SqlDataSource>

</div>
</form>
```

You also need to define the connection string in the web.config file, like this:

```
<connectionStrings>
  <add name="NorthWind"
    connectionString="Data Source=localhost;
    Integrated Security=SSPI;Initial Catalog=Northwind"
    providerName="System.Data.SqlClient" />
</connectionStrings>
```

This code displays the screen show in Figure 5-10.

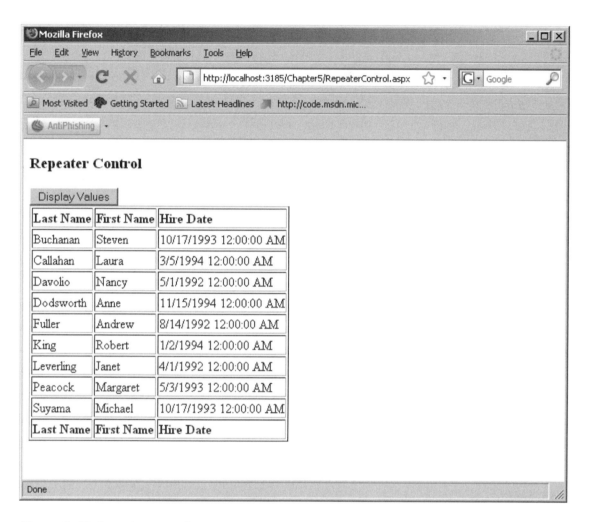

Figure 5-10. Repeater control

Here, the control is defined with a data source set to a SELECT command from the old reliable Northwind database. The <headertemplate> tag defines the headers for each column of data before the repeater starts, and the <footertemplate> tag defines what appears for each column when the data source has been iterated and the repeater ends. The <itemtemplate> is the most interesting. This is what is displayed for each row in the Repeater control. In this example, it's nothing too exciting— simply a row in an HTML table. Suppose you took it a bit further and embedded some edit controls here.

Extracting data from a repeater control is a matter of iterating its Item and Control collection. The Item collection contains a series of RepeaterItem objects. Each RepeaterItem object has a Controls collection that contains the individual data fields. The code in Listing 5-17 shows how to extract the data from the Repeater control shown in Figure 5-11 and present it back to the user in an HTML table.

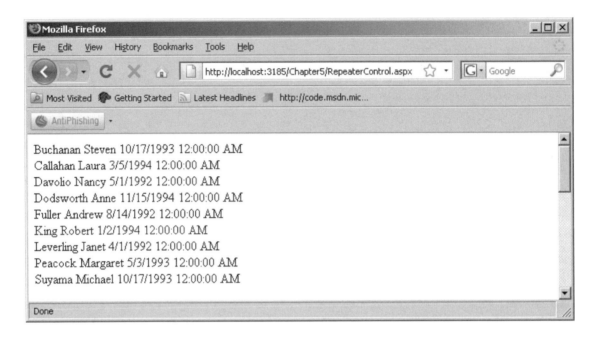

Figure 5-11. Data from a Repeater Control

Listing 5-17. Displaying the Contents of a Repeater Control

```
Repeater oRepeater = ((Repeater)Page.FindControl("Repeater1"));

foreach (RepeaterItem oRepeaterItem in oRepeater.Items)
{
    foreach (Control oControl in oRepeaterItem.Controls)
    {
        if (oControl is DataBoundLiteralControl)
        {
            Response.Write(((DataBoundLiteralControl)oControl)
.Text + "<br>");
        }

    }
}
```

Although not shown in this example, you can determine exactly which row of data you're on by storing the primary key in a hidden field for each of the items displayed.

Practical Solutions

By way of example, let's examine some practical examples in which data-driven techniques can be particularly useful. You look at how to create data-driven criteria pages. The techniques to persist filters and grid layouts are nearly identical to their WinForms counterparts covered in the previous chapter, and there is no need to review them again here.

Dynamic Criteria Controls

Suppose you want to display a list box to users that allows them to select no items, one item, or multiple items. You can accomplish this with the following two lines of code:

```
oDT = GetDepartments();
ShowListBox(Criteria.Department, oDT, "DictionaryID",
  "Description", 10, 20, 200, 180, "Departments");
```

This code displays the web page shown in Figure 5-12.

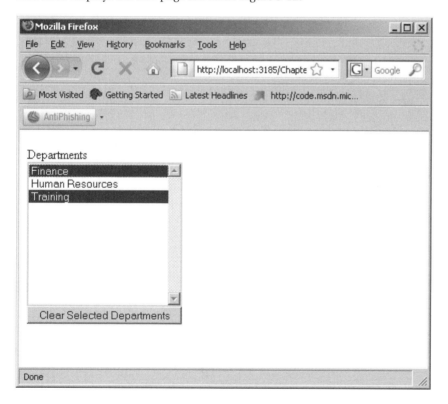

Figure 5-12. Filtering departments

This example examines the data-driven techniques for creating web `ListBox` controls on the fly. You aren't using a `CheckBoxList` control because the ID values that are assigned to it through the `ListItem` object don't persist client-side and therefore can't be retrieved through JavaScript. Microsoft KnowledgeBase article Q309338 explains this in more detail.

The goal is to retrieve the user selections client-side only because you can always pass the values to the server via hidden controls. Because of the increasing popularity of asynchronous JavaScript (AJAX), more and more developers are avoiding postbacks for tasks such as report generation. By retrieving the user selections client-side and invoking an on-demand reporting web service asynchronously, you can display the report output with minimal server hits. This approach also simplifies the UI code because you don't need to maintain state between postbacks. Like its WinForms counterpart, the `ShowListBox()` method invokes additional methods that display the `Label`, `ListBox`, and `Button` objects that make up the set of controls. These controls are managed in the classes shown in Listing 5-18.

Listing 5-18. ControlManager and ListBoxManager Classes

```
public enum Criteria
{
    Department = 0
}

abstract class ControlManager
{
    private Criteria iIndex;
    private Label oLabelControl;

    public Criteria Index
    {
        get { return iIndex; }
        set { iIndex = value; }
    }

    public Label LabelControl
    {
        get { return oLabelControl; }
        set { oLabelControl = value; }
    }
}

class ListBoxManager : ControlManager
{
    private System.Web.UI.WebControls.ListBox oListBoxControl;
    private Button oButtonControl;

    public System.Web.UI.WebControls.ListBox ListBoxControl
    {
        get { return oListBoxControl; }
```

```
      set { oListBoxControl = value; }
   }

   public Button ButtonControl
   {
      get { return oButtonControl; }
      set { oButtonControl = value; }
   }
}
```

To display the control, you need to pass the Criteria enumerator to the ShowListBox() method (see Listing 5-19) along with the data source information, the dimensions of the list box, and the caption. ShowListBox() instantiates an object of type ListBoxCollection that receives the instantiated objects of the Label, ListBox, and Button types. These controls are then added to the properties of the ListBoxCollection objects.

Listing 5-19. ShowListBox() Method

```
private void ShowListBox(Criteria iIndex,
   DataTable oDT,
   string szID,
   string szDescription,
   int iLeft,
   int iTop,
   int iWidth,
   int iHeight,
   string szCaption)
{
   ListBoxManager oListBoxManager;

   oListBoxManager = new ListBoxManager();
   oListBoxManager.Index = iIndex;

   oListBoxManager.LabelControl =
   AddDynamicLabel(iIndex, iLeft, iTop, szCaption);

   oListBoxManager.ListBoxControl =
   AddDynamicListBox(iIndex, iLeft, iTop + 20, iWidth, iHeight);

   oListBoxManager.ButtonControl =
      AddDynamicListBoxButton(iIndex, iLeft,
      iTop + iHeight + 20, iWidth, 23, szCaption);

   LoadListBox(oListBoxManager.ListBoxControl, oDT,
      "DictionaryID", "Description", false);
}
```

The AddDynamicLabel() method (see Listing 5-20) instantiates a Label object and assigns its location via the Style() method. The new control is then added to the Controls collection of the owner Panel object that displays it to the user.

Listing 5-20. *AddDynamicLabel() Method*

```
private Label AddDynamicLabel(Criteria iIndex,
    int iLeft,
    int iTop,
    string szCaption)
{
    Label oLabel;

    oLabel = new Label();
    oLabel.Style[HtmlTextWriterStyle.Position] = "absolute";
    oLabel.Style[HtmlTextWriterStyle.Left] = iLeft.ToString() + "px";
    oLabel.Style[HtmlTextWriterStyle.Top] = iTop.ToString() + "px";
    oLabel.Text = szCaption;

    Panel1.Controls.Add(oLabel);

    return oLabel;
}
```

The ListBox control is displayed in a similar fashion, as illustrated in the AddDynamicListBox() method shown in Listing 5-21. The SelectionMode property is always set to multiple selections; otherwise, a combo box would suffice.

Listing 5-21. *AddDynamicListBox() Method*

```
private System.Web.UI.WebControls.ListBox AddDynamicListBox(Criteria iIndex,
    int iLeft,
    int iTop,
    int iWidth,
    int iHeight)
{
    System.Web.UI.WebControls.ListBox oListBox;
    oListBox = new System.Web.UI.WebControls.ListBox();
    oListBox.ID = "ListBox" + ((int) iIndex);
    oListBox.Style["position"] = "absolute";
    oListBox.Style["left"] = iLeft.ToString() + "px";
    oListBox.Style["top"] = iTop.ToString() + "px";
    oListBox.Style["height"] = iHeight.ToString() + "px";
    oListBox.Style["width"] = iWidth.ToString() + "px";
    oListBox.BorderStyle = BorderStyle.Solid;
    oListBox.SelectionMode = ListSelectionMode.Multiple;
```

```
    Panel1.Controls.Add(oListBox);
    return oListBox;
}
```

The Button control is created and displayed in a fashion similar to the Label and ListBox, as shown in Listing 5-22.

Listing 5-22. *AddDynamicListBoxButton() Method*

```
private Button AddDynamicListBoxButton(Criteria iIndex,
    int iLeft,
    int iTop,
    int iWidth,
    int iHeight,
    string szCaption)
{
    Button oButton;
    oButton = new Button();
    oButton.Style["position"] = "absolute";
    oButton.Style["left"] = iLeft.ToString() + "px";
    oButton.Style["top"] = iTop.ToString() + "px";
    oButton.Style["width"] = iWidth.ToString() + "px";
    oButton.Text = "Clear Selected " + szCaption;
    oButton.Attributes.Add("onclick",
    "return DeselectAll('ListBox" + ((int) iIndex) + "')");
    Panel1.Controls.Add(oButton);

    return oButton;
}
```

The Button control triggers JavaScript code—that is, when clicked, it must clear the selections in the list box with which it's associated. The generic JavaScript function that clears the select options in the ListBox is shown in Listing 5-23. The button's OnClientClick event property is wired to this JavaScript function using the Attributes.Add() method.

Listing 5-23. *DeselectAll Method*

```
function DeselectAll(szListBox)
{
    var oListBox = document.getElementById(szListBox);
    for (i=0; i < oListBox.options.length; i++)
    oListBox.options[i].selected = false;
    return false;
}
```

151

Extracting the User Selections

After the user has completed entering their report criteria, the Get Data button can generically retrieve the information one control at a time. In the code shown in Listing 5-24, the selected departments are retrieved and displayed in an alert box.

Listing 5-24. *Retrieving the User Selections*

```
function GetData()
{
   var szDepartments = "Departments: " + ParseIt("ListBox6", false, true) + "\n";
   alert(szDepartments);
   return false;
}
```

The JavaScript `ParseIt()` function shown in Listing 5-25 performs the same task as its WinForms counterpart. It receives as parameters the name of the list box, and Boolean values to indicate whether quotes should surround each item, and whether only the selected values should be returned.

Listing 5-25. *JavaScript `ParseIt()` Function*

```
function ParseIt(szListBox, bQuotes, bCheckedOnly)
{
   var oListBox = document.getElementById(szListBox);
   var szResult = new String('');
   var szQuotes = '';
   var szValue = '';

   if (bQuotes)
      szQuotes = "'";

   for (i=0; i < oListBox.options.length; i++)
   {
      szValue = oListBox.options[i].value;

      if (bCheckedOnly)
      {
         if (oListBox.options[i].selected)
            szResult += szQuotes + szValue + szQuotes + ",";
      }
      else
         szResult += szQuotes + szValue + szQuotes + ",";

      if (szResult.length > 0)
         szResult = szResult.substring(0, szResult.length - 1);

   return szResult;
}
```

Summary

In this chapter, you reviewed data-driven programming for web applications. You saw the differences between this environment and WinForms applications. Specifically, you looked at when controls enter the control tree and when their individual events fire relative to the owner page. In addition, you looked at a few practical examples of how to build survey forms and report criteria screens using data-driven techniques. Coming up, you apply these same techniques to WPF applications.

CHAPTER 6

■■■

Dynamic WPF

The introduction of Windows Presentation Foundation (WPF) in the .NET 3.0 Framework presented a major paradigm shift for the development of both desktop and web-based applications. Over the years, the user interface development community has largely split into two camps: desktop and web developers. Although the database access and business layer code is the same, the technologies used to develop the interfaces are vastly different, each requiring its own level of expertise.

WPF attempts to bridge this gap by offering a similar programming architecture for both platforms. Using XAML to create the UI, you can create both desktop-based applications as well as web applications that run in a browser. Unfortunately, the user interfaces of these WPF web applications, known as XBAP applications, aren't as independent of the .NET Framework as ASP.NET pages are. Users must have the Framework installed on their machines in order to run them. Although it's not a perfect solution, its user interface is still vastly superior to executing HTML and JavaScript in a browser. This chapter discusses the specifics of using data-driven techniques with WPF. First, though, you review the technologies that make WPF happen.

XAML

Extensible Application Markup Language (XAML) is often spoken of in the same breath as WPF. XAML is to WPF what HTML is to ASP.NET. It allows the user interface to remain separate from the code that drives it. Unlike HTML, however, XAML is completely optional. Anything you can accomplish in XAML, you can accomplish in source code. Thus, the user interface designer can focus on what they do best: creating user interfaces. Developers can work separately to create the code that brings the user interface to life.

WPF: Beyond the Hype

This separation of the user interface/graphics design roles from the development role may sound like a Microsoft pipe dream or at least marketing hype. Admittedly, you've had the ability to do this since .NET was released. WinForms Designer files hold the source code to instantiate the controls that make up a form. XAML files hold the declarative markup to instantiate the controls that make up a form. Is there truly a difference? With the introduction of the Microsoft Expression tools, real graphic designers can create UIs using a tool that is very familiar to them. Expression Blend provides a user experience much like the Adobe tools that designers have been using for years. On the other hand, I've heard it argued that XML/XAML is a Microsoft legal maneuver that allows the company to argue that its technology is really open source and therefore Microsoft can't possibly be monopolizing the market for any given technology.

Where WPF will ultimately wind up, only time and the marketplace will tell.

The first thing you should know about data-driven XAML is that it's much easier to accomplish than data-driven Win and WebForms. The main reason is that it's already, by its very nature, data-driven. In the chapters on Win and WebForms, you examined how to iterate the `Controls` collection of a `Form` (or `Page`) to build an XML representation of the control hierarchy. The beauty of WPF is that XAML is already an XML representation of the control hierarchy. As for instantiating code at runtime, that is also easy, because you can embed the source code directly in the XAML itself.

Nevertheless, an understanding of XAML is absolutely vital to developing any user interface in WPF. When you create a WPF form visually, the IDE generates the XAML to define the window. For example, suppose you lay out a form like the one shown in Figure 6-1.

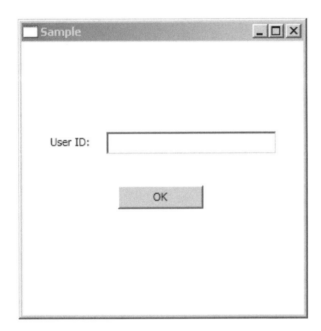

Figure 6-1. *WPF window*

The IDE generates the XAML shown in Listing 6-1.

Listing 6-1. *XAML for a Simple WPF Window*

```xml
<Window x:Class="DataDrivenWPF.Sample"
    xmlns="http://schemas.microsoft.com/winfx/2006/xaml/presentation"
    xmlns:x="http://schemas.microsoft.com/winfx/2006/xaml"
    Title="Sample" Height="300" Width="300">
    <Grid>
        <Label Height="28" Margin="24,88,0,0" Name="label1"
                VerticalAlignment="Top" HorizontalAlignment="Left"
```

```
            Width="57">User ID:</Label>
        <Button Margin="99,0,104,106" Name="cmdOK" Height="23"
                VerticalAlignment="Bottom">OK</Button>
        <TextBox Height="23" Margin="87,90,28,0" Name="txtUserID"
                VerticalAlignment="Top" />
    </Grid>
</Window>
```

This XAML is user editable, and you'll likely find it faster to make your immediate property changes—naming elements, setting Content properties, and so on—directly in the XAML rather than in the properties dialog.

XAML is simply XML, and it must follow the rules for XML with respect to naming and structure. You can open and manipulate XAML files using .NET's XML classes. Therefore, you can do the following:

```
XmlDocument oXmlDocument = new XmlDocument();

oXmlDocument.Load(@"C:\temp\GridDemo.xaml");
```

If the XmlDocument object can't load the XAML, then you don't have properly formed XAML. If you wish, you can even generate XAML at runtime and execute it in lieu of runtime-compiled controls. You will see how to accomplish this later in the chapter.

Layout

There are significant differences between screen layouts in WinForms and WPF. WPF is more akin to ASP.NET than to WinForms, and you must bear these considerations in mind when creating dynamic applications. Rather than simply instantiating controls and displaying them at fixed positions on a form, you need to store them in appropriate layout controls. Moreover, you must consider additional properties that either don't exist in WinForms development or aren't as important as they are in WPF.

One difference with WPF is that relative positioning is preferred over the absolute positioning that is typical of WinForms development. Each WPF Window requires that you use a layout control in order to usefully display multiple controls within it, because a WPF window is designed to hold only one element. If you choose, for example, to drag a control directly on a window, it positions itself in the center of the form and you can't do anything else with it. The form shown in Figure 6-2 contains a Button. Nothing else can be added to it. You can't add any additional controls, because you just used up your one element with the Button.

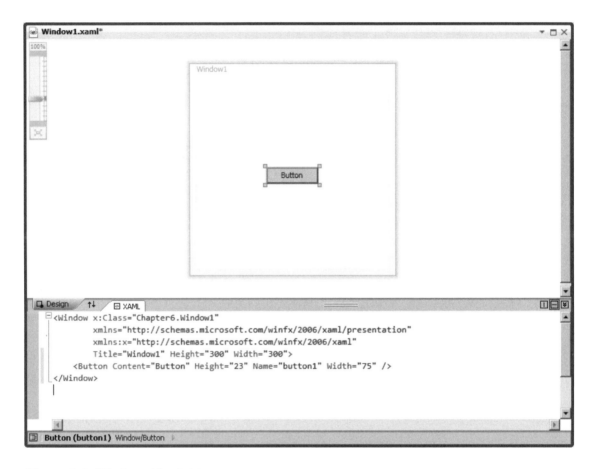

Figure 6-2. Window with a Button

Several layout controls are available for displaying controls on a WPF form, each of which may be nested several layers deep. The following sections look at each one individually.

Canvas

The Canvas container allows you to lay out forms using an absolute coordinate-based system. This is generally discouraged in WPF because the design philosophy is to use relative positioning to achieve a richer user interface where controls size to one another. Microsoft intended the Canvas for vector graphics use only. Listing 6-2 shows some controls displayed at absolute positions in a Canvas container.

Listing 6-2. XAML for a Canvas

```
<Window x:Class="DataDrivenWPF.Canvas"
    xmlns="http://schemas.microsoft.com/winfx/2006/xaml/presentation"
    xmlns:x="http://schemas.microsoft.com/winfx/2006/xaml"
```

```
        Title="Canvas" Height="300" Width="300">
        <Canvas Height="230" Name="canvas1" Width="261">
            <Button Canvas.Left="82" Canvas.Top="128" Height="23" Name="cmdSave"
                    Width="75">Save</Button>
            <Label Canvas.Left="10" Canvas.Top="10" Height="28" Name="label1"
                    Width="85">Last Name:</Label>
            <Label Canvas.Left="10" Canvas.Top="39" Height="28" Name="label2"
                    Width="85">First Name:</Label>
            <Label Canvas.Left="12" Canvas.Top="68" Height="28" Name="label3"
                    Width="83">City:</Label>
            <TextBox Canvas.Left="101" Canvas.Top="10" Height="23" Name="textBox1"
                    Width="120" />
            <TextBox Canvas.Left="101" Canvas.Top="39" Height="23" Name="textBox2"
                    Width="120" />
            <TextBox Canvas.Left="101" Canvas.Top="68" Height="23" Name="textBox3"
                    Width="120" />
        </Canvas>
</Window>
```

The output of this code is shown in Figure 6-3.

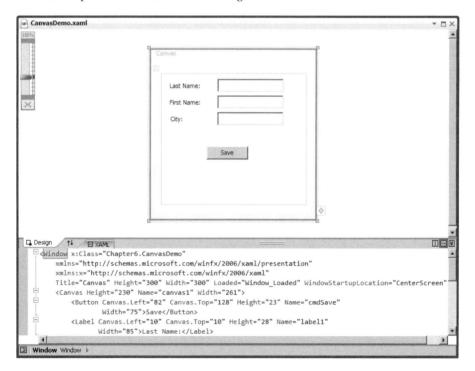

Figure 6-3. A Canvas

■ **Note** WPF supports complex graphic rendering using DirectX. Using fixed-pixel coordinates causes display problems when font sizes or the screen resolution change. It's best to use the `Alignment` and `Margin` properties to position elements in a container control. Also, use the `Auto` settings rather than specified `Width` and `Height` values to set size.

Grid

Each of the layout controls previously discussed can be used as an element of another to create hierarchies of containers and elements. For example, you may wish to place your Add, Save, Delete, and Cancel buttons in a `StackPanel` to line them up one atop the other, and then place this `StackPanel` in a `Grid`. When you're working with WPF controls, you need to think about several design considerations. First, controls aren't intended to be explicitly sized. The idea is to position a control in a starting location and let the `Content` property determine its size; the control adjusts itself to fit the content. Second, controls are positioned relatively, not absolutely. Your chosen container determines the layout. If you need to position elements in specific areas of a `Window`, use a `Grid`. ASP.NET developers have been using this approach for years via HTML tables.

A `Grid` is the most versatile layout control. When you first create a `Window`, it contains a set of default `Grid` tags. If you then drop a `Button` on the `Window`, you see XAML similar to the following:

```
<Grid>
    <Button Margin="101,89,102,0" Name="button1" Height="26"
            VerticalAlignment="Top">Button</Button>
</Grid>
```

The `Margin` property shows the button's relative position to the parent grid in the order left, top, right, and bottom. A series of controls like the ones shown in Figure 6-4 produce the XAML shown in Listing 6-3.

Listing 6-3. XAML for a Grid

```
 <Grid>
        <Button Name="button1" Height="26" VerticalAlignment="Top"
Margin="20,76,126,0">Button</Button>
        <CheckBox Height="20" Margin="20,50,138,0" Name="checkBox1"
VerticalAlignment="Top">CheckBox</CheckBox>
        <ComboBox Height="23" Margin="64,21,94,0"
Name="comboBox1" VerticalAlignment="Top" />
        <Label Height="28" Margin="12,21,0,0" Name="label1" VerticalAlignment="Top"
HorizontalAlignment="Left" Width="46">State:</Label>
 </Grid>
```

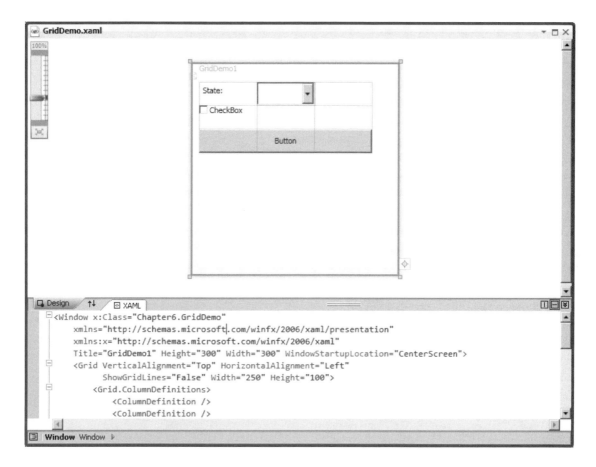

Figure 6-4. *Grid control positions*

You can achieve a similar effect by adding rows and columns to the grid and then positioning the control elements in specific row/column positions as shown in Listing 6-4 which creates a grid with three rows and three columns. The Row and Column properties of the Grid object are attached properties. These properties can be used to alter the layout of controls nested under the Grid control without having any the knowledge of how layout is performed in the Grid class.

Listing 6-4. *Grid Definition*

```
<Window x:Class="DataDrivenWPF.GridDemo1"
    xmlns="http://schemas.microsoft.com/winfx/2006/xaml/presentation"
    xmlns:x="http://schemas.microsoft.com/winfx/2006/xaml"
    Title="GridDemo1" Height="300" Width="300">
    <Grid VerticalAlignment="Top" HorizontalAlignment="Left"
        ShowGridLines="False" Width="250" Height="100">
      <Grid.ColumnDefinitions>
```

```
        <ColumnDefinition />
        <ColumnDefinition />
        <ColumnDefinition />
    </Grid.ColumnDefinitions>
    <Grid.RowDefinitions>
        <RowDefinition />
        <RowDefinition />
        <RowDefinition />
    </Grid.RowDefinitions>

    <Label Name="label1" Grid.Row="0" Grid.Column="0">State:</Label >
    <ComboBox  Name="comboBox1" Grid.Row="0" Grid.Column="1"></ComboBox >
    <CheckBox Name="checkBox1" Grid.Row="1" Grid.Column="0">CheckBox</CheckBox>
    <Button Name="button1" Grid.ColumnSpan="3" Grid.Row="2">Button</Button>

    </Grid>
</Window>
```

You can further refine an element's position with a grid cell by using the `Margin` property. For example, if you adjust the `State` label like this

```
<Label Name="label1" Margin="30,0,0,0" Grid.Row="0" Grid.Column="0">State:</Label >
```

its position nudges to the right because you've increased the left margin. If you adjust it like this

```
<Label Name="label1" Margin="30,16,0,0" Grid.Row="0" Grid.Column="0">State:</Label
>
```

it drops down so far that it half disappears below the bottom of the cell. The positions specified by Margin are relative to the cell containing the object. Therefore, if you position the object too low, it will position itself relative to its cell container and thus appear below that container's border.

StackPanel

As the name suggests, a `StackPanel` displays its contents one next to the other, as shown in Figure 6-5. By default, the contained elements appear one atop the other. To add spaces between them, use the `Margin` property.

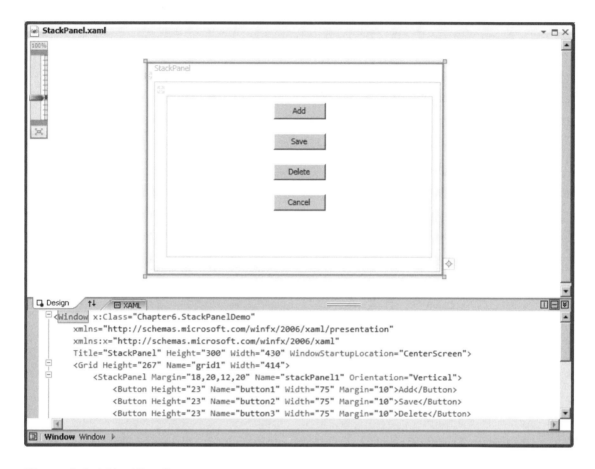

Figure 6-5. A StackPanel

Listing 6-5 shows the XAML to generate this window.

Listing 6-5. XAML for a StackPanel

```
<Window x:Class="Chapter6.StackPanelDemo"
    xmlns="http://schemas.microsoft.com/winfx/2006/xaml/presentation"
    xmlns:x="http://schemas.microsoft.com/winfx/2006/xaml"
    Title="StackPanel" Height="300" Width="430"
      WindowStartupLocation="CenterScreen">
    <Grid Height="267" Name="grid1" Width="414">
        <StackPanel Margin="18,20,12,20" Name="stackPanel1" Orientation="Vertical">
            <Button Height="23" Name="button1" Width="75"
                Margin="10">Add</Button>
            <Button Height="23" Name="button2" Width="75"
```

```
                Margin="10">Save</Button>
            <Button Height="23" Name="button3" Width="75"
                Margin="10">Delete</Button>
            <Button Height="23" Name="button4" Width="75"
                Margin="10">Cancel</Button>
        </StackPanel>
    </Grid>
</Window>
```

The image shows a list of buttons arranged together. In fact, grouping command buttons is probably the most common use of the StackPanel. A StackPanel doesn't just position elements vertically. By setting the Orientation property to Horizontal, you can change the layout as shown in Figure 6-6.

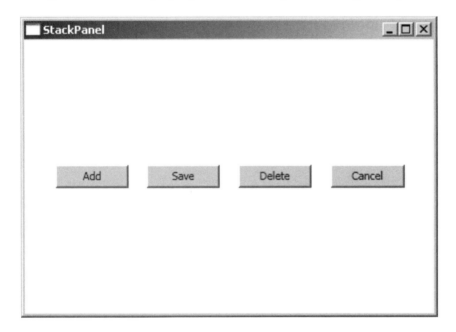

Figure 6-6. *Horizontal StackPanel*

WrapPanel

A WrapPanel container (Listing 6-6) displays controls adjacent to one another as space permits. When it reaches the right edge of the container, or the bottom if the Orientation is vertical, it places the next control on the next line (or the next column). Figure 6-7 shows this effect with a Horizontal Orientation property.

Listing 6-6. *XAML for a WrapPanel*

```
<Window x:Class="DataDrivenWPF.WrapPanel"
```

```
      xmlns="http://schemas.microsoft.com/winfx/2006/xaml/presentation"
      xmlns:x="http://schemas.microsoft.com/winfx/2006/xaml"
      Title="WrapPanel" Height="300" Width="315">
      <WrapPanel Margin="20,12,12,12" Name="wrapPanel1" Orientation="Horizontal">
          <Button Height="23" Name="button1" Width="75" Margin="5">Button</Button>
          <Button Height="23" Name="button2" Width="75" Margin="5">Button</Button>
          <Button Height="23" Name="button3" Width="75" Margin="5">Button</Button>
          <Button Height="23" Name="button4" Width="75" Margin="5">Button</Button>
          <Button Height="23" Name="button5" Width="75" Margin="5">Button</Button>
          <Button Height="23" Name="button6" Width="75" Margin="5">Button</Button>
          <Button Height="23" Name="button7" Width="75" Margin="5">Button</Button>
      </WrapPanel>
</Window>
```

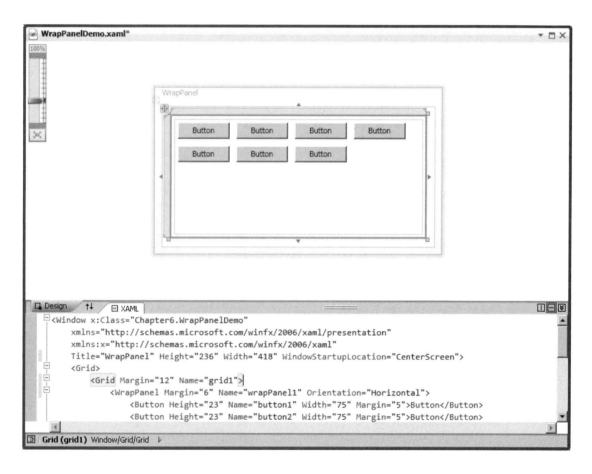

Figure 6-7. Horizontal WrapPanel

Figure 6-8 shows a vertical `WrapPanel`.

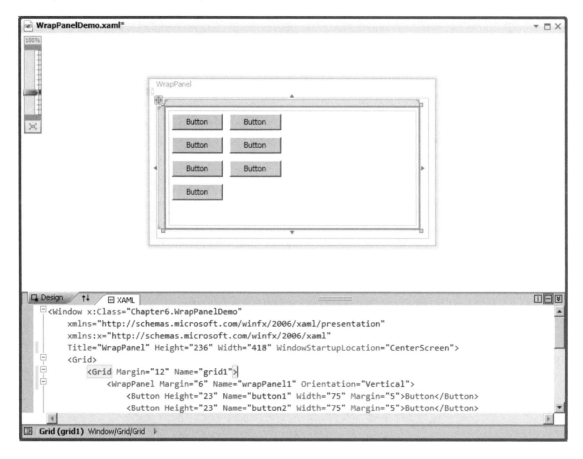

Figure 6-8. Vertical WrapPanel

DockPanel

The `DockPanel` container displays a collection of controls relative to one another. You can control this relationship by setting the `Dock` property in the child element. The code in Listing 6-7 displays the window in Figure 6-9.

Listing 6-7. XAML for a DockPanel

```
<Window x:Class="DataDrivenWPF.DockPanelDemo"
    xmlns="http://schemas.microsoft.com/winfx/2006/xaml/presentation"
    xmlns:x="http://schemas.microsoft.com/winfx/2006/xaml"
    Title="DockPanel" Height="300" Width="300">
```

```
    <DockPanel Margin="12" Name="dockPanel1" LastChildFill="False">
        <Button DockPanel.Dock="Left" Name="cmdA">A</Button>
        <Button DockPanel.Dock="Top" Name="cmdB">B</Button>
        <Button DockPanel.Dock="Right" Name="cmdC">C</Button>
        <Button DockPanel.Dock="Bottom" Name="cmdD">D</Button>
    </DockPanel>
</Window>
```

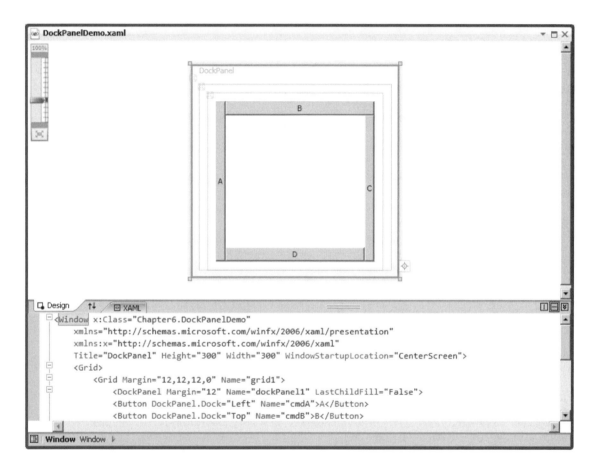

Figure 6-9. *A* DockPanel

The LastChildFill property determines whether the last control added to the DockPanel control fills the remaining space. In the preceding example, it's set to False. Figure 6-10 shows what happens when it's set to True.

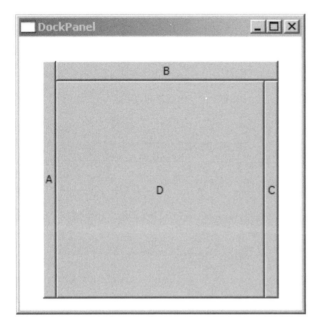

Figure 6-10. *DockPanel with LastChildFill set to True*

Runtime Instantiation

Instantiating WPF controls at runtime is functionally similar to doing so for WinForms controls. You still need to declare a variable and the set the properties as shown here:

```
TextBox oTextBox = new TextBox();
oTextBox.Name = "txtFirstName";
oTextBox.Width = 100;
```

This code example creates a new TextBox object named txtFirstName. Its Width property is set to 100 device-independent units, with a default of pixels, where each unit is 1/96 inch.

What to do with this object constitutes the main difference with WinForms. To display this control, you need to make it a child of one of the container controls discussed in the previous section. Here, you make it a part of a Grid control, because this will likely be the container you use most often.

You can position the TextBox by using the Margin property, as shown in Listing 6-8.

Listing 6-8. *Instantiating a TextBox*

```
TextBox oTextBox = new TextBox();
oTextBox.Name = "txtFirstName";
oTextBox.Width = 100;
oTextBox.Text = "Hello";
```

```
oTextBox.Margin = new Thickness(30, 0, 0, 240);
```

You can also position it by employing the `SetRow()` and `SetColumn()` methods of the parent `Grid`. You have better control if you use the column and row approach. The following code places the `TextBox` in the second cell of the first row:

```
Grid.SetRow(oTextBox, 0);
Grid.SetColumn(oTextBox, 1);
```

After the `Textbox` control has been positioned, you add it to the `Grid`'s `Children` collection like this:

```
oGrid.Children.Add(oTextBox);
```

When all the controls have been added to the `Grid`, you can add it to the `Content` property of the owner `Window` as follows:

```
this.Content = oGrid;
```

The code in Listing 6-9 shows the full source for creating a `Grid`, adding rows and columns, instantiating controls, positioning them within the `Grid`, and then adding the `Grid` to the `Window`'s `Content` property.

Listing 6-9. *Instantiating and Configuring a Grid in Source Code*

```
ColumnDefinition oColumnDefinition;
RowDefinition oRowDefinition;
Label oLabel;
TextBox oTextBox;
ComboBox oComboBox;
Button oButton;

//Create two columns and add them to the grid
oColumnDefinition = new ColumnDefinition();
Grid1.ColumnDefinitions.Add(oColumnDefinition);

oColumnDefinition = new ColumnDefinition();
Grid1.ColumnDefinitions.Add(oColumnDefinition);

//Create a row and add it to the grid
oRowDefinition = new RowDefinition();
oRowDefinition.Height = GridLength.Auto;
Grid1.RowDefinitions.Add(oRowDefinition);

//... then add the controls for that row
oLabel = new Label();
oLabel.Content = "Last Name:";
```

```
Grid.SetRow(oLabel, 0);
Grid.SetColumn(oLabel, 0);
Grid1.Children.Add(oLabel);

oTextBox = new TextBox();
oTextBox.Name = "txtLastName";
oTextBox.Width = 100;
Grid.SetRow(oTextBox, 0);
Grid.SetColumn(oTextBox, 1);
Grid1.Children.Add(oTextBox);

//Create another row
oRowDefinition = new RowDefinition();
oRowDefinition.Height = GridLength.Auto;
Grid1.RowDefinitions.Add(oRowDefinition);

// ...and add controls here as well
oLabel = new Label();
oLabel.Content = "Salutation:";
Grid.SetRow(oLabel, 1);
Grid.SetColumn(oLabel, 0);
Grid1.Children.Add(oLabel);

oComboBox = new ComboBox();
oComboBox.Name = "cmbSalutation";
oComboBox.Width = 100;
oComboBox.Items.Add("Mr.");
oComboBox.Items.Add("Mrs.");
oComboBox.Items.Add("Dr.");
Grid.SetRow(oComboBox, 1);
Grid.SetColumn(oComboBox, 1);
Grid1.Children.Add(oComboBox);

//Add one more row
oRowDefinition = new RowDefinition();
oRowDefinition.Height = GridLength.Auto;
Grid1.RowDefinitions.Add(oRowDefinition);

//...and add a Button control wired to an event handler
oButton = new Button();
oButton.Width = 100;
oButton.Content = "Get Data";
oButton.Click += new RoutedEventHandler(this.cmdGetData_Click);
Grid.SetRow(oButton, 2);
Grid.SetColumn(oButton, 1);
Grid1.Children.Add(oButton);
```

```
//Add this grid to the owner window
this.Content = Grid1
```

This code produces the screen shown in Figure 6-11.

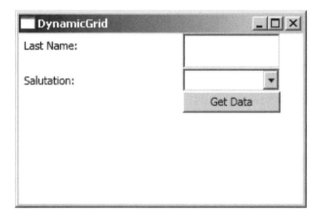

Figure 6-11. *Dynamically generated* `Grid`

Accessing Child Controls

There are a number of parallels here between WPF and WinForms/ASP.NET. Because a `Window` is a `ContentControl`, it may contain only one child element. This element is most likely a layout control, which in turn can contain other elements and/or other container controls. Therefore, there is no `Controls` collection of the parent `Window` object. In the previous example, after the `Grid` object is instantiated and constructed, it's set to the `Content` property of the `Window`. The `Content` property is an object data type because it may contain various control types. You can determine the type of controls by using the `GetType()` method like this:

```
?this.Content.GetType().Name
```

In the example in Listing 6-9, it returns "Grid". If you cast the `Content` property to a `Grid` object, you can iterate through the `Children` collection just like you do the `Controls` collection on Win and WebForms. The code in Listing 6-10 shows this in action.

Listing 6-10. *Iterating through the* `Children` *Collection*

```
Grid oGrid;
string szData;

oGrid = ((Grid)this.Content);
```

171

```
foreach (UIElement oElement in oGrid.Children)
{
    switch (oElement.GetType().Name)
    {
        case "TextBox":
            szData = ((TextBox)oElement).Text;
            break;

        case "ComboBox":
            szData = ((ComboBox)oElement).Text;
            break;
    }
}
```

This is a rather simple example that shows how a layout control may contain elements. Real-life applications use container controls that contain elements, but also other container controls that in turn may contain elements and still more container controls nested several levels deep. You examine this nesting in the next section.

Nested Controls

Like the Controls collection in a Win or WebForms, WPF controls have an ownership hierarchy. A Window may own a GroupBox, and that GroupBox may own a CheckBox, and so on. Suppose you were to lay out this interface using the visual designer. The XAML looks like Listing 6-11.

Listing 6-11. XAML for Nested Containers

```
<Window x:Class="DataDrivenWPF.GridDemo"
    xmlns="http://schemas.microsoft.com/winfx/2006/xaml/presentation"
    xmlns:x="http://schemas.microsoft.com/winfx/2006/xaml"
    Title="Grid" Height="300" Width="300">
    <Grid>
        <Button Height="23" Margin="101,0,102,12" Name="cmdGetData"
                VerticalAlignment="Bottom"
                    Click="cmdGetData_Click">Get Data</Button>
        <GroupBox Header="My Data" Margin="38,46,34,73" Name="groupBox1">
            <Grid>
                <CheckBox Margin="44,54,30,54" Name="checkBox1">Check Me</CheckBox>
            </Grid>
        </GroupBox>
    </Grid>
</Window>
```

And the window looks like Figure 6-12.

Figure 6-12. *Nested containers*

Note the hierarchy in the XAML. The Window contains a Grid that contains a GroupBox that contains another Grid that contains a CheckBox. To iterate through this hierarchy, you need to resort to recursion. You must bear in mind a few considerations about recursing through a WPF control tree. As noted in the previous section, the owner Window doesn't have a Controls collection. Rather, it has a Content property. This property is of type object, and it must be cast to a specific container control object in order to access its Children property. You can accomplish this using the method shown in Listing 6-12.

Listing 6-12. *Referencing Child Control Collections*

```
private UIElementCollection GetUIElementCollection(object oContent)
{
    UIElementCollection oUIElementCollection = null;

    switch (oContent.GetType().Name)
    {
        case "Grid":
            oUIElementCollection = ((Grid) oContent).Children;
            break;

        case "StackPanel":
            oUIElementCollection = ((StackPanel) oContent).Children;
            break;
```

```
            case "DockPanel":
                oUIElementCollection = ((DockPanel) oContent).Children;
                break;

            case "Canvas":
                oUIElementCollection = ((Canvas) oContent).Children;
                break;
        }

        return oUIElementCollection;
}
```

After the type of the child container has been determined, you can iterate through its component elements. If one of these elements is an owner to many controls—say, like a GroupBox—then you can cast its Content property to the appropriate container object and continue the recursion. When you draw a GroupBox on a Window, for example, it automatically displays with a Grid container inside it. Because a GroupBox is intended to hold multiple controls, you therefore need a container like a Grid to handle the content. Thus, to iterate through a series of nested controls on a Window, you can use the recursive IterateControls() method shown in Listing 6-13.

Listing 6-13. *IterateControls() Method*

```
private void IterateControls(UIElementCollection oUIElementCollection)
{
    Grid oGrid = null;
    GroupBox oGroupBox = null;
    StackPanel oStackPanel = null;

    foreach (UIElement oElement in oUIElementCollection)
    {
        switch (oElement.GetType().Name)
        {
            case "TextBox":
                szData += ((TextBox) oElement).Text + "\n";
                break;

            case "ComboBox":
                szData += ((ComboBox)oElement).Text + "\n";
                break;

            case "CheckBox":
                szData += ((CheckBox)oElement).Content.ToString() + "\n";
                break;

            case "Button":
                szData += ((Button)oElement).Content.ToString() + "\n";
```

```
                break;

        case "GroupBox":
            oGroupBox = ((GroupBox) oElement);
            szData += oGroupBox.Header + "\n";
            IterateControls(GetUIElementCollection(oGroupBox.Content));
            break;

        case "Grid":
            oGrid = ((Grid) oElement);
            IterateControls(oGrid.Children);
            break;

        case "StackPanel":
            oStackPanel = ((StackPanel) oElement);
            IterateControls(oStackPanel.Children);
            break;
    }

    }

}
```

This method iterates through the elements in a `UIElementCollection` object. After the object type is determined, you can use the appropriate property to extract its value. If the object type is a container, the property that references it `UIElementCollection` object is passed to `IterateControls()`, and the recursion continues.

XamlWriter/XamlReader

In the chapters 4 and 5, covering dynamic Win and WebForms, respectively, you examined how to iterate the `Controls` collection to produce an XML image of the Form's hierarchy. With WPF, an XML image is part and parcel of the technology itself. XAML is XML that defines your `Window` as you create it with the visual designer. Just as WinForms and WebForms applications generate the source code to instantiate, initialize, and position the controls you draw on them, WPF does the same via XAML. No source code is generated when `Windows` are visually designed—only XAML. Because the screen layout is stored in an XML format already, you can design your forms and then store the XAML in a database for later retrieval.

Visual Studio provides two classes from the `System.Windows.Markup` namespace to handle this for you: `XamlWriter` and `XamlReader`. Suppose you wish to persist the layout of the `Window` shown in Figure 6-11. You can extract the XAML and save it to a file as follows:

```
string szXAML = XamlWriter.Save(this.Content);

File.WriteAllText(@"c:\temp\griddemo.xaml", szXAML);
```

The XAML looks like Listing 6-14.

Listing 6-14. XAML for Window Layout

```
<Grid xmlns="http://schemas.microsoft.com/winfx/2006/xaml/presentation"
xmlns:s="clr-    namespace:System;assembly=mscorlib">
   <Grid.ColumnDefinitions>
      <ColumnDefinition />
      <ColumnDefinition />
   </Grid.ColumnDefinitions>
   <Grid.RowDefinitions>
      <RowDefinition Height="Auto" />
      <RowDefinition Height="Auto" />
      <RowDefinition Height="Auto" />
   </Grid.RowDefinitions>
   <Label Grid.Column="0" Grid.Row="0">Last Name:</Label>
   <TextBox Name="txtLastName" Width="100" Grid.Column="1"
      Grid.Row="0" xml:space="preserve" />
   <Label Grid.Column="0" Grid.Row="1">Salutation:</Label>
   <ComboBox Name="cmbSalutation" Width="100"
         Grid.Column="1" Grid.Row="1">
      <s:String>Mr.</s:String>
      <s:String>Mrs.</s:String>
      <s:String>Dr.</s:String>
   </ComboBox>
   <Button Width="100" Grid.Column="1" Grid.Row="2">Get Data</Button>
</Grid>
```

To re-create a window from this data, you can use the XamlReader as shown in Listing 6-15.

Listing 6-15. Recreating a Window from XAML Using XamlReader

```
string szXAML = File.ReadAllText(@"c:\temp\griddemo.xaml");

this.Content = XamlReader.Parse(szXAML);
```

Persisting Objects

XamlWriter and XamlReader aren't limited to working with user interface elements. You can persist any object using these tools, in effect creating a form of XAML-based object serialization. For example, suppose you have the non–user interface class Dog shown in Listing 6-16.

Listing 6-16. Dog Class

```
public class Dog
{
    public string Name { get; set; }
    public string Breed { get; set; }
```

176

```
    public string Bark()
    {
        return "Woof, woof!";
    }
}
```

If you instantiate this object, you can serialize it using `XamlWriter` and `XamlReader`, as shown in Listing 6-17.

Listing 6-17. *Instantiating a Dog Object*

```
Dog oDog = new Dog();
oDog.Breed = "Pit Bull";
oDog.Name = "Elke";

string szXAML = XamlWriter.Save(oDog);

MessageBox.Show(szXAML);
```

The variable `szXAML` holds the following string, which indicates the class's property settings and its host assembly:

```
<Dog Name=\"Elke\" Breed=\"Pit Bull\" xmlns=\"clr-
namespace:DataDrivenWPF;assembly=DataDrivenWPF\" />
```

You can then reverse this process by extracting the XAML definition and casting it to an object of type `Dog` like this:

```
Dog oMyDog = ((Dog)XamlReader.Parse(szXAML));
```

IsAncestorOf/IsDescendantOf

Two very useful methods for determining the hierarchical relationship of two controls are `IsAncestorOf()` and `IsDescendantOf()`. In the screen image shown in Figure 6-13, a `Window` directly owns a `StackPanel`, a `GroupBox`, and a `Button`. The `StackPanel` owns Save and Cancel buttons, and the `GroupBox` owns a `CheckBox`.

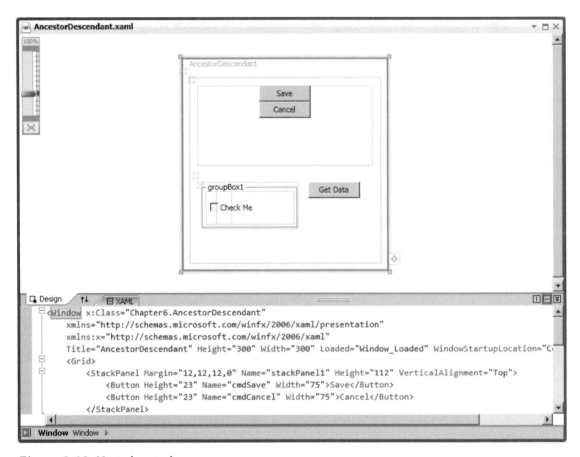

Figure 6-13. Nested controls

The code shown in Listing 6-18 indicates which controls owns which other controls in their genealogical relationship.

Listing 6-18. IsAncestorOf() and IsDescendantOf()

```
bool bIsAncestorOf;
bool bIsDescendantOf;

bIsAncestorOf = grpMyData.IsAncestorOf(chkCheckMe);  //returns true
bIsAncestorOf = grpMyData.IsAncestorOf(cmdGetData);  //returns false
bIsAncestorOf = cmdSave.IsAncestorOf(cmdCancel);  //returns false
bIsAncestorOf = stackPanel1.IsAncestorOf(cmdCancel);  //returns true

bIsDescendantOf = chkCheckMe.IsDescendantOf(grpMyData);  //returns true
bIsDescendantOf = cmdSave.IsDescendantOf(stackPanel1);  //returns true
bIsDescendantOf = cmdSave.IsDescendantOf(chkCheckMe);  //returns false
```

Wiring Events

You can wire events either through code or through XAML. Suppose you wish to display the contents of a TextBox called txtUserID using the event handler shown in Listing 6-19.

Listing 6-19. *Button Event Handler*

```
private void cmdOK_Click(object sender, RoutedEventArgs e)
{
    MessageBox.Show(txtUserID.Text);
}
```

You can accomplish this through XAML by wiring the event handler by name to the Click property like this:

```
<Button Margin="99,0,104,106" Name="cmdOK" Height="23"
        VerticalAlignment="Bottom" Click="cmdOK_Click">OK</Button>
```

Or you can accomplish it in code by assigning a delegate to the event handler:

```
cmdOK.Click += new RoutedEventHandler(this.cmdOK_Click);
```

This event-wiring approach is exactly the same as with Win and WebForms.

XAML does offer one additional possibility for storing source code and associating it with an event. You can store the source code in the XAML itself in a CDATA section using an x:Code directive element. CDATA sections are part of XML, not just XAML, and are used to inform the parser that the text contained within the section isn't XML markup and therefore shouldn't be interpreted as such. Here you can store a block of .NET source code that will compile at compile time, not at runtime like the examples shown in Chapter 2. When the XAML file is compiled, the code contained within the x:Code element is placed in a partial class in the Window1.g.cs file. This is a C# code file with suffix .g.cs, the g being short for "generated". This code can be embedded in the XAML as shown in Listing 6-20.

Listing 6-20. *CDATA Section*

```
<Button Margin="86,122,91,117" Name="cmdCodeInXAML"
        Click="cmdCodeInXAML_Click">Code In XAML</Button>
<x:Code>
    <![CDATA[
    void cmdCodeInXAML_Click(object sender, RoutedEventArgs e)
    {
        MessageBox.Show("You clicked me!");
    }
  ]]>
</x:Code>
```

Data-Driven .Menus

To illustrate how easy data-driven programming is with WPF, compare this section to its counterpart in Chapter 4. Creating data-driven menus in WinForms and wiring them to events takes a bit of work. Using WPF, you need only re-create the XAML within a `Window` to do this. Examine the code shown in Listing 6-21.

Listing 6-21. *XAML for a Menu*

```
<Window x:Class="DataDrivenWPF.MenuDemo"
    xmlns="http://schemas.microsoft.com/winfx/2006/xaml/presentation"
    xmlns:x="http://schemas.microsoft.com/winfx/2006/xaml"
    Title="Menu" Height="300" Width="300">
    <Grid>
        <StackPanel Margin="12,12,11,11" Name="stackPanel1">
            <Menu xmlns="http://schemas.microsoft.com/winfx/2006/xaml/presentation"
    xmlns:x="http://schemas.microsoft.com/winfx/2006/xaml">
                <MenuItem Header="File">
                    <MenuItem Header="Customers" Click="Menu_Click"/>
                    <MenuItem Header="Vendors" Click="Menu_Click"/>
                    <MenuItem Header="Accounts" Click="Menu_Click"/>
                </MenuItem>
                <MenuItem Header="Reports">
                    <MenuItem Header="Personnel" Click="Menu_Click"/>
                    <MenuItem Header="Invoice Register" Click="Menu_Click"/>
                    <MenuItem Header="Aging Schedule" Click="Menu_Click"/>
                </MenuItem>
            </Menu>
        </StackPanel>
    </Grid>
</Window>
```

This code produces the menus shown in Figure 6-14.

Figure 6-14. *XAML-generated menu*

Each menu item is wired to the event handler shown in Listing 6-22.

Listing 6-22. *MenuItem Event Handler*

```
private void Menu_Click(object sender, RoutedEventArgs e)
{
    MenuItem oMenuItem = ((MenuItem)sender);

    MessageBox.Show(oMenuItem.Header.ToString());
}
```

You could just have easily read the menu definition from a XAML file (or an XML file, because the two are one and the same) and then display it in the Window.

Suppose you save the XAML for the menus to a separate file, leaving only the definition for the Window and the Grid as shown in Listing 6-23. I've added a Window_Loaded() event handler because you'll need that in a bit.

Listing 6-23. *Code Stub for a Window*

```
<Window x:Class="DataDrivenWPF.MenuDemo"
    xmlns="http://schemas.microsoft.com/winfx/2006/xaml/presentation"
    xmlns:x="http://schemas.microsoft.com/winfx/2006/xaml"
    Title="Menu" Height="300" Width="300" Loaded="Window_Loaded">
    <Grid Name="Grid1">
    </Grid>
</Window>
```

You can then try to instantiate this code at runtime and assign it to the Children collection of the Grid container, as shown in Listing 6-24.

Listing 6-24. *Loading XAML for the Menu Programmatically*

```
using (FileStream oFileStream = new FileStream("Menu.xaml", FileMode.Open))
{
    Menu oMenu = XamlReader.Load(oFileStream) as Menu;

    if (oMenu != null)
        this.Grid1.Children.Add(oMenu);
}
```

I say "try to" because compiling this code triggers an error message similar to the following:

```
Must compile XAML file that specifies events. Line '4' Position '50'.
```

The reason is that the XAML has no knowledge of the Menu_Click event compiled within the Window object. Therefore, it can't resolve the reference to it within the XAML. Your options at this point are to include the event code in the XAML by including a CDATA tag as described previously, or remove the event-handler references from the XAML and wire them up after the Window is loaded. You can accomplish the latter task using the recursive routine shown in Listing 6-25.

Listing 6-25. Recursing Menu Structures and Assigning Event Handlers

```
private void Window_Loaded(object sender, RoutedEventArgs e)
{

    using (FileStream oFileStream = new FileStream("Menu.xaml", FileMode.Open))
    {
        Menu oMenu = XamlReader.Load(oFileStream) as Menu;

        if (oMenu != null)
        {
            this.Grid1.Children.Insert(0, oMenu);

            WireMenus(oMenu.Items);
        }

    }

}

private void WireMenus(ItemCollection oItemCollection)
{
    foreach (MenuItem oMenuItem in oItemCollection)
    {
        if (oMenuItem.HasItems)
            WireMenus(oMenuItem.Items);
        else
            oMenuItem.Click += new RoutedEventHandler(Menu_Click);
    }
}
```

Summary

In this chapter, you reviewed data-driven programming for WPF applications. You saw the differences between this environment and WinForms/WebForms applications. Specifically, you looked at how elements related to containers and how to iterate these hierarchies. You also looked at how XAML is essentially a data-driven format in itself, thus making dynamic programming using WPF rather easy. Coming up, you apply data-driven techniques to reporting.

■ ■ ■

Reporting

The purpose of this chapter is to show you how to generate dynamic reports at runtime. The goal is not to show how to build a reporting interface to enable users to design their own reports. Such a task would be way too ambitious a project and can best be served by providing users with end-user reporting and business intelligence tools and training them on their use.

As a rule, traditional report writing tools like Crystal Reports and SQL Server Reporting Services are intended to create design-time reports. If you know what your report will look like and what data fields it will use at design time, you can lay out this format, and these tools will serve their purpose well. Because you're looking at the data-driven aspects of report development, however, such tools may not be the best approach for you. In this chapter, you examine the pros and cons of each tool and how to employ them in data-driven applications.

SQL Server Extended Properties

SQL Server offers a feature called *extended properties* that you can use to add metadata to your data objects. You can do this visually by right-clicking the object, as shown in Figure 7-1. Select the Extended Properties entry on the left side of the tab, and you see a simple data-entry form where you can name properties and enter values for them in a key/value pair relationship.

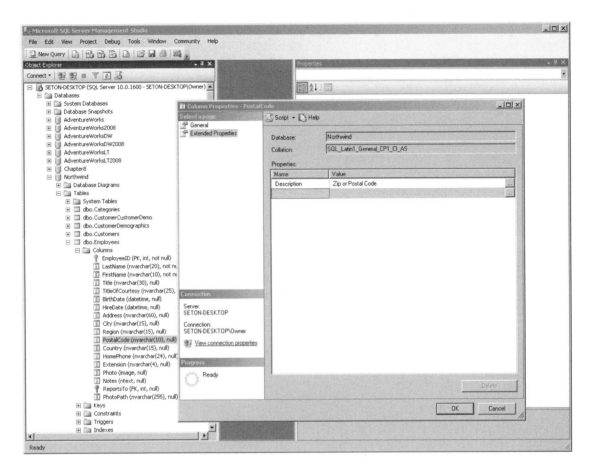

Figure 7-1. *Creating extended properties*

this same task programmatically via the `sp_addextendedproperty` stored procedure. The code in Listing 7-1 shows how to add an extended property to the `PostalCode` column of the `Employees` table, which is owned by the schema `dbo`.

Listing 7-1. *Adding an Extended Property to a Column*

```
exec sp_addextendedproperty
'Description',
'Zip or Postal Code',
'schema',
'dbo',
'table',
'Employees',
'column',
```

```
'PostalCode'
```

To add a descriptive property to the Employees table itself, you can use the stored procedure call in Listing 7-2.

Listing 7-2. Adding an Extended Property to a Table

```
exec sp_addextendedproperty
'Description',
'List of Employees and Consultants',
'schema',
'dbo',
'table',
'Employees',
Null,
Null
```

The syntax for this stored procedure is very simple. It follows the pattern in Listing 7-3.

Listing 7-3. sp_addextendedproperty Parameters

```
exec sp_addextendedproperty
<Name of extended property>,
<Value of extended property>,
'schema',
<name of schema, commonly 'dbo'>,
'table',
<Name of table>,
' Your Description Here ',
<Name of column>
```

You can also modify existing extended properties with the sp_updateextendedproperty stored procedure. This uses the same parameter structure as sp_addextendedproperty. An example is shown in Listing 7-4, where the Description property of the Employees table is changed.

Listing 7-4. Modifying a Table's Extended Property

```
exec sp_updateextendedproperty
'Description',
'List of Employees, Consultants, and Temps',
'schema',
'dbo',
'table',
'Employees',
Null,
Null
```

After you've entered a series of extended properties, you need some way of retrieving them. This is the job of the fn_listextendedproperty function. Using fn_listextendedproperty, you can retrieve the name and type of the database object along with the name and value of the extended property. For example, the following call retrieves the extended properties for the Employees table:

```
SELECT *
FROM fn_listextendedproperty (Null, 'schema', 'dbo',
'table', 'Employees', Null, Null);
```

The results are shown here:

Objtype	objname	name	value
TABLE	Employees	Description	List of Employees, Consultants, and Temps

Retrieving the extended properties for the individual columns is just as easy:

```
SELECT *
FROM fn_listextendedproperty (Null, 'schema', 'dbo',
'table', 'Employees', 'column', Null);
```

This call returns the results shown here:

Objtype	objname	name	value
COLUMN	LastName	Description	Last Name
COLUMN	FirstName	Description	First Name
COLUMN	Title	Description	Title
COLUMN	TitleOfCourtesy	Description	Prefix
COLUMN	BirthDate	Description	Date of Birth
COLUMN	HireDate	Description	Date of Hire
COLUMN	PostalCode	Description	Zip or Postal Code

Creating extended properties is all well and good, but how can this feature be used practically? Suppose you have a web-based personnel-management application containing a general personnel report that can display an employee's name and up to one dozen out of several hundred columns of information stored in an employee table. Each user may be interested in creating a custom report that includes only certain pieces of relevant information. One user may wish to create an emergency contact list and therefore request off-site contact addresses and phone numbers. Another user may be looking to determine space and resource utilization and request building, floor, desk, extension, and e-mail within an office complex. You could create a report that displayed each data element for each staff member, and hide the unwanted columns by passing in parameters at runtime. This approach would clearly be unwieldy. Instead, you can offer the user a CheckedListBox containing all these several data elements, and the user can select the ones they wish. Such an interface might look like Figure 7-2.

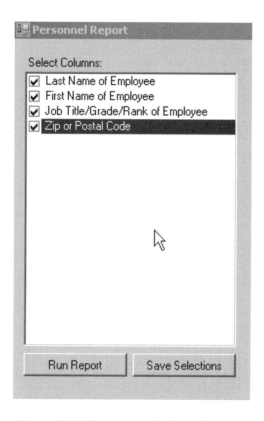

Figure 7-2. User-selectable data elements

This CheckedListBox can be populated with the employee table's metadata returned from the stored procedure shown in Listing 7-5.

■ **Note** Understand that this routine only returns columns that have extended properties assigned. Therefore, using extended properties for this purpose is an all-or-nothing proposition.

Listing 7-5. *Retrieving Extended Properties*

```
ALTER PROCEDURE [dbo].[spc_GetFieldList]

AS

SELECT * FROM fn_listextendedproperty (Null, 'schema', 'dbo',
'table', 'Employees', 'column', Null);
```

The column name (such as PostalCode) is assigned to the ValueMember property, and the plain language name (such as Zip or Postal Code) is assigned to the DisplayMember. When the user makes their selection and clicks Run Report, the code shown in Listing 7-6 retrieves the values and creates a SQL statement.

Listing 7-6. *Building a SQL Statement from the User Selections*

```
StringBuilder oSQL = new StringBuilder("SELECT ");

//iterate the checked items and add them to the column list
foreach (object oItem in lstColumns.CheckedItems)
{
    oSQL.Append((oItem).Value);
    oSQL.Append(", ");
}

//Remove the trailing comma
oSQL.Remove(oSQL.Length - 2, 2);

oSQL.Append(" FROM Employees");
```

The resulting SQL looks something like this:

```
SELECT LastName, FirstName, BirthDate, PostalCode FROM Employees
```

These selections can then be persisted to an XML structure and stored in an XML column in your database. With a simple iteration through the CheckedItems collection, as shown in Listing 7-7, you can create an XML mapping of each user's selections.

Listing 7-7. *Storing User Selections as XML*

```
XmlDocument oXmlDocument = new XmlDocument();
XmlNode oXMLMainNode;
XmlNode oXMLNode;
XmlAttribute oXmlAttribute;

oXmlDocument.CreateXmlDeclaration("1.0", "UTF-8", null);
```

```
oXMLMainNode = oXmlDocument.CreateNode(XmlNodeType.Element,
    "Columns", string.Empty);
oXmlDocument.AppendChild(oXMLMainNode);

//iterate the checked items and add them to the column list
foreach (object oItem in lstColumns.CheckedItems)
{
    oXMLNode = oXmlDocument.CreateNode(XmlNodeType.Element,
      "ColumnName", string.Empty);
    oXMLMainNode.AppendChild(oXMLNode);

    oXmlAttribute = oXmlDocument.CreateAttribute("name");
    oXmlAttribute.Value = ((ListItem)oItem).Value;
    oXMLNode.Attributes.Append(oXmlAttribute);
}

oXmlDocument.Save(@"c:\temp\columns.xml");
```

This code produces the XML shown in Listing 7-8.

Listing 7-8. *XML Output*

```
<Columns>
  <ColumnName name="LastName" />
  <ColumnName name="FirstName" />
  <ColumnName name="BirthDate" />
  <ColumnName name="HireDate" />
</Columns>
```

Now that you've offered the user a selection of columns and allowed them to persist those columns to a database, you can examine the various export formats available for dynamic report creation.

Microsoft Excel

Even when not working with data-driven applications, I've long believed that there is no better reporting tool than a well-written stored procedure and a copy of Excel. When used properly, a report writer is just a data-formatting tool. All the intelligence is (or at least should be, in my opinion) stored in the stored procedure, or business class, that feeds raw data to the reporting tool. The stored procedure should provide the detail data in the format it will appear in, minus any totals and subtotals. It should even provide calculated columns. If you need to show this year's and last year's expenses for a series of line items in your report and wish to display the percentage changes between these two data elements, the stored procedure can calculate this for you. As a rule, the more work that can be done in the stored procedure, the better.

Formatting in a Stored Procedure

I once worked with a developer who took a very creative approach to deploying data-driven reports. Not only did he create the data set in the stored procedure, but he established the display attributes there as well. He did this by creating virtual column names that consisted of a comma-delimited list of visual settings. For example, he would have a SQL statement that looked like this:

```
SELECT
LastName [Last Name, 1000, B, L],
FirstName [First Name, 1000, N, L],
Title [Title, 1500, N, L],
HireDate [Date of Hire, 600, N, L, MM/DD/YYYY]
FROM Employees
ORDER BY LastName, FirstName
```

This SQL would tell the reporting engine (and the data grids) to give the first column a caption of Last Name, make it 1000 twips wide, display it in Bold (as opposed to Normal or Italic), and display the data left justified. This way, if the developer needed to change a visual attribute, he could do so in the stored procedure and not need to redistribute a new EXE.

I like Microsoft Excel for two primary reasons. First, its cell-and-column format is perfect for reporting. Second, its nature as a spreadsheet makes it a powerful interactive tool for users to perform analysis. You can facilitate this by outputting calculated columns as formulas. Instead of displaying raw numbers for totals and subtotals, formulas allow summary values to change as the user manipulates the detail when performing "what-if" analysis.

One of the most frequent requests I've received over the years from clients is to create report output in Microsoft Excel. Commonly, the users only want their reports in Excel, because no other format matters to them. With its row-and-column architecture and data-analysis functionality, it's a natural venue for report delivery.

Still another reason you may wish to consider Excel is to handle reports in which users select the columns that appear. Because report writers by their nature are intended for design-time report creation, you can't possibly anticipate all the permutations a user may desire. Moreover, because you have full control over what's going into each cell, you can specify what appears as formulas and what appears as raw data.

If you want to create a server-based reporting solution, the creation of XLS files with Microsoft Excel itself isn't a viable solution. Excel, and the rest of the Microsoft Office suite, still requires the use of COM Interop. Although .NET 4.0 offers many new features for working with COM objects, especially the new `dynamic` type, they're not everyone's primary choice of development tools. The Excel object model has a large memory footprint and was intended to be instantiated individually on desktop machines, not potentially hundreds of times simultaneously on servers. No technical barriers preclude you from doing this, but the solution isn't scalable, and you'll soon eat up your server's memory. Simply put, Excel was never intended to be used this way. Moreover, if you aren't careful about cleaning up and destroying your objects when you're finished, stray Excel instantiations remain in memory, and you have to destroy them through Task Manager or with a reboot. Excel objects are also very slow, and even after the stored procedure executes, outputting the information to a spreadsheet can take several minutes for a report with a few thousand rows. Still, a surprising number of people take this approach. At a recent Microsoft TechEd conference, one of the speakers asked how many people were instantiating Excel directly on a server, and at least two dozen of the 80 or so people in the room raised their hands.

Fortunately, there are two third-party solutions designed specifically as scalable, server-based replacements for Excel: Essential XlsIO from Syncfusion and OfficeWriter for Excel from SoftArtisans. Both have object models similar to that of Excel, so if you know VBA programming, you can pick up either of these tools very quickly. They're also dramatically faster than Microsoft Excel; in timing studies I've done, both products created sample spreadsheets anywhere between 10 and 100 times faster than Microsoft Excel. I cover these tools in the next sections.

Syncfusion's Essential XlsIO

Syncfusion's (www.syncfusion.com) Essential XlsIO is written completely in .NET code (C#) and optionally comes with the source code. This product offers `PageSetup` objects, row height settings, page breaks, document property settings, data validation, conditional formatting, comments, rich text, autofilters, charts, hyperlinks, PivotTables, and images. Essential XlsIO offers everything but macros, but it preserves them if they're present in template spreadsheets. Listing 7-9 shows how to create a simple spreadsheet.

Listing 7-9. Setting Up Syncfusion Essential XlsIO Code

```
//Instantiate the spreadsheet creation engine
oExcelEngine = new ExcelEngine();
//Create a workbook

oWorkBook = oExcelEngine.Excel.Workbooks.Create();
//Reference the first worksheet
oWS = oWorkBook.Worksheets[0];

//Set orientation and paper size
oWS.PageSetup.Orientation = ExcelPageOrientation.Portrait;
oWS.PageSetup.PaperSize = ExcelPaperSize.PaperLetter;

//Set margins
oWS.PageSetup.LeftMargin = 0.25;
oWS.PageSetup.RightMargin = 0.25;
oWS.PageSetup.TopMargin = 1.25;
oWS.PageSetup.BottomMargin = 1.0;

//Set the first row to print at the top of every page
oWS.PageSetup.PrintTitleRows = "$A$1:$IV$1";

//Set header and footer text
oWS.PageSetup.LeftFooter = "Page &P of &N\n&D &T";
oWS.PageSetup.CenterHeader = "Sample Report";

//Set column widths
oWS.SetColumnWidth(1, 20);
oWS.SetColumnWidth(2, 10);
```

```
//Set workbook's summary and custom document properties
oWorkBook.BuiltInDocumentProperties.Author = "Essential Essential XlsIO";
oWorkBook.CustomDocumentProperties["Today"].DateTime = DateTime.Today;
```

You need to instantiate the spreadsheet-creation engine first and then reference the existing workbook and worksheet as you would in Excel. The `PageSetup` object encapsulates the same settings as its Excel counterpart, and Essential XlsIO provides its own enumerated values to refer to such properties as `Orientation` and `PaperSize`. Headers and footers are set as you expect. Finally, you set the workbook's summary and custom document properties. Listing 7-10 shows how the cells are filled with data from the data source.

Listing 7-10. *Populating the Cells*

```
//Set column headers
oWS.Range[sRow, 1].Text = "Product";
oWS.Range[sRow, 2].Text = "Sales";

//Display headers in bold, centered, with a yellow background
oWS.Range[sRow, 1, sRow, 2].CellStyle.Color = Color.Yellow;
oWS.Range[sRow, 1, sRow, 2].CellStyle.HorizontalAlignment =
ExcelHAlign.HAlignCenter;
oWS.Range[sRow, 1, sRow, 2].CellStyle.Font.Bold = true;
sRow++;

//Get sample data as a DataTable object, move through the results,
//and write data to cells
oDT = GetData();

foreach(DataRow oDR in oDT.Rows)
{
    oWS.Range[sRow, 1].Text = oDR["Product"].ToString();
    oWS.Range[sRow, 2].Value = oDR["Sales"].ToString();
    sRow++;
}
sRow++;

//Display total line via formula in bold
oWS.Range[sRow, 1].Text = "Grand Total";
oWS.Range[sRow, 2].Formula = "SUM(B2:B" + (sRow - 1).ToString() + ")";
oWS.Range[sRow, 1, sRow, 2].CellStyle.Font.Bold = true;

//Format Sales column
oWS.Range[2, 2, sRow, 2].NumberFormat = "0.00";
oWorkBook.SaveAs(@"c:\temp\sample.xls");
oWorkBook.Close();
```

Rather than refer to individual cells, Essential XlsIO refers to ranges. As in Excel, you can use range references to apply data formats and cell attributes like color and font. You can even use ranges to assign values. The last printed page of the spreadsheet produced by this code is shown in Figure 7-3.

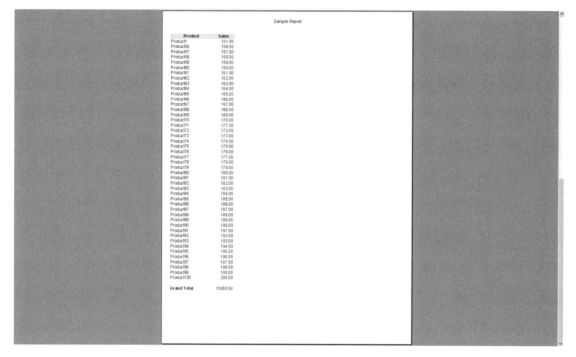

Figure 7-3. Spreadsheet output from Essential XlsIO

You can also use several helper methods like the worksheet object's `ImportDataTable()` method that make importing ADO.NET data sources like `Array`, `DataTable`, `DataColumn`, and `DataView` easier than iterating through the data source.

In addition to creating Excel reports purely using code, it's also possible to use existing spreadsheets as templates for report generation. Often, it's easier to design the look and feel of the report using the Excel GUI and then use XlsIO to dynamically fill data during runtime. Using this approach, you can also embed elements like macros in your report that Essential XlsIO doesn't directly support but retains on resaving if they're present in the template spreadsheet. Listing 7-11 shows how to generate a report based on a template spreadsheet.

Listing 7-11. Report Based on Spreadsheet Templates

```
//Instantiate the spreadsheet creation engine
oExcelEngine = new ExcelEngine();

//Create a workbook
oWorkBook = oExcelEngine.Excel.Workbooks.
   Open(@"..\..\Data\Template.xls", ExcelOpenType.Automatic);
```

```
//Reference the first worksheet
oWS = oWorkBook.Worksheets[0];

//Get sample data
oDT = GetTable();

//Import DataTable into worksheet
oWS.ImportDataTable(oDT,false,2,1,-1,-1,false);

//Display total line via formula in bold
oWS.Range[oDT.Rows.Count+1, 1].Text = "Grand Total";
oWS.Range[oDT.Rows.Count+1, 2].Formula =
    "SUM(B2:B" + (oDT.Rows.Count - 1).ToString() + ")";
oWS.Range[oDT.Rows.Count+1, 1, oDT.Rows.Count+1, 2].CellStyle.Font.Bold = true;
```

After the workbook is loaded into memory using the Open() method, all the elements in the workbook become accessible through the Essential XlsIO API. This makes it possible to read data from existing spreadsheets that users may upload back to the server after making modifications on their local machines. It's also possible to read and write the spreadsheets to streams, which can be convenient at times. No temporary files are generated on the server when saving to a stream. It only requires medium-trust security settings so the stream an be deployed on shared hosting environments and cloud computing environments like Windows Azure.

Essential XlsIO also has support for another variant of the template-based approach for report generation, whereby the end user can design the template and place special markers in it that are replaced with data dynamically during runtime.

In addition, Essential XlsIO can read and write SpreadsheetML files, which are Excel-compatible XML files; XLSX files, which are the default file format for Excel 2007; and CSV files; in addition to the default Excel (97-2003) binary format.

SoftArtisans' OfficeWriter for Excel

SoftArtisans' (www.softartisans.com) OfficeWriter for Excel tool produces native Excel files (Office 97, 2000, XP, 2003, and 2007) without instantiating Excel. For use on high-request web server environments, OfficeWriter is a lean tool designed specifically to generate Excel and Word documents on a server. There are two versions of this product: the Enterprise Edition and the Standard Edition.

The application object in the Enterprise product offers an unlimited number of spreadsheets with full programmatic functionality, including PivotTables, VBA, charts, and macros. The programmatic control allows you to add flexibility to your applications by instantly modifying reports based on runtime data or your users' requests.

The Standard Edition preserves all of the Excel features in a template or existing spreadsheet. With limited exposure to the OfficeWriter application object in the Standard Edition, features such as cell merging and column and row autofitting aren't available at runtime.

Listing 7-12 shows how to create a spreadsheet using SoftArtisans' OfficeWriter. The output is the same as that shown in Figure 7-3. If you've ever created a spreadsheet with VBA code, this should all be familiar territory.

Listing 7-12. Creating a Spreadsheet Using SoftArtisans' OfficeWriter for Excel

```
ExcelApplication oExcelApplication;
Workbook oWB;
Worksheet oWS;
GlobalStyle oGlobalStyle;
Area oArea;
DataTable oDT;
int sRow = 0;

//Create a workbook
oExcelApplication = new ExcelApplication();
oWB = oExcelApplication.Create();

//Reference the first worksheet
oWS = oWB.Worksheets[0];

//Set orientation and paper size
oWS.PageSetup.Orientation = PageSetup.PageOrientation.Portrait;
oWS.PageSetup.PaperSize = PageSetup.PagePaperSize.Letter;

//Set margins
oWS.PageSetup.LeftMargin = 0.25;
oWS.PageSetup.RightMargin = 0.25;
oWS.PageSetup.TopMargin = 1.25;
oWS.PageSetup.BottomMargin = 1.0;
oWS.PageSetup.Zoom = 100;

//Set the first row to print at the top of every page
oWS.PageSetup.SetPrintTitleRows(0, 2);

//Set header and footer text
oWS.PageSetup.LeftFooter = "Page &P of &N\n&D &T";
oWS.PageSetup.CenterHeader = "Sample Report";

//Set column widths
oWS.GetColumnProperties(0).Width = 100;
oWS.GetColumnProperties(1).Width = 50;
```

OfficeWriter instantiates an object of type `ExcelApplication` that is the equivalent of `Excel.Application`. Then, you can create a new workbook and refer to the first worksheet in that workbook. The `PageSetup` interface mirrors Excel's closely.

You populate the cells by setting the properties of the `Cells` objects, as shown in Listing 7-13.

195

Listing 7-13. Populating the Cells

```
//Set column headers
oWS.Cells[sRow, 0].Value = "Product";
oWS.Cells[sRow, 1].Value = "Sales";
//Display headers in bold, centered, with a yellow background
oWS.Cells[sRow, 0].Style.BackgroundColor = Color.SystemColor.Yellow;
oWS.Cells[sRow, 0].Style.HorizontalAlignment = Style.HAlign.Center;
oWS.Cells[sRow, 0].Style.Font.Bold = true;
oWS.Cells[sRow, 1].Style.BackgroundColor = Color.SystemColor.Yellow;
oWS.Cells[sRow, 1].Style.HorizontalAlignment = Style.HAlign.Center;
oWS.Cells[sRow, 1].Style.Font.Bold = true;
sRow++;

//Get sample data, move through the results, and write data to cells
oDT = GetData();
foreach(DataRow oDR in oDT.Rows)
{
   oWS.Cells[sRow, 0].Value = oDR["Product"].ToString();
   oWS.Cells[sRow, 1].Value = int.Parse(oDR["Sales"].ToString());
  sRow++;
}
sRow++;

//Display total line via formula in bold
oWS.Cells[sRow, 0].Value = "Grand Total";
oWS.Cells[sRow, 1].Formula = "=SUM(B2:B" + (sRow - 1).ToString() + ")";
oWS.Cells[sRow, 0].Style.Font.Bold = true;
oWS.Cells[sRow, 1].Style.Font.Bold = true;

//Format Sales column
oGlobalStyle = oWB.CreateStyle();
oGlobalStyle.NumberFormat = "0.00";
oArea = oWS.CreateArea(1, 1, sRow, 1);
oArea.SetStyle(oGlobalStyle);
oExcelApplication.Save(oWB, @"c:\temp\sample.xls");
oDT.Dispose();
```

Formatting is performed by creating a GlobalStyle object and determining what the style attributes are. In this example, it sets the NumberFormat to 0.00 but can also set fonts and colors. Then, an Area object, which is similar to a Range object in Excel, uses the SetStyle() method to apply the new style to the designated area.

In addition to creating and formatting spreadsheets, SoftArtisans offers its Hot-Cell Technology within Excel. This feature allows you to specify dynamic cells that are linked to and update data sources on the server. Just by modifying a report on a client machine, users can use Excel as a rich front end. With the ability to retrieve or update data on a web server, all end users can now access the same centralized location for up-to-date business information.

PDF

Adobe Portable Data Format (PDF) has been a standard for document distribution for many years. Although Adobe Reader is free and Adobe publishes the specification for PDF documents, using this specification to develop your own output is a major development task. Therefore, this section examines two third-party products that can do the job for you: iTextSharp and Syncfusion's Essential PDF.

Although you can certainly create a report in the PDF format directly, it can be a bit cumbersome to do so. PDF is more frequently a format for export existing reports *to*, not a format you develop *in* directly. Nevertheless, you can directly output using these PDF tools, and the next sections tell you how.

iTextSharp

iTextSharp is an open source freeware library available at `http://sourceforge.net/projects/itextsharp/`. The tool consists of one .NET assembly called `iTextSharp.DLL`. You can use iTextSharp to create free-form text documents, multicolumn newsletters, and just about anything else you can think of. The sample code shown in Listing 7-14 illustrates how to export a `DataTable` to a columnar report.

Listing 7-14. Creating a Report Using iTextSharp

```
Document oDocument = new Document();
PdfWriter oPdfWriter;
PdfPTable oPdfPTable;

oDT = GetData();

oPdfWriter = PdfWriter.GetInstance(oDocument,
    new FileStream(@"c:\temp\Chap0101.pdf", FileMode.Create));

//Assign instance of object which handles page events
oPdfWriter.PageEvent = new PDFPageEvent();

oDocument.Open();

//Create a PdfPTable with enough columns to handle the
//columns in the DataTable
oPdfPTable = new PdfPTable(oDT.Columns.Count);

//Add the data to the PdfPTable dynamically
foreach (DataRow oDR in oDT.Rows)
{
    foreach (DataColumn oDC in oDT.Columns)
    {
        oPdfPTable.AddCell(oDR[oDC.ColumnName].ToString());
    }
}
```

197

```
//Add the table to the document object
oDocument.Add(oPdfPTable);

oDocument.Close();
```

This code dynamically iterates through a DataTable and places its contents in the cells of a table that is rendered to the report. To handle the page headers, you need to create a PDFPageEvent class that implements the IPdfPageEvent interface. This interface imports a number of methods to trap the various events that arise in the creation of a PDF document. The code for the PDFPageEvent class is shown in Listing 7-15.

Listing 7-15. *Displaying Headers Using Page Events*

```
public class PDFPageEvent : IPdfPageEvent
{
    private void DisplayHeader(PdfWriter oWriter, Document oDocument)
    {
        PdfPTable oPdfPTable = new PdfPTable(oDT.Columns.Count);

        foreach (DataColumn oDC in oDT.Columns)
        {
            oPdfPTable.AddCell(oDC.ColumnName.ToString());
        }

        oDocument.Add(oPdfPTable);
    }

    public void OnOpenDocument(PdfWriter oWriter, Document oDocument)
    {
    }

    public void OnStartPage(PdfWriter oWriter, Document oDocument)
    {
        DisplayHeader(oWriter, oDocument);
    }

    public void OnEndPage(PdfWriter oWriter, Document oDocument)
    {
    }

    public void OnCloseDocument(PdfWriter oWriter, Document oDocument)
    {
    }

    public void OnParagraph(PdfWriter oWriter, Document oDocument,
        float paragraphPosition)
    {
```

```
    }

    public void OnParagraphEnd(PdfWriter oWriter, Document oDocument,
        float paragraphPosition)
    {
    }

    public void OnChapter(PdfWriter oWriter, Document oDocument,
        float paragraphPosition, Paragraph title)
    {
    }

    public void OnChapterEnd(PdfWriter oWriter, Document oDocument,
        float paragraphPosition)
    {
    }

    public void OnSection(PdfWriter oWriter, Document oDocument,
        float paragraphPosition, int depth, Paragraph title)
    {
    }

    public void OnSectionEnd(PdfWriter oWriter, Document oDocument,
        float paragraphPosition)
    {
    }

    public void OnGenericTag(PdfWriter oWriter, Document oDocument,
        Rectangle rect, string text)
    {
    }
}
```

Here, the DisplayHeader() method outputs a table at the top of every page. Instead of displaying the data, it displays the column names. This code produces the report shown in Figure 7-4.

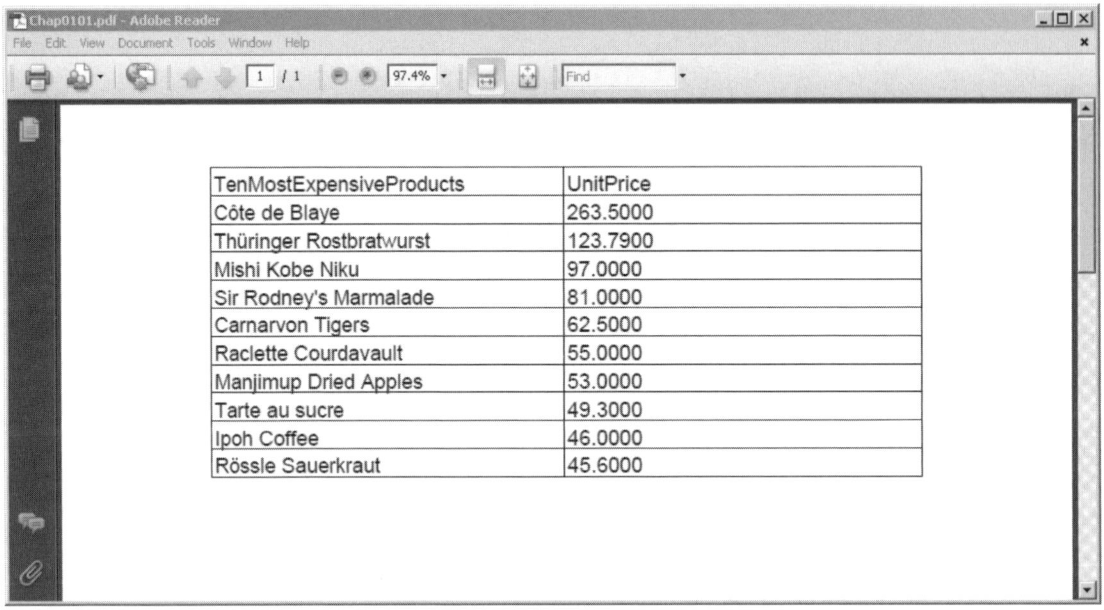

TenMostExpensiveProducts	UnitPrice
Côte de Blaye	263.5000
Thüringer Rostbratwurst	123.7900
Mishi Kobe Niku	97.0000
Sir Rodney's Marmalade	81.0000
Carnarvon Tigers	62.5000
Raclette Courdavault	55.0000
Manjimup Dried Apples	53.0000
Tarte au sucre	49.3000
Ipoh Coffee	46.0000
Rössle Sauerkraut	45.6000

Figure 7-4. *iTextSharp report output*

Syncfusion's Essential PDF

Syncfusion's Essential PDF (`www.syncfusion.com`) is distributed either as an individual tool or bundled with its Essential BackOffice Studio. Unlike iTextSharp, it comes with full documentation and technical support. And, as you'd expect in a licensed product, it has many more features.

To display a `DataTable` dynamically in PDF, you use the `PdfLightTable` object, which is designed precisely for that purpose. The code shown in Listing 7-16 performs the same task in Essential PDF that the code in Listing 7-14 does with iTextSharp.

Listing 7-16. *Displaying a `DataTable` in Syncfusion's Essential PDF*

```
PdfDocument oPdfDocument = new PdfDocument();
PdfPage oPdfPage = oPdfDocument.Pages.Add();
PdfLightTable oPdfLightTable = new PdfLightTable();
PdfLayoutFormat oPdfLayoutFormat = new PdfLayoutFormat();

//Get the data
oPdfLightTable.DataSource = GetData();

//Dynamically add the header...
oPdfLightTable.Style.ShowHeader = true;

//made up of the column names...
```

```
oPdfLightTable.Style.HeaderSource = PdfHeaderSource.ColumnCaptions;

//and repeat on every page
oPdfLightTable.Style.RepeatHeader = true;

//Set layout properties
oPdfLayoutFormat.Break = PdfLayoutBreakType.FitElement;

//Draw table
oPdfLightTable.Draw(oPdfPage, new PointF(0, 10), oPdfLayoutFormat);

//Save to disk
oPdfDocument.Save("Sample.pdf");

System.Diagnostics.Process.Start("Sample.pdf");
```

This code displays the report shown in Figure 7-5. As you can see, it's the same as the one generated by iTextSharp.

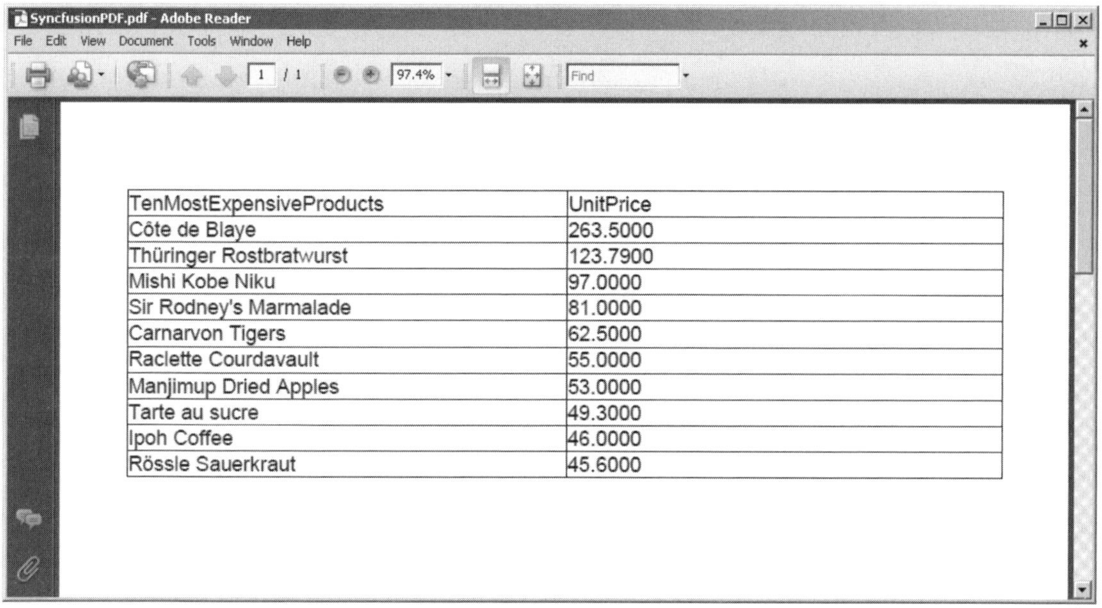

TenMostExpensiveProducts	UnitPrice
Côte de Blaye	263.5000
Thüringer Rostbratwurst	123.7900
Mishi Kobe Niku	97.0000
Sir Rodney's Marmalade	81.0000
Carnarvon Tigers	62.5000
Raclette Courdavault	55.0000
Manjimup Dried Apples	53.0000
Tarte au sucre	49.3000
Ipoh Coffee	46.0000
Rössle Sauerkraut	45.6000

Figure 7-5. Syncfusion's PDF report output

SAP/Business Objects: Crystal Reports

Crystal Reports is still the 800-pound gorilla of the reporting world. It has been around since 1991 and is currently in its thirteenth incarnation. Crystal Reports has an SDK called the Report Application Server (RAS) that allows you to create reports at runtime. Two types of RAS SDK models are available. One ships with the Crystal Reports 2008 Advanced Edition and is known as the *unmanaged RAS*, and the other ships with BusinessObjects Enterprise XI and is called the *managed RAS. Unmanaged* refers to the direct access the programming language provides to Crystal report files on disk. *Managed* refers to reports that are managed within the InfoStore repository of the server product. A detailed analysis of the Enterprise object model is beyond the scope of this book, so this section focuses on the unmanaged RAS. For the managed RAS, I refer you to my previous Apress book, *Pro Crystal Enterprise/BusinessObjects XI Programming.*

Embedded vs. Nonembedded Reports

When you develop a report using the version of Crystal Reports that ships with Visual Studio, you have a choice of creating separate RPT files or embedding the reports directly in your compiled application. The advantage of embedding reports directly is that .NET creates a class wrapper for you to interact with your reports, and you no longer need to deal with the disk file programmatically. The report itself is embedded within the compiled application assembly and doesn't function as a separate RPT.

The downside to this approach is that every time you wish to update a report, you need to recompile and distribute an EXE rather than just a separate RPT file. Moreover, getting an individual RPT file through your company's change-control process for installation on a production box is usually much easier than pushing through a full EXE.

Dynamic Crystal Reports

There are two ways to create Crystal reports dynamically: using preset columns and using the Crystal SDK. Both have their advantages and disadvantages, which you learn in the sections that follow.

Preset Columns

Using preset columns is the easier way to create a data-driven Crystal report. It's also cruder. By creating a report file and binding it to a typed `DataSet` with, say, ten columns, you can bind up to ten selected data elements chosen by the user. You need to create ten parameter fields as well to serve as column headers. Both the `DataSet` columns and the parameters fields are given consistent names such as `DColumn1, DColumn2..DColumn`*n*. Then, using the code in Listing 7-17, you can use SQL virtual column names to return a result set where the columns are named `DColumn1, DColumn2..DColumn`*n.*

Listing 7-17. Dynamic Crystal Reports Using Preset Columns

```
private string DynamicCrystalReports()
{
    DynamicCrystalReport oDynamicCrystalReport;
    ParameterFields oParameterFields;
    ParameterField oParameterField;
    ParameterDiscreteValue oParameterDiscreteValue;
```

```
    StringBuilder oSQL = new StringBuilder("SELECT ");
    DataSet1 oDS = new DataSet1();
    SqlConnection oSqlConnection;
    SqlDataAdapter oSqlDataAdapter;
    SqlCommand oSqlCommand;
    int iColumn = 1;
    int iColCnt = 1;

    oDynamicCrystalReport = new DynamicCrystalReport();
    oParameterFields = new ParameterFields();

    //Assign the description text to the parameter objects for the selected
    //fields. The iColumn variable assigns the parameters in sequence based on
name.
    foreach (object oItem in lstColumns.CheckedItems)
    {
        oParameterField = new ParameterField();
        oParameterField.Name = "DataColumn" + iColumn.ToString();
        oParameterDiscreteValue = new ParameterDiscreteValue();
        oParameterDiscreteValue.Value = ((ListItem)oItem).Text;
        oParameterField.CurrentValues.Add(oParameterDiscreteValue);
        oParameterFields.Add(oParameterField);

        oSQL.Append(((ListItem)oItem).Value + " AS DColumn" + iColumn.ToString());
        oSQL.Append(", ");

        iColumn++;
    }

    //There are 10 hard-coded columns in this report. Place an empty string
    //in the header fields for the unused columns
    iColCnt = oDynamicCrystalReport.ParameterFields.Count;

    for (int i = iColumn; i <= iColCnt; i++)
    {
        oParameterField = new ParameterField();
        oParameterField.Name = "DataColumn" + iColumn.ToString();
        oParameterDiscreteValue = new ParameterDiscreteValue();
        oParameterDiscreteValue.Value = string.Empty;
        oParameterField.CurrentValues.Add(oParameterDiscreteValue);
        oParameterFields.Add(oParameterField);

        iColumn++;
    }

    //Pass in the collection of 10 named parameter objects
    crystalReportViewer1.ParameterFieldInfo = oParameterFields;
```

203

```
//Whack the trailing comma
oSQL.Remove(oSQL.Length - 2, 2);

oSQL.Append(" FROM Employees");

//Execute the SQL
oSqlConnection = new
  SqlConnection("Data Source=SETON-NOTEBOOK; "+
  "Initial catalog=Northwind;"+
  "Integrated security=SSPI;Persist security info=False");
oSqlConnection.Open();

oSqlDataAdapter = new SqlDataAdapter();
oSqlCommand = new SqlCommand();

oSqlCommand.CommandText = oSQL.ToString();
oSqlCommand.Connection = oSqlConnection;
oSqlDataAdapter.SelectCommand = oSqlCommand;

//Make sure the table name matches the one used in DataSet1.Designer.cs.
//DataTable1 is the default name. If you fail to name it properly, the
//headers will appear but the report data will not.
oSqlDataAdapter.Fill(oDS, "DataTable1");

//Assign the DataTable to the report
oDynamicCrystalReport.SetDataSource(oDS);
crystalReportViewer1.ReportSource = oDynamicCrystalReport;

return oSQL.ToString();
}
```

The results can be seen in Figure 7-6.

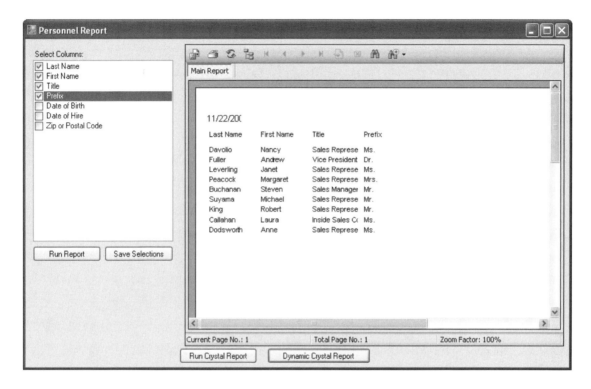

Figure 7-6. Crystal reports output

Using the Crystal SDK

If you have Crystal Reports 2008, you can also create a report using its SDK's object model. Just as in Word or Excel VBA, for example, anything you can do with Crystal Reports from the designer interface you can also accomplish programmatically via the SDK. Using the same interface shown in the previous section, you can build a report using the code shown in Listing 7-18.

Listing 7-18. Dynamic Crystal Report Using SDK

```
CrystalDecisions.CrystalReports.Engine.ReportDocument oReportDocument;
ISCDReportClientDocument oReportClientDocument;
Section oSection;
FontColor oDetailHeaderTextFont;
FontColor oDetailHeaderFieldFont;
System.Data.DataSet oDS;
string szSQL;
int iLeft = 10;
int iTop = 1;
int iWidth = 2000;
```

```
int iHeight = 200;

//Define font objects
oDetailHeaderTextFont = CreateFont("Arial", 10, false, true,
    false, false, System.Drawing.Color.Black);
oDetailHeaderFieldFont = CreateFont("Arial", 10, false, false,
    false, false, System.Drawing.Color.Black);

//Create a new ReportDocument
oReportDocument = new CrystalDecisions.CrystalReports.Engine.ReportDocument();

//Access the ReportClientDocument in the ReportDocument
oReportClientDocument = oReportDocument.ReportClientDocument;

//create new report document
oReportClientDocument.New();

//Iterate through the selected columns to build an SQL string
szSQL = BuildSQL();

//Add the data source to the report. This is needed so the data
//structure is available when the field objects are added.
oDS = AddTable(oReportClientDocument,
               szConnectString,
               szSQL);

//Iterate through the selected columns
foreach (object oItem in lstColumns.CheckedItems)
{
    //Obtain a reference to the page header section
    oSection = oReportClientDocument.ReportDefinition.PageHeaderArea.Sections[0];

    //Add a text object as a column header
    AddTextField(oReportClientDocument, oSection, oDetailHeaderTextFont,
        CrAlignmentEnum.crAlignmentLeft, ((ListItem)oItem).Text,
        iLeft, iTop, iWidth, iHeight);

    //Obtain a reference to the report details section
    oSection = oReportClientDocument.ReportDefinition.DetailArea.Sections[0];

    //Add the data field bound to a data source column
    AddField(oReportClientDocument, oSection, oDetailHeaderFieldFont,
        CrAlignmentEnum.crAlignmentLeft, "Table", ((ListItem)oItem).Value,
        iLeft, iTop, iWidth, iHeight);

    iLeft += (iWidth + 20);
```

```
}

oReportDocument.SetDataSource(oDS);

crystalReportViewer1.ReportSource = oReportDocument;
```

This code iterates through the user-selected columns, creates a SQL statement pulling only that data, instantiates a report object, adds the column headers and data columns to it, sets the data source, and displays it in the Crystal viewer. This report doesn't need to persist to disk. If you wish to do this, you can use the code shown in Listing 7-19.

Listing 7-19. *Writing a Dynamically Created Report to a Disk File*

```
object oTarget = @"c:\temp";

oReportClientDocument.SaveAs(@"myreport.rpt", ref oTarget,
((int)CdReportClientDocumentSaveAsOptionsEnum.
cdReportClientDocumentSaveAsOverwriteExisting));

oReportDocument.Load(@"c:\temp\myreport.rpt");
```

Because the SQL is generated at runtime, you can bind it to the report object using the code shown in Listing 7-20. Doing so at the beginning of the process is necessary so the data structures are available to the reports as data columns are added.

Listing 7-20. *AddTable() Method*

```
private System.Data.DataSet AddTable(ISCDReportClientDocument
oReportClientDocument,
                                    string szConnectString,
                                    string szSQL)
{
    SqlDatabase oSqlDatabase = new SqlDatabase(szConnectString);
    ISCRDataSet oISCRDataSet;
    System.Data.DataSet oDS;

    using (DbCommand oDbCommand = oSqlDatabase.GetSqlStringCommand(szSQL))
    {
        oDS = oSqlDatabase.ExecuteDataSet(oDbCommand);
    }

    oISCRDataSet = CrystalDecisions.ReportAppServer.
        DataSetConversion.DataSetConverter.Convert(oDS);
    oReportClientDocument.DatabaseController.AddDataSource(oISCRDataSet);

    return oDS;
}
```

You add data fields one by one using the AddField() method shown in Listing 7-21.

Listing 7-21. AddField() method

```
private void AddField(ISCDReportClientDocument oReportClientDocument,
                      Section oSection,
                      FontColor oFontColor,
                      CrAlignmentEnum sAlignmentEnum,
                      string szTableName,
                      string szFieldName,
                      int iLeft,
                      int iTop,
                      int iWidth,
                      int iHeight)
{
    ISCRTable oISCRTable;
    ISCRField oField;
    ISCRReportObject oISCRReportObject;
    FieldObject oFieldObject;
    CrystalDecisions.ReportAppServer.DataDefModel.Table oTable;

    oISCRTable = oReportClientDocument.Database.
        Tables.FindTableByAlias(szTableName);

    //Extract the table or stored procedure and cast it to a Table object
    oTable = ((CrystalDecisions.ReportAppServer.DataDefModel.Table)oISCRTable);

    //Cast this field reference to a Field object
    oField = ((Field)oTable.DataFields.FindField(szFieldName,
        CrFieldDisplayNameTypeEnum.crFieldDisplayNameName,
        CrystalDecisions.ReportAppServer.DataDefModel.
        CeLocale.ceLocaleUserDefault));

    ////Instantiate a FieldObject and set the properties
    ////and display the data and position on the page.
    oFieldObject = new FieldObject();
    oFieldObject.Kind = CrReportObjectKindEnum.crReportObjectKindField;
    oFieldObject.DataSource = oField.FormulaForm;
    oFieldObject.Left = iLeft;
    oFieldObject.Top = iTop;
    oFieldObject.Width = iWidth;
    oFieldObject.Height = iHeight;
    oFieldObject.FieldValueType = oField.Type;
    oFieldObject.FontColor = oFontColor;
    oFieldObject.Format.HorizontalAlignment = sAlignmentEnum;
```

```
    oISCRReportObject = ((ISCRReportObject)oFieldObject);

    ////Add the field to the report
    oReportClientDocument.ReportDefController.ReportObjectController.
        Add(oISCRReportObject, oSection, 0);

}
```

You can add column headers in the form of TextObjects. Working with TextObjects is one of the less intuitive parts of the Crystal Reports object model. Adding a text field (shown in Listing 7-22) is a rather convoluted process involving a number of objects—five to be exact—just to display a piece of text on the report. First you need a ParagraphTextElement object that contains the text you wish to display, which you then need to add to a ParagraphElements collection object. This collection is then added to the ParagraphElements property of a Paragraph object, which in turn is added to a Paragraphs collection. Finally, the Paragraphs collection object is added to the Paragraphs property of a TextObject. The TextObject is the visual element that holds settings for size and position.

Listing 7-22. AddTextField() method

```
private void AddTextField(ISCDReportClientDocument oReportClientDocument,
    Section oSection,
    FontColor oFontColor,
    CrAlignmentEnum sAlignmentEnum,
    string szText,
    int iLeft,
    int iTop,
    int iWidth,
    int iHeight)
{
    TextObject oTextObject;
    ISCRReportObject oISCRReportObject;
    Paragraphs oParagraphs;
    Paragraph oParagraph;
    ParagraphElements oParagraphElements;
     ParagraphTextElement oParagraphTextElement;

     //Instantiate the necessary objects
     oTextObject = new TextObject();
     oParagraphs = new Paragraphs();
     oParagraph = new Paragraph();
    oParagraphElements = new ParagraphElements();
    oParagraphTextElement = new ParagraphTextElement();

   //Set the displayed text to the ParagraphTextElement object
    oParagraphTextElement.Text = szText;
    oParagraphTextElement.Kind = CrParagraphElementKindEnum.
```

```
        crParagraphElementKindText;

    //Add the ParagraphTextElement to the ParagraphElements collection
    oParagraphElements.Add(oParagraphTextElement);

    //Set the ParagraphElements collection to the ParagraphElements
    //property of the Paragraph object and set the text alignment
    oParagraph.ParagraphElements = oParagraphElements;
    oParagraph.Alignment = sAlignmentEnum;

    //Add the Paragraph object to the Paragraphs collection
    oParagraphs.Add(oParagraph);

    //Set up the TextObject by assigning the Paragraphs collection object to
    //its Paragraphs property. Also, set the size and position.
    oTextObject.Kind = CrReportObjectKindEnum.crReportObjectKindText;
    oTextObject.Paragraphs = oParagraphs;
    oTextObject.Left = iLeft;
    oTextObject.Top = iTop;
    oTextObject.Width = iWidth;
    oTextObject.Height = iHeight;
    oTextObject.FontColor = oFontColor;

    oISCRReportObject = ((ISCRReportObject) oTextObject);

    //Finally, add the TextObject to the report
    oReportClientDocument.ReportDefController.ReportObjectController.
        Add(oISCRReportObject, oSection, -1);
}
```

You can take this process much further by adding sections, groups, formulas, and parameters all at runtime to produce a data-driven report completely customized to your needs.

SQL Server Reporting Services

SQL Server Reporting Services (SSRS) has slowly made headway into the report-writing market. Today, it rivals the major report-writing tools like Crystal Reports, Cognos, and Actuate. Unlike Crystal Reports, SSRS uses an XML-based RDL format to store its report definitions. Therefore, any tool that can generate ASCII or manipulate XML can also generate an SSRS report.

Using RDL

RDL can be rather verbose. Simply generating a report showing last name and first name requires some 483 line of RDL.

Listing 7-23 shows a small segment of the RDL for this report.

Listing 7-23. RDL Code Snippet

```
<TableRow>
  <TableCells>
    <TableCell>
      <ReportItems>
        <Textbox Name="LastName_Header">
          <Value>Last Name</Value>
          <CanGrow>true</CanGrow>
          <UserSort>
            <SortExpression>=Fields!LastName.Value</SortExpression>
            <SortExpressionScope>table_Employee</SortExpressionScope>
          </UserSort>
          <Style>
            <Color>White</Color>
            <BackgroundColor>#528ae7</BackgroundColor>
            <FontSize>8pt</FontSize>
            <PaddingLeft>2pt</PaddingLeft>
            <PaddingRight>2pt</PaddingRight>
            <PaddingTop>2pt</PaddingTop>
            <PaddingBottom>2pt</PaddingBottom>
            <BorderColor>
               <Default>#c0c0c0</Default>
            </BorderColor>
            <BorderStyle>
               <Default>Solid</Default>
            </BorderStyle>
            <FontFamily>Tahoma</FontFamily>
            <FontWeight>Bold</FontWeight>
            <Language>en-US</Language>
          </Style>
        </Textbox>
      </ReportItems>
```

As you can see, this is pure XML. You can save the RDL for any report to a file with an XML extension and better examine it with your favorite web browser. If you're allowing users to dynamically build simple columnar reports, wrapping methods around the RDL isn't a difficult task. For something more complicated, you need to consult the RDL specification, which you can find at `http://www.microsoft.com/downloads/details.aspx?FamilyID=2A20C7AF-52E8-4882-BD24-9479B3C7517D&displaylang=en`.

___

■ **Note** Although there was discussion of delivering an RDL object model with SQL Server 2008, this didn't come to pass. The RDL object model (RDLOM) is available in the `Microsoft.ReportingServices.RdlObjectModel.dll` assembly, but its direct use by developers isn't supported. Teo Lachev discusses how to exploit the object model in his book *Applied Microsoft SQL Server 2008 Reporting Services* (Prologika Press). There, you learn how to create a wrapper class for the RDLOM, but be forewarned that this is no small undertaking. Moreover, there is no guarantee that it will be compatible with a future release.

Dynamic Rdl

One option for creating dynamic SQL Server Reporting Services reports is to use a third-party library called Dynamic Rdl, which you can find on the Web at www.dynamicrdl.com. This tool provides a class wrapper around the RDL object model as described in the previous section. Dynamic Rdl objects are transformed into their XML-based RDL representations automatically, so you don't need to create and validate RDL manually. Suppose you've constructed the following SQL based on user selections:

```
SELECT LastName, FirstName
FROM Employees
ORDER BY LastName, FirstName
```

The object wrappers offered by Dynamic Rdl allow you to dynamically create an SSRS report from this SQL. In the following code examples, you see how to set up a dynamic report.

The code in Listing 7-24 sets up the object variables and shows how to extract the data for the report. In addition to the SQL, the only other parameter you need is the connection string.

Listing 7-24. Connecting the Report to a Data Source

```
Report oReport;
ReportItemsType oReportItemsType;
TableType oTableType;
StyleType oTitleStyle;
StyleType oHeaderStyle;
StyleType oDetailsStyle;
TableRowsType oTableRowsType;
TableRowType oTableRowType;
TableCellType oTableCellType;

// Derive a list of DataSet columns names from the dynamic SQL
IList<string> oColumnList = base.GetQueryFieldNames(szSQL, szConnect);

// Instantiate a report object and set the width
oReport = new Report { Width = oColumnList.Count + "in" };

// Connect to the data source
oReport.DataSources = new DataSourcesType { DataSource = new DataSourceType[1] };
oReport.DataSources.DataSource[0] =
    new DataSourceType { Name = "NorthWind",
```

```
        ConnectionProperties = new ConnectionPropertiesType() };
oReport.DataSources.DataSource[0].ConnectionProperties.ConnectString = szConnect;
oReport.DataSources.DataSource[0].ConnectionProperties.DataProvider = "SQL";

// Execute the SQL and return a DataSet
oReport.DataSets = new
DataSetsType { DataSet =
    base.CreateDataSet(szSQL, "NorthWind", "DataSet", szConnect) };
```

Listing 7-25 shows the page setup and creation of the main header that spans the columns. It also illustrates how to instantiate the TableType object that serves as a container for the report detail. Each column in the report is set to a standard width.

Listing 7-25. *Performing Page and Table Setup*

```
// Perform the page setup
oReport.LeftMargin = "0.5in";
oReport.RightMargin = "0.5in";
oReport.TopMargin = "0.5in";
oReport.BottomMargin = "0.5in";
oReport.PageWidth = (oColumnList.Count*COLUMN_WIDTH + 1) + "in";
oReport.InteractiveWidth = (oColumnList.Count*COLUMN_WIDTH + 1) + "in";

// Body
oReport.Body = new BodyType { Height = "0.5in" };

// Report Items
oReportItemsType = new ReportItemsType();
oReport.Body.ReportItems = oReportItemsType;

// Set up a table
oTableType = new TableType();
oTableType.Name = "Table1";
oTableType.KeepTogether = true;
oTableType.DataSetName = "DataSet";
oTableType.Top = "0.0in";
oReportItemsType.Table = oTableType;

//...and dynamically define the table's columns
oTableType.TableColumns = new TableColumnsType();
oTableType.TableColumns.TableColumn = new TableColumnType[oColumnList.Count];

for (int i = 0; i < oColumnList.Count; i++)
{
    oTableType.TableColumns.TableColumn[i] = new TableColumnType();
    oTableType.TableColumns.TableColumn[i].Width = COLUMN_WIDTH + "in";
}
```

213

```
oTitleStyle =
    new StyleType { FontSize = "12pt", FontWeight = "Bold", TextAlign = "Center" };
oHeaderStyle =
    new StyleType { BackgroundColor = "SteelBlue",
        Color = "White", FontWeight = "Bold" };

// Create a table header
oTableType.Header = new HeaderType();
oTableType.Header.RepeatOnNewPage = true;
oTableRowsType = new TableRowsType();
oTableType.Header.TableRows = oTableRowsType;
oTableRowsType.TableRow = new TableRowType[2];

// Create a header that spans the columns
oTableRowType = new TableRowType();
oTableRowsType.TableRow[0] = oTableRowType;
oTableRowType.Height = "0.3in";
oTableRowType.TableCells =
    new TableCellsType { TableCell = new TableCellType[1] { new TableCellType() }
};
oTableRowType.TableCells.TableCell[0].ColSpan = (uint)oColumnList.Count;
oTableRowType.TableCells.TableCell[0].ReportItems =
    new ReportItemsType { Textbox =
        CreateTextBox("TextBoxTitle", true, true, oTitleStyle, "Dynamic Report") };
```

The code in Listing 7-26 shows how to iterate the DataSet, create the individual columns headers, and then populate the columns with data. You see that this code produces a template to be executed by SSRS. Unlike the earlier Excel example, you're not populating every cell in every row with data.

Listing 7-26. *Setting Up the Detail Section*

```
// Create the individual column headers
oTableRowType = new TableRowType();
oTableRowsType.TableRow[1] = oTableRowType;
oTableRowType.Height = "0.25in";
oTableRowType.TableCells =
    new TableCellsType { TableCell = new TableCellType[oColumnList.Count] };

for (int i = 0; i < oColumnList.Count; i++)
{
    oTableCellType = new TableCellType();
    oTableRowType.TableCells.TableCell[i] = oTableCellType;
    oTableCellType.ReportItems =
        new ReportItemsType { Textbox = CreateTextBox("TextBoxHeader" + i,
                                          true,
                                          true,
```

```
                            oHeaderStyle,
                            oColumnList[i]) };
    oTableCellType.ReportItems.Textbox.Width = COLUMN_WIDTH + "in";
}

// Iterate through the DataSet and populate the detail section of the report
oDetailsStyle = new StyleType { FontSize = "9pt" };

oTableType.Details = new DetailsType();
oTableRowsType = new TableRowsType();
oTableType.Details.TableRows = oTableRowsType;
oTableRowsType.TableRow = new TableRowType[1];
oTableRowType = new TableRowType();
oTableRowsType.TableRow[0] = oTableRowType;
oTableRowType.Height = "0.2in";
oTableRowType.TableCells =
    new TableCellsType { TableCell = new TableCellType[oColumnList.Count] };

for (int i = 0; i < oColumnList.Count; i++)
{
    oTableCellType = new TableCellType();
    oTableRowType.TableCells.TableCell[i] = oTableCellType;
    oTableCellType.ReportItems =
        new ReportItemsType { Textbox = CreateTextBox("TextBoxDetails" + i,
        true,
        true,
        oDetailsStyle,
        "=Fields!" + oColumnList[i] + ".Value") };
    oTableCellType.ReportItems.Textbox.Width = COLUMN_WIDTH + "in";
}
```

After the Report template object has been created, it needs data to populate it. The code shown in Listing 7-27 executes the SQL statement, binds it to the report, and displays its ReportViewer control in local processing mode.

Listing 7-27. Extracting the Data and Binding It to the Report

```
using (SqlConnection oSqlConnection =
    new SqlConnection(szConnectString))
{
    using (SqlCommand oSqlCommand = new SqlCommand(szSQL, oSqlConnection))
    {
        using (SqlDataAdapter oSqlDataAdapter = new SqlDataAdapter(oSqlCommand))
        {
            oDS = new DataSet("DataSet");
            oSqlDataAdapter.Fill(oDS);
```

```
using (MemoryStream oMemoryStream = new MemoryStream())
{
    oXmlSerializer = new XmlSerializer(typeof(Report));

    // Serialize the report into the MemoryStream
    oXmlSerializer.Serialize(oMemoryStream, oReport);

    bytes = oMemoryStream.ToArray();

    // Encoding ensures a correctly formed XML
    //document is loaded for the report.
    oUTF8Encoding = new System.Text.UTF8Encoding();

    using (StringReader oStringReader =
        new StringReader(oUTF8Encoding.GetString(bytes)))
    {
        ReportViewer.LocalReport.LoadReportDefinition(oStringReader);
        ReportViewer.LocalReport.DataSources.Add(
            new ReportDataSource("DataSet", oDS.Tables[0]));
    }
}
}
}
}
```

If you try to use column aliasing (for example, LastName AS [Last Name]) to obtain better column headers, you receive an error informing you that SSRS dataset field names must be CLS complaint. Therefore, no spaces can be used. You need to pass another parameter to the main method containing a mapping between the column names used in the query and report headers. A class implementing an IDictionary interface for name-value pairs does the trick nicely. You can find more examples of how to use Dynamic Rdl at http://www.dynamicrdl.com/download/Dynamic.Rdl.Samples.zip.

Summary

This chapter covered how to create data-driven reports. You looked at the features of Microsoft Excel and how to create PDF files. You also examined the two most popular reporting tools on the market: Crystal Reports and SQL Server Reporting Services. Coming up, you see what's involved in creating a user interface for users to design their own screens.

■ ■ ■

Database Design

This chapter discusses database design considerations for data-driven applications. When developing a data-driven application, you're certainly not bound to any particular entity structure by virtue of your application's data-driven nature. Still, certain database techniques can make your application more flexible, depending on how and why you introduced data-driven technology.

Data Storage

You can most easily extend your application to handle runtime-created data elements by using the Data Definition Language (DDL) commands of your RDBMS. Before you continue any further, though, you need to be aware of one caveat right away: after you release your application, you can't control the permissions that the application has when it connects to the database—and DDL commands require an administrator privilege. If the application connects to the RDBMS through a user ID that doesn't have administrator privileges, these commands will fail. Because corporate security policies are understandably very rigid, you can't expect to insist that your customers grant administrator rights to the user ID for your application just so it can execute the occasional DDL command.

As I said, the easiest way to store new column and table structures is by creating new columns and tables using DDL. Although this may seem obvious, in the next section you look at an alternative approach. Using the personnel-management system example I've been beating to death all along in the book, if you have a table that stores `LastName`, `FirstName`, and `DateOfBirth`, you can add a new column defined by the user by executing this command:

```
ALTER TABLE Employees ADD FavoriteBeer varchar(100)
```

Previous chapters covered how to instantiate the form control objects to edit this new column. By tying this database column to a `TextBox` control, you can now track the favorite brand of beer for all your employees.

Most likely, though, you want to select such a series of options from a dictionary so users don't need to type in their favorite brand of beer free-form, leaving you to deal with all the various misspellings of *Michelob* and *Budweiser*. In this case, you can maintain a dictionary table to standardize the options. When the administrator decides to store this data, they can require that the end users select it from a dictionary, thereby requiring the use of a `ComboxBox` rather than a `TextBox`. They need to define *Beer Brands* as a dictionary type and can store this new type in the `DictionaryType` table:

```
DictionaryTypeID int
Description varchar(100)
```

Each type of entry in `DictionaryType` corresponds to one or more entries in the `Dictionary` table, which has the following structure:

```
DictionaryID int
Description varchar(100)
DictionaryType int
```

When you define the Favorite Beer entry, you can insert its title into the `DictionaryType` table. The unique ID—`DictionaryTypeID`, which in the following example has a value of 3—is then used as the foreign key in the `Dictionary` table to determine that all entries with this designation belong to the beer list. The table data looks something like Tables 8-1 and 8-2.

Table 8-1. *DictionaryType Table*

DictionaryTypeID	Description
1	State
2	Department
3	Favorite Beer

Table 8-2. *Dictionary Table*

DictionaryID	Description	DictionaryTypeID
1	New Jersey	1
2	California	1
3	Texas	1
4	Finance	2
5	Sales	2
6	IT	2
7	Michelob	3
8	Budweiser	3

Now you can present the user with a combo box that is populated by one routine that pulls its data using the `DictionaryTypeID` value as a parameter:

```
SELECT DictionaryID, Description
```

```
FROM Dictionary
WHERE DictionaryTypeID = @DictionaryType
ORDER BY Description
```

■ **Note** Even if you're not building a data-driven application, using such a storage mechanism for simple dictionary entries makes sense. You only need to maintain one table and one set of SELECT, INSERT, UPDATE, and DELETE stored procedures. I once had to maintain an application that had 76 tables of the same structure as the one you just saw—a full one-fourth of all the tables in the application.

Building a front end to allow a user the ability to create and configure their own data columns is easy. Look at the screen in Figure 8-1.

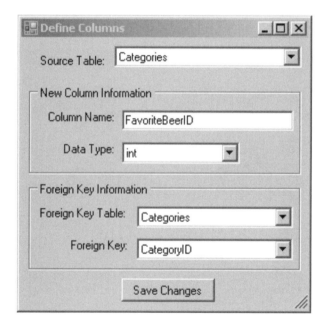

Figure 8-1. User interface to create custom columns and foreign key relationships

the source and foreign table combo boxes with the following SQL, which extracts the metadata from the INFORMATION_SCHEMA view:

```
SELECT TABLE_NAME
FROM INFORMATION_SCHEMA.TABLES
WHERE TABLE_TYPE = 'BASE TABLE'
ORDER BY TABLE_NAME
```

219

After a table is selected, its associated key combo box is populated with this SQL, which uses the table name as a parameter:

```
SELECT COLUMN_NAME
FROM INFORMATION_SCHEMA.COLUMNS
WHERE TABLE_NAME = <tablename>
AND DATA_TYPE = 'int'
ORDER BY ORDINAL_POSITION
```

The assumption here is that only integer type columns are used in primary and foreign key relationships.

You can determine the available data types in your SQL Server installation by extracting them from the sys.types table as shown here:

```
SELECT name
FROM sys.types
ORDER BY name
```

Each version of the RDBMS has slightly different data types. SQL Server 2008, for example, introduced a *date* and a *time* data type. Therefore, a hard-coded list of options won't work well.

Ultimately, the goal is to generate the text of the necessary DDL commands, as shown in Listing 8-1.

Listing 8-1. *DDL Commands to Add a Column and Create a Foreign Key Relationship*

```
ALTER TABLE Employees ADD BeerID int

ALTER TABLE Employees
ADD CONSTRAINT FK_Employees_FavoriteBeerID FOREIGN KEY (FavoriteBeerID)
REFERENCES Dictionary (DictionaryID)
```

The code to generate this DDL is shown in Listing 8-2.

Listing 8-2. *Generating DDL Commands*

```
string szSQL;
string szSourceTable = cmbSourceTable.Text;
string szSourceTableColumn = txtColumnName.Text;
string szForeignKeyTable = cmbForeignKeyTable.Text;
string szForeignKeyColumn = cmbForeignKey.Text;
string szDataType = cmbDataType.Text;

szSQL = "ALTER TABLE " + szSourceTable + " ADD " +
    szSourceTableColumn + " " + szDataType;

ApplySQL(szSQL);

szSQL = "ALTER TABLE " + szSourceTable +
```

```
            " ADD CONSTRAINT FK_" + szSourceTable + "_" + szSourceTableColumn +
            " FOREIGN KEY (" + szSourceTableColumn + ") " +
            " REFERENCES " + szForeignKeyTable + " (" + szForeignKeyColumn + ")";

ApplySQL(szSQL);
```

■ **Note**   You can distribute your applications with a series of additional columns in every table to handle future custom data elements created by users. I've seen applications in which each table has columns named Field1Varchar...Field*n*Varchar, Field1Int...Field*n*Int, Field1DateTime...Field*n*DateTime, and so on. The additional step with this technique is the need for a special table to associate a label with each data element defined by the user. Programmatically, this approach is very easy to implement and allows you to keep a normalized structure while avoiding DDL commands. However, it does present a cumbersome database design, and you need to limit the number of additional data elements the users may add.

Committing Data to the Database

Instantiating controls and modifying data structures at runtime is a nice feature, but it won't get you very far unless you can tie those controls to a data source. Normally, controls created at design time pass their values to stored procedures that are crafted to accept a static list of values as parameters. If you have admin rights to the server, you can form the text for a stored procedure, create it at runtime, execute it, and then delete it. Of course, doing this doesn't obtain for you the performance benefits of precompilation that you normally get in a stored procedure, because you never cache the execution plan. It's just used and deleted.

If you don't have admin rights, you can create an INSERT or UPDATE statement and pass it to a stored procedure that does nothing but accept a SQL statement and execute it. This very simple stored procedure is shown in Listing 8-3.

Listing 8-3. Executing SQL Strings

```
CREATE PROCEDURE spc_ExecuteSQL

@SQL varchar(max)

AS

EXEC (@SQL)
```

To execute this code, you need to construct a SQL statement in a string variable and pass it to the stored procedure like this:

```
spc_ExecuteSQL 'SELECT * FROM DataDictionary'
```

■ **Note** A stored procedure that is designed to execute SQL statements is a definite security risk. To prevent unauthorized users from ever invoking it outside of your application and wreaking havoc—think DELETE FROM Employees—you can pass a second variable containing an encrypted string as an authorization code. If the code doesn't match the contents of an internal security table, the stored procedure won't execute. Even if you offer to do this, your client's security policy may forbid such an approach under any circumstances. Therefore, proceed cautiously before relying on this technique.

When you instantiate a control at runtime, the name of its corresponding table column can be assigned to the Tag property or to a custom property that you can add by subclassing the control. By selecting the values of each control based on its object type, you can marry them to column names and create a series of UPDATE and INSERT statements using a StringBuilder object. Listing 8-4 shows how to accomplish this.

Listing 8-4. *Creating INSERT and UPDATE Statements*

```
StringBuilder oUPDATE = new StringBuilder();
StringBuilder oINSERT = new StringBuilder();
StringBuilder oINSERTColumns = new StringBuilder();
StringBuilder oINSERTValues = new StringBuilder();
int iPrimaryKeyID = 12;
string szTag = this.Tag.ToString();

oINSERT.AppendFormat("INSERT INTO {0} (", szTag.Substring(0, szTag.IndexOf("|")));
oUPDATE.AppendFormat("UPDATE {0} SET ", szTag.Substring(0, szTag.IndexOf("|")));

GetSQL(panel1.Controls, oUPDATE, oINSERTColumns, oINSERTValues);

//Remove the trailing comma
oUPDATE.Remove(oUPDATE.Length - 2, 2);

oUPDATE.AppendFormat(" WHERE {0} = {1}",
    szTag.Substring(szTag.IndexOf("|") + 1),
    iPrimaryKeyID.ToString());

//Remove the trailing comma
oINSERTColumns.Remove(oINSERTColumns.Length - 2, 2);
oINSERTValues.Remove(oINSERTValues.Length - 2, 2);

oINSERT.AppendFormat("{0} ) VALUES ( {1} )",
    oINSERTColumns.ToString(),
    oINSERTValues.ToString());

MessageBox.Show(oUPDATE.ToString());
MessageBox.Show(oINSERT.ToString());
```

This code generates both the `INSERT` and `UPDATE` statements for the table to which the owner `Form` object is bound. The `Tag` property of the `Form` object holds a pipe-delimited string indicating the table name and primary key column of the data table. Optionally, you can subclass the `Form` object into your own `Form` class and add `TableName` and `PrimaryKeyColumnName` properties yourself. The remainder of the code uses the `StringBuilder` class to create the SQL. To associate the column name and control value together, the `GetSQL()` method recursively iterates the controls collection. This method is shown in Listing 8-5.

Listing 8-5. *Iterating the Controls Collection to Obtain the Column Names and Associated Values*

```
private void GetSQL(System.Windows.Forms.Control.
ControlCollection oControls,
    StringBuilder oUPDATE,
    StringBuilder oINSERTColumns,
    StringBuilder oINSERTValues)
{
    string szControlType;
    string szColumnName;

    //iterate through every control in the control
    //collection of the owner object
    foreach (Control oSubControl in oControls)
    {
        //Get the name of the control type - ListBox, CheckBox, etc.
        szControlType = oSubControl.GetType().Name;

        //Find the control's saved data in the XML
        if (oSubControl.Tag != null)
        {
            szColumnName = oSubControl.Tag.ToString();

            oUPDATE.Append(szColumnName);
            oUPDATE.Append(" = ");

            oINSERTColumns.Append(szColumnName);

            switch (szControlType)
            {
                case "TextBox":
                    oUPDATE.Append("'");
                    oUPDATE.Append((SubControl).Text);
                    oUPDATE.Append("'");

                    oINSERTValues.Append("'");
                    oINSERTValues.Append((oSubControl).Text);
                    oINSERTValues.Append("'");
```

```
                        break;

                case "CheckBox":
                    oUPDATE.Append(((CheckBox)oSubControl).Checked ? "1" : "0");
                    oINSERTValues.Append(((CheckBox)oSubControl).
                        Checked ? "1" : "0");
                    break;
            }

            oUPDATE.Append(", ");
            oINSERTValues.Append(", ");
            oINSERTColumns.Append(", ");
        }

        //Perform recursion to handle child controls
        if (oSubControl.HasChildren)
            GetSQL(oSubControl.Controls, oUPDATE, oINSERTColumns, oINSERTValues);
    }
}
```

Any control with a Tag property that isn't null is assumed to be in play. When you click the Get SQL button in the screen shown in Figure 8-2, you see the SQL statements shown in Listing 8-6.

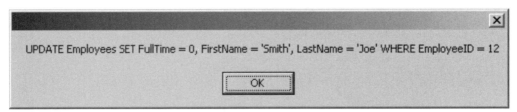

Figure 8-2. *SQL generation*

Listing 8-6. *Generated SQL Statements*

```
UPDATE Employees
SET FullTime = 0,
FirstName = 'Carl',
```

```
LastName = 'Smith'
WHERE EmployeeID = 1

INSERT INTO Employees
(FullTime, FirstName, LastName)
VALUES
(0, 'Carl', 'Ganz')
```

Using Inverted Tables

Performing runtime modifications of a database may not always be possible due to your client's security policy. Some organizations may not even permit the existence of a stored procedure whose sole purpose is to execute SQL commands. You can avoid DDL commands completely by storing your dynamic structures in an inverted table.

Structuring Inverted Data

Think of a typical table that may contain a primary key, LastName, FirstName, BirthDate, DeptID, and Salary columns. Translating this into an inverse table relationship provides a more flexible approach to storing data where existing tables never need to be modified via DDL. This approach requires two tables to identify the columns. The first is a DataDictionary table, and the second is a DataStorage table. The DataDictionary table defines the various columns referenced in DataStorage and looks like the structure shown in Figure 8-3.

	Column Name	Data Type	Allow Nulls
▶	DataDictionaryID	int	☐
	ColumnName	varchar(100)	☐
	DataType	varchar(20)	☐
			☐

Figure 8-3. DataDictionary table

Each primary key in DataDictionary references a DataDictionaryID column in DataStorage. DataStorage holds the individual values of data elements under a primary key. Thus, storing the values of LastName, FirstName, BirthDate, DeptID, and Salary requires five rows in DataStorage. Because such disparate data—strings, numerics, and so on—needs to be stored in this table, the DataValue column is a varchar. The actual data type is stored in DataDictionary, and conversions are performed at runtime. Figure 8-4 shows the DataStorage table.

	Column Name	Data Type	Allow Nulls
▶	DataStorageID	int	☐
	DataDictionaryID	int	☐
	DataValue	varchar(100)	☐
	DataElementID	int	☑
			☐

Figure 8-4. *DataStorage table*

Using this approach, a data set that traditionally looks like this

EmployeeID	LastName	FirstName	BirthDate	Salary	DeptID
1	Gates	Bill	1955-01-01 00:00:00.000	500000.00	7
2	Jobs	Steve	1956-06-01 00:00:00.000	90000.00	8

will now look like this:

DataStorageID	DataElementID	DataDictionaryID	DataValue
1	1	1	Bill
2	1	2	Gates
3	1	3	1955-01-01
4	1	4	500000
5	1	5	7
6	2	1	Steve
7	2	2	Jobs
9	2	3	1956-06-01
10	2	4	90000
11	2	5	8

The definitions of the data columns are stored in the `DataDictionary` table and look like this:

DataDictionaryID	ColumnName	DataType
1	LastName	varchar
2	FirstName	varchar
3	HireDate	date
4	DeptID	int
5	Salary	money

Although the DataDictionary/DataStorage approach is the most flexible, the code to support it is a bit more complex and the data is more cumbersome to work with. The biggest advantage here is that no DDL is required to alter the structure. Simply INSERT a row into the DataDictionary table, and you can immediately begin storing data associated with that entry in the DataStorage table.

■ **Note**   I've seen this database design approach used when an application requires search capabilities on a large number of data elements. I know of one company that sold securities information that consisted of a ticker symbol and a trading date as the unique key. For each security on a given day, the company had to store the opening, high, low, and closing prices; the CUSIP number; the P/E ratio; and more than 100 other data elements. Because each data element needed to be searchable by the users, it wasn't practical to store them in the 100-plus table columns that would have been needed. After all, it's not possible to have more than 100 indices on a table, and that's what would have been required to permit efficient searching. Moreover, millions of combinations of ticker symbol/dates were stored in the table. By creating an inverted table and indexing the Ticker Symbol, Date, DataDictionary, and DataValue columns only, users could easily narrow down a given data element and search it quickly.

Extracting Inverted Data

As you'd guess, storing data in this fashion requires some change in thinking and in structuring your SQL. Normally, to extract all records where the LastName is 'Gates' and the salary is greater than $90,000 per year, you execute this rather intuitive SQL:

```
SELECT EmployeeID
FROM Employees
WHERE Salary > 90000
AND LastName = 'Gates'
```

However, to extract it from the inverted table, you need to do this:

```
SELECT EmployeeID
FROM DataStorage
WHERE DataDictionaryID = 4
AND Value > 90000
INTERSECT
SELECT EmployeeID
FROM DataStorage
WHERE DataDictionaryID = 2
AND Value = 'Gates'
```

This example retrieves only one matching data element: the EmployeeID. Because you're performing an INTERSECT of the different data elements, it's not possible to pull all the data at once. To access the available data fields for a given employee, you need to create a list of EmployeeIDs and then retrieve the matching data elements, as shown in Listing 8-7.

Listing 8-7. *Retrieving Inverted Data*

```
CREATE PROCEDURE spc_GetInvertedData

AS

CREATE TABLE #temp
(
    EmployeeID int
)

INSERT INTO #temp
    SELECT DataElementID
    FROM DataStorage
    WHERE DataDictionaryID = 5
    AND DataValue >= 90000
    INTERSECT
    SELECT DataElementID
    FROM DataStorage
    WHERE DataDictionaryID = 1
    AND DataValue = 'Gates'

SELECT ColumnName, DataType
FROM DataDictionary
ORDER BY DataDictionaryID

SELECT ds.DataStorageID, ds.DataDictionaryID, ds.DataElementID,
ds.DataValue, dd.ColumnName, dd.DataType
FROM DataStorage ds
```

```
INNER JOIN DataDictionary dd ON ds.DataDictionaryID = dd.DataDictionaryID
WHERE ds.DataElementID IN
    (SELECT EmployeeID
     FROM #temp)
ORDER BY ds.DataElementID, ds.DataDictionaryID
```

Converting Inverted Data to a Normalized Structure

This SQL code returns two data sets. The first is the structure of the data itself so you can create the `DataTable` object to receive the normalized data. The second is the inverted data. Because the traditional approach uses one row for every entity (here, employee), it makes sense to convert the inverted structure to a normalized structure that can be more easily manipulated. Because you never know what the structure will be at any given point in time, you can't create classes to encapsulate your data. The properties are always changing. In theory, you can generate the class code at runtime, perform a runtime compilation, and then use reflection to access the properties and methods, but that's probably more trouble than it's worth. The code in Listing 8-8 shows how to load the inverted employee data into a normalized structure.

Listing 8-8. *Loading Inverted Data into a Normalized Structure*

```
DataSet oDS = GetInvertedData();
DataTable oStructureDT = oDS.Tables[0];
DataTable oInvertedDT = oDS.Tables[1];
DataTable oNormalDT = new DataTable();
DataRow oNewDR = null;
int iPrimaryKeyID;

if (oInvertedDT.Rows.Count == 0)
    return;

//Create the normalized structure
foreach (DataRow oDR in oStructureDT.Rows)
{
    oNormalDT.Columns.Add(new DataColumn(oDR["ColumnName"].ToString(),
        ConvertType(oDR["DataType"].ToString())));
}


iPrimaryKeyID = 0;

//Iterate the inverted data set
foreach (DataRow oDR in oInvertedDT.Rows)
{
    //When the primary key changes, you can add the new row...
    if (iPrimaryKeyID != int.Parse(oDR["DataElementID"].ToString()))
    {
```

```
        //...except the first time through
        if (iPrimaryKeyID != 0)
            oNormalDT.Rows.Add(oNewDR);

        //Create a new row object and set the primary key value
        oNewDR = oNormalDT.NewRow();

        iPrimaryKeyID = int.Parse(oDR["DataElementID"].ToString());
    }

    //Add the data to the named column
    oNewDR[oDR["ColumnName"].ToString()] = oDR["DataValue"].ToString();

}

oNormalDT.Rows.Add(oNewDR);

dataGridView1.DataSource = oNormalDT;
```

Because there is no direct mapping between the data types available in .NET and those in SQL Server (and Oracle and every other RDBMS, for that matter), a conversion from SQL Server data types to .NET data types must happen when assigning the data type of the DataColumn objects. The ConvertType() method shown in Listing 8-9 performs this for some of the major data types.

Listing 8-9. Converting SQL Server Data Types to .NET

```
private Type ConvertType(string szSQLServerType)
{
    Type oType = null;
    string szDotNetType = string.Empty;

    switch (szSQLServerType)
    {
        case "nvarchar":
        case "nchar":
        case "char":
        case "varchar":
            oType = typeof(string);
            break;

        case "datetime":
        case "date":
        case "time":
            oType = typeof(DateTime);
            break;
```

```
        case "int":
            oType = typeof(int);
            break;

        case "money":
            oType = typeof(decimal);
            break;
    }

    return oType;
}
```

Executing this code produces the screen shown in Figure 8-5.

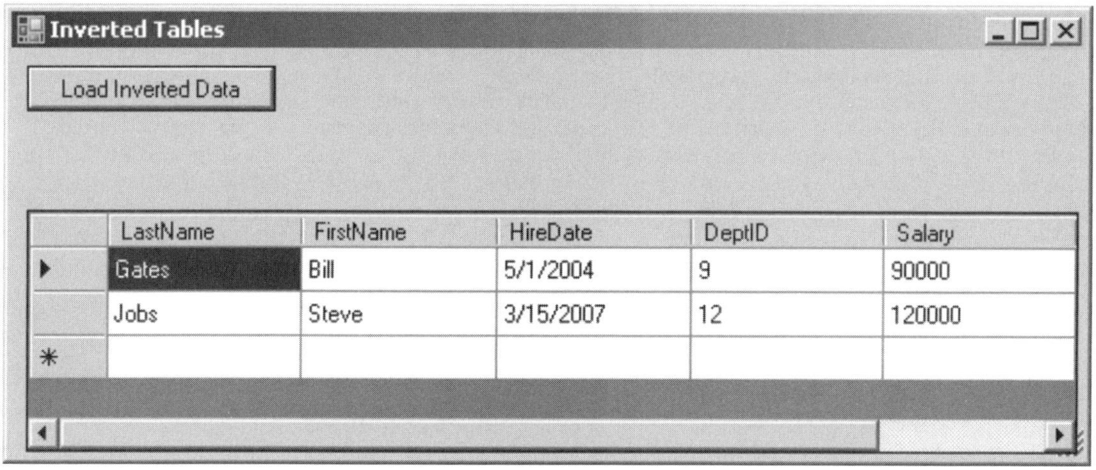

Figure 8-5. *Normalizing inverted data*

One variant to the inverted approach is to use typed `DataValue` columns so as to avoid type conversions in SQL. For example, you can have a `DataStorage` table that looks like Figure 8-6.

Column Name	Data Type	Allow Nulls
▶ TypedDataStorageID	int	☐
DataDictionaryID	int	☐
DataElementID	int	☐
DataValueVarchar	varchar(100)	☐
DataValueInt	int	☐
DataValueDate	date	☐
DataValueMoney	money	☐
		☐

Figure 8-6. Typed DataStorage table

Then, you store your data in the column specific to its data type.

Mixing Normalized and Inverted Tables

If you wish to employ a traditional normalized database design in your data-driven application, you may certainly do so. In the personnel-management system example, you've likely created a series of data-collection fields for the employee's personal information that you store in a series of normalized tables. Yet you realize that you can't possibly anticipate all the data elements a user may wish to collect. To remedy this, you can create a one-to-many table that stores an unlimited number of data-driven columns. The DataElementID column in the DataStorage table references the EmployeeID in the Employee table. Here, you need to perform JOINs in a stored procedure using dynamic SQL. The stored procedure code shown in Listing 8-10 illustrates how to convert inverted data to a normalized structure and then JOIN it with an existing table.

Listing 8-10. Extracting the Inverted Data

```
DECLARE @SQL varchar(max)
DECLARE @ColumnName varchar(100)
DECLARE @DataValue varchar(100)
DECLARE @DataType varchar(100)
DECLARE @Cnt int
DECLARE @x int
DECLARE @ID int
DECLARE @DataElementID int
DECLARE @DataElementIDPrev int

--Store the employee IDs that match the criteria
CREATE TABLE #IDtemp
(
    EmployeeID int
)

--Put all matching employeeIDs into the temp table
INSERT INTO #IDtemp
```

```
    SELECT DataElementID
    FROM DataStorage
    WHERE DataDictionaryID = 5
    AND DataValue >= 90000

--Pull all the inverted data whose primary key is found in the temp table
SELECT ds.DataElementID, ds.DataValue, dd.ColumnName, dd.DataType
INTO #DataStoragetemp
FROM DataStorage ds
INNER JOIN DataDictionary dd ON ds.DataDictionaryID = dd.DataDictionaryID
WHERE ds.DataElementID IN
    (SELECT EmployeeID
     FROM #IDtemp)
ORDER BY ds.DataElementID, ds.DataDictionaryID

DROP TABLE #IDtemp

--Add a unique key to facilitate iteration
ALTER TABLE #DataStoragetemp ADD ID int IDENTITY
```

The first section of this code is very similar to Listing 8-11. You need to extract a list of the matching primary key values and then pull the detail data based on those values. The tricky part is shown in Listing 8-11. Here, a normalized temporary table is built from the structure held in the DataDictionary. Then, the primary key value is INSERTed into it, and all subsequent values are UPDATEd one column at a time. The result is a normalized table that can be joined with the Employees table.

Listing 8-11. Converting an Inverted Table to a Normalized One

```
--Create a temp table to hold the normalized data
CREATE TABLE #Datatemp
(
    DataElementID int
)

--Add columns to the normalized data table by extracting them
--from the data dictionary
SELECT 'ALTER TABLE #Datatemp ADD ' +
ColumnName + ' ' +
CASE
    WHEN DataType = 'varchar' THEN DataType + '(max)'
    ELSE DataType
END AS ColumnName
INTO #Structuretemp
FROM DataDictionary

SET @Cnt = @@ROWCOUNT
```

```
--Add a unique key to facilitate iteration
ALTER TABLE #Structuretemp ADD ID int IDENTITY

SET @x = 1

WHILE @x <= @Cnt
    BEGIN
        SELECT @SQL = ColumnName
        FROM #Structuretemp
        WHERE ID = @x

        SET @x = @x + 1

        EXEC (@SQL)
    END

DROP TABLE #Structuretemp

SET @x = 1
SET @ID = 0
SET @DataElementIDPrev = 0

SELECT @Cnt = COUNT(*) FROM #DataStoragetemp

--Iterate through the inverted data and create INSERT and
--UPDATE statements to populate the normalized temp table
WHILE @x <= @Cnt
    BEGIN
        SELECT @DataElementID = DataElementID,
        @DataValue = DataValue,
        @ColumnName = ColumnName,
        @DataType = DataType
        FROM #DataStoragetemp
        WHERE ID = @x

        IF @DataType = 'varchar' OR @DataType = 'date'
            SET @DataValue = '''' + @DataValue + ''''

        IF @DataElementID <> @DataElementIDPrev
            BEGIN
                SET @SQL = 'INSERT INTO #Datatemp (DataElementID, ' + @ColumnName +
                ') VALUES (' +
                CONVERT(varchar, @DataElementID) + ', ' + @DataValue + ')'

                -- INSERT INTO #Datatemp (DataElementID, LastName) VALUES (1, 'Gates')
                EXEC (@SQL)
```

```
            SET @DataElementIDPrev = @DataElementID
        END
    ELSE
        BEGIN
            SET @SQL = 'UPDATE #Datatemp SET ' + @ColumnName + ' = ' +
            @DataValue + ' WHERE DataElementID = ' +
            CONVERT(varchar, @DataElementID)

            -- UPDATE #Datatemp SET FirstName = 'Bill' WHERE DataElementID = 1
            EXEC (@SQL)
        END

    SET @x = @x + 1
  END

--Join the permanent normalized table to the temp normalized
--table to prove this really works
SELECT e.LastName, e.FirstName, t.*
FROM Employees e
INNER JOIN #Datatemp t ON e.EmployeeID = t.DataElementID
ORDER BY e.LastName, e.FirstName

DROP TABLE #DataStoragetemp
DROP TABLE #Datatemp
```

Summary

In this chapter, you reviewed the various data structures to store information entered through a dynamic interface. You examined the pros and cons of using DDL to modify the existing structures while also looking at how to store information in tables flexible enough to handle whatever data elements a user wishes to create. You also examined how to bind dynamic controls to data columns and create INSERT and UPDATE statements.

Index

▓ E

▓ F

■S

You Need the Companion eBook

Your purchase of this book entitles you to buy the companion PDF-version eBook for only $10. Take the weightless companion with you anywhere.

We believe this Apress title will prove so indispensable that you'll want to carry it with you everywhere, which is why we are offering the companion eBook (in PDF format) for $10 to customers who purchase this book now. Convenient and fully searchable, the PDF version of any content-rich, page-heavy Apress book makes a valuable addition to your programming library. You can easily find and copy code—or perform examples by quickly toggling between instructions and the application. Even simultaneously tackling a donut, diet soda, and complex code becomes simplified with hands-free eBooks!

Once you purchase your book, getting the $10 companion eBook is simple:

❶ Visit **www.apress.com/promo/tendollars/**.

❷ Complete a basic registration form to receive a randomly generated question about this title.

❸ Answer the question correctly in 60 seconds, and you will receive a promotional code to redeem for the $10.00 eBook.

THE EXPERT'S VOICE™

233 Spring Street, New York, NY 10013

Offer valid through 6/10.